The Fund Raiser's Guide to the Internet

The NSFRE/Wiley Fund Development Series

Beyond Fund Raising: New Strategies for Nonprofit Innovation and Investment by Kay Sprinkel Grace

Critical Issues in Fund Raising edited by Dwight F. Burlingame

Fund-Raising Cost Effectiveness: A Self-Assessment Workbook by James M. Greenfield

A Guide to the Creation and Use of Investment Policies by Charitable Organizations by Robert P. Fry

The Nonprofit Handbook: Fund Raising, Second Edition edited by James M. Greenfield

The NSFRE Fund-Raising Dictionary by National Society of Fund Raising Executives

The Universal Benefits of Volunteering: A Practical Workbook for Nonprofit Organizations, Volunteers, and Corporations by Walter P. Pidgeon, Jr.

The NSFRE/Wiley Fund Development Series

The NSFRE/Wiley Fund Development Series is intended to provide fund development professionals and volunteers (including board members and others interested in the not-for-profit sector) with top-quality publications that help advance philanthropy as voluntary action for the public good. Our goal is to provide practical, timely guidance and information on fund raising, charitable giving, and related subjects. NSFRE and Wiley each bring to this innovative collaboration unique and important resources that result in a whole greater than the sum of its parts.

The National Society of Fund-Raising Executives

The NSFRE is a professional association of fund-raising executives which advances philanthropy through its more than 18,000 members in 149 chapters throughout the United States, Canada, and Mexico. Through its advocacy, research, education, and certification programs, the Society fosters development and growth of fund-raising professionals, works to advance philanthropy and volunteerism, and promotes high ethical standards in the fund-raising profession.

1997 NSFRE Publishing Advisory Council

The Fund Raiser's Guide to the Internet

Michael Johnston

JOHN WILEY & SONS, INC.
New York • Chichester • Weinheim • Brisbane • Singapore • Toronto

Copyright © 1999 by Michael Johnston. All rights reserved. Published by John Wiley & Sons, Inc.

Published simultaneously in Canada.

Library of Congress Cataloging-in-Publication Data:
Johnston, Michael W., 1963–
    The fund raiser's guide to the Internet / Michael Johnston.
        p.   cm. — (NSFRE/Wiley fund development series)
    Includes bibliographical references and index.
    ISBN 0-471-25365-0 (pbk./disk)
    1. Fund raising—Computer network resources.   2. Nonprofit organizations—Computer network resources.   3. Internet (Computer network)   I. Title.   II. Series.
    HV41.2.J64   1998
    025.06'3617'0681—dc21   98-8021
                                                                 CIP

Printed in the United States of America.

10 9 8 7 6 5 4 3 2 1

About the Author

Michael Johnston, President of Hewitt and Johnston Consultants, a full service fundraising consulting firm, was a senior consultant from 1988 to 1991 with Stephen Thomas Associates, the first direct mail fundraising firm in Canada to work exclusively with nonprofit organizations.

His clients have ranged from sports organizations for the disabled to political parties in Canada, the U.S., and the UK. In 1991, he was a political fundraising consultant for the Australian Labour Party in Canberra and Melbourne.

Michael's volunteer experience is extensive, having served on several boards and committees. He is currently a board member and chair of Fundraising for the Sunshine Centre for Seniors in downtown Toronto.

He has also been a volunteer fundraising leader with the United Way in their Management Assistance Program where he has assisted agencies in developing strategic fundraising solutions.

He is a past board member and current member of the National Society of Fundraising Executives (NSFRE), sits on the NSFRE's Volunteer Online Council, and has been a past member of the Ethics Committee of the Canadian Society of Fundraising Executives (CSFRE).

He has worked with a wide range of educational institutions in the United States, including Seton Hall University and LaSalle University, lecturing on the Internet and the nonprofit sector.

Contents

Foreword xi

Acknowledgments xiii

1 Introduction 1

2 Who Is on the Net: Demographics 27

3 Seeing Is Believing: How People Read Online 47

4 The Electronic Tablet: How People Write Online 65

5 The Reply Device 91

6 Security: Safeguarding Your Homestead on the Electronic Frontier 121

7 Members Only: Value—Added Areas for Members 139

8 Inviting People to Action: Campaigning 161

9 Getting Your Message to Stand Out: Marketing Online 197

Index 225

About the Disk 233

▼ Foreword

Congratulations. Since you are about to read this book, you don't need to be convinced that your organization needs a presence on the World Wide Web. Unfortunately, there are still tens of thousands of organizations where leadership is either afraid to take the plunge or for some uninformed reason has decided an organizational Web site is unnecessary.

There is only one thing worse than a nonprofit without a Web site. What's worse is an organization with a boring site that was slapped together without a plan and without an understanding of who will see and use it.

Many nonprofits are accomplishing great things on the Internet. One thing that most are not doing—yet—is making large sums of money. While fund raising is the ultimate goal of a Web site, the real purpose is communication with donors. Once that communication is established, the dollars will come. And don't be surprised if those dollars come via the traditional method—a first class stamp.

Who is on the Net? Just about everyone who your organization wants to reach. Who is using the Internet to its greatest potential? My guess is about 25 percent of the population. For example, I have been "net enabled" for several years and still fumble around in cyberspace. That is probably the case with a good percentage of your donors.

And, while encryption technology has gotten more secure, a sizable block of people—including me—still won't purchase something with a credit card over the Internet. If they don't buy a book from Amazon.com because of security concerns, they certainly will not donate via the Web.

That is why the World Wide Web should be all things to all donors. It should provide information for the wary and also be a place for commerce—whether it is the purchase of a wildlife calendar or for a straight donation.

Sometimes the obvious has to be mentioned for everything to make sense. Nonprofits hope that donors will respond to a direct-mail appeal. In the case of donor acquisition, the charity has spent time and money selecting the names of people who the direct marketing managers believe will be most receptive to an appeal.

On the Internet, an organization has absolutely no control over who visits. The visit could come at 1 o'clock in the afternoon or 1 o'clock in the morning. The person visiting online is someone who is curious but maybe not yet convinced that they want to donate. And, chances are, the visitor doesn't meet the carefully crafted profile developed to select the list used for the direct-mail campaign. Simply put, a Web site should be user-driven, versus organizationally-driven.

A charity's Web site has to provide the opportunity for relationship building. It must provide communication. It must be entertainingly interactive and it must provide an opportunity to give. The site must provide many avenues for that gift and for information that could eventually lead to major gifts and planned giving. That's right—planned giving. The stereotype of the geeky kid with Cheetos and a keyboard is giving way to a mainstream user. That new demographic includes people who were computer-phobic, were forced to learn how to use a computer at work, and now can't live without one. Here is the translation—they are in the 50s and have money and are starting to think about estate planning.

Every nonprofit executive knows that the best source of revenue is generated soliciting from the house donor file. They also know that the charity's greatest resource is made of flesh and blood—staff and volunteers. Many nonprofits are using the Net to keep these valuable resources connected via Intranets and members-only sections of the Web site. It is a natural fit. Volunteers and donors feel an affinity for organizations where they give their time and money. Making them feel special via restricted areas binds them more tightly to your organization.

But simply building it won't make them come (apologies to Kevin Costner). Marketing the site and campaigning on-line are just as vital as the construction.

These days, consultants who hold themselves out as Internet experts are more numerous than Milton Berle one-liners. Unfortunately, the results are often far from humorous. There are but a handful of people who understand the World Wide Web and fund raising. Michael Johnston is one of the best. His knowledge is universal, having worked with nonprofit organizations in the United States, Canada, Europe, and Africa. This book is a great foundation from which any organization can build an Internet presence.

PAUL CLOLERY
Editor-in-Chief, The NonProfit Times

Acknowledgments

Throughout the late eighties and early nineties, I worked as a nonprofit fundraising consultant, happily raising money for organizations through the mail, telephone, and person-to-person. And then the Internet arrived. I was introduced to the Net in the early nineties by a friend and colleague, George Irish. He began to explain and demonstrate the huge potential that lay in this new medium for the nonprofit sector. Over the past five years, his vision, technical knowledge, and layperson's touch for the Internet has helped shape many of my ideas. This book simply wouldn't have happened without him.

In addition to George, I owe a debt of gratitude to a number of wonderful friends, colleagues, and family who helped make this book mature and useful to the nonprofit reader.

In 1995, at the International NSFRE Fundraising Conference in Chicago, I began to insist that delegates take a more critical and disciplined approach to this new medium. I believed we could take our nonprofit fundraising and management skills and apply them to the Internet. Jennifer Herman, a fund raiser from Minneapolis, listened to me, thought I was making some sense, and introduced me to the editor of *The NonProfit Times*, Paul Clolery. I wanted to thank Jennifer for believing in my vision, and insisting that other people listen to me. Paul heard what I had to say, and I began writing freelance articles about nonprofits and the Internet for his magazine. Paul has always been a constructive critic in my work about the Internet, and I thank him for being so honest in his help and criticism.

This book has coalesced throughout the past four years—a result of sharing, listening, and questioning nonprofit organizations about their online experiences.

ACKNOWLEDGMENTS

One of the best environments for me to learn from nonprofits online has been at Seton Hall University. Miriam Lyons Frolow, Assistant Director, Nonprofit Resource Sector Institute of NJ at Seton Hall University, has consistently been a gracious host for a number of my teaching sessions. Likewise, John Bouza, a fund-raising consultant in Canada, Steve Morgan and Marc Nohr in the United Kingdom, as well as the staff at the NonProfit Centre at La Salle University, have helped make my lectures rich learning experiences for me.

I also wanted to thank Howard Lake for being an early explorer in the area of fund raising and the Internet. His commitment to the sector is helping many of our European colleagues understand the online nonprofit world.

It has been a considerable challenge to write this book while running a consulting firm. I've had to rely on the excellent research of George Irish and Victoria Boyd Bell to ensure the book is as thorough as it is. Allyson Hewitt, my business partner, has been a thorough reader of a number of chapters, and has given me solid advice on how to write more effectively for nonprofit managers and decision-makers.

I also wanted to thank the numerous nonprofit (and commercial) organizations who have shared their online experiences, good and bad. This book has been made infinitely more useful with their selfless participation. I especially wanted to thank Rosemary Oliver and Jennifer Good of Greenpeace Canada, Jane Pratt of the American Red Cross, Larry Short of World Vision USA, Susan Thorning at the Ontario Community Support Association, David Housley of World Wildlife Fund USA, Jeff Kenney of World Wildlife Canada, Rob McCue of Yahooligans, Sue Schneider of Interactive Gaming News, Brian Erman of Keybuy.com, and so many more. I apologize for not including everyone here, but the reader will see clearly in the book just which organizations helped us. All of these organizations have been extraordinarily generous in helping us make this book for the nonprofit sector.

I also want to thank the staff at John Wiley and Sons in New York. Martha Cooley has always believed in this project, and that's why it is in front of you today. Thanks also to Anne Brunell and John Lapuz, who have helped make a book that I believe is easy to read and understand.

One final note. The National Society of Fundraising Executives has been an integral support in getting this material to print. Their belief in my approach, research, and communicating on the Internet led to John Wiley approaching me to write this book. I thank them for their commitment to educational resources for our sector.

Finally, I wanted to thank my brother, Mark, for being my best reader, part-time researcher, project manager and cheerleader. It has been a pleasure to work with someone who can provide such insightful comments yet be tough enough to push me to make a deadline. This book is especially dedicated to you.

MIKE JOHNSTON
Toronto, Canada
hjc@ican.net

The Fund Raiser's Guide to the Internet

▼1 Introduction

FUND RAISING ON THE NET

As a nonprofit fund raiser, one does not want to be left behind by other practitioners when a new fund-raising medium comes on to the scene. Yet, the pressure of being forced to master a new fund-raising medium, when one is still working on the "ins and outs" of direct mail, telephone, and television fund raising, is stress one does not need.

Now, with the frenzied press coverage of the Internet, one is being asked (or is about to be!) by staff, volunteers, and board members about the fund-raising potential of this new electronic medium.

This chapter will show that there are as many fund-raising opportunities online as there are in the "real world." Fund raisers have never been stumped for new fund-raising ideas—and it will be no different online.

There are three questions that nonprofit managers, staff, and volunteers should be asking about the Internet:

- Should we get online?
- What are other groups doing on the Internet?
- Will it be profitable to our organization to use the Internet for fund-raising purposes?

The answers are yes, a lot, and with time.

There is no doubt that almost every nonprofit organization has to get online. There are just too many people on the Internet now, and in the future, to ignore. It

1

is a new medium that nonprofit organizations are already using to reach a wider audience to help them accomplish their mission and mandate—including new ways to raise money. Every nonprofit organization should make the small investment to have it as a part of their media mix.

The World Wide Web

The World Wide Web (WWW) is the fastest growing part of the Internet. It is the place nonprofit organizations are going to raise money. On the Web, pages of hypertext can be browsed, almost like flipping through the pages of a magazine—complete with pictures, graphics, and even sound and video clips. Individuals and organizations can publish their own home pages by storing them on a computer that is connected to the Internet and letting interested individuals come and browse the site.

The WWW, because of its capabilities and ease of use, appears destined to become the future of the Internet—for a while anyway. The WWW is a place where organizations are publishing for a wider audience as well as for their own niche constituencies. The majority of new Internet users are coming online and are using the WWW to find information, browse, research, chat, and now, to make donations to their favorite charities.

Because other fund-raising media are becoming more competitive and cluttered with solicitations, every fundraising professional is looking to gain the competitive edge. The reader can get there first. Now it is time to explain what is being accomplished on the Internet so the reader can begin to plan how he or she will participate successfully.

This chapter will outline Internet fund-raising activities in the following way:

• Direct donations online (Members and Donors)
• Pledges online
• Merchandise sales
• Online auctions
• Online lotteries
• Online fund-raising behavior (part of Greenpeace Canada study)

Now, just what are nonprofit organizations around the world doing on the Internet to raise money?

DIRECT DONATIONS

A) Membership Fundraising Online

Is it possible for nonprofit organizations to find online members? The evidence from the World Wildlife Fund (WWF) USA is a cautious, but tantalizing, yes.

The World Wildlife Fund USA has created an online membership opportunity for visitors. In the bottom right hand corner of the home page, the text "join" takes visitors to a membership form (**https://www.newmedium.com/wwfus/credit_cardform.html**) that presents the visitor with the following offer:

> *Your membership donation of $15 or more entitles you to 12 months of benefits including WWF's bimonthly newsletter FOCUS with reports from the field and an annual WWF Members Travel Issue.*
>
> *When you join, you will also receive by mail the WWF members' only Panda T-shirt pictured at right, one size (XL) fits all.*
>
> *To join, either fill out the credit card form below or select from the other join options at right.*

The online visitor can make an immediate online membership donation or call the 1-800 number. For a further exploration of online membership issues please turn to chapter seven. For an in-depth discussion of online response forms turn to chapter five.

World Wildlife Fund USA has a slowly growing membership response online. For its first year of electronic solicitation (from March 1996 until April 1996), WWF had 312 individuals take out a membership through an online credit card transaction. That's an average of 26 people per month. From April of 1997 until April of 1998, there have been 836 online memberships (with an average donation of $35). That's an average of 70 memberships per month. In one year there's been a 270% growth in membership donations!

In what other medium are nonprofit organizations experiencing a 270% increase in membership donations with little or no extra effort? Probably none. WWF's experience proves this new and growing medium demands that nonprofit organizations start to invest in online membership and donor cultivation and solicitation.

B) Online Donations

Nonprofit managers might be willing to believe that online visitors may take out a membership (with resulting benefits and privileges), but are probably skeptical that online visitors will make online credit card donations. The experience of the American Red Cross should make everyone drop their skepticism and begin looking more seriously at online credit card donations via the Internet.

No nonprofit organization has taken more online credit card donations than the American Red Cross. Since July of 1996 until the end of April 1998, they had received 1,004 online donations for a total of $128,074.55. That's an average donation of $127.56. However, if you eliminate all gifts over $1,000, then the Red Cross has raised $78,674.55 though 982 online gifts. That's an average donation of $80.12, which is considerably higher than the $36 average gift the American Red Cross receives for its direct mail appeals.

C) Large Gifts Online

Many nonprofit managers are skeptical that nonprofit organizations can receive large gifts via the Internet. The experience of the American Red Cross since November of 1996 shows otherwise.

From November of 1996 until April of 1998, The American Red Cross has received 22 online credit card donations that total $49,400. That is an astounding $2,245.45 per donation! The online credit card gifts went from a low of $1,000 to as high as $12,000. These were not pledges. These were not donations that needed to be confirmed by the donor. They were simply electronic transactions with the prospective donor entering their information online, sending it to The American Red Cross and with the nonprofit organization finally processing the gift. It's important to realize that online consumers do not make transactions of this size when buying consumer goods. It may be easier for citizens to make large transactions online if they involve helping a charity instead of buying goods.

At a minimum, these findings dictate that nonprofit organizations should offer website visitors the opportunity to make large gifts. Most web site gift arrays do not provide online donors with a chance to choose a $1,000 gift option, but the findings from the American Red Cross show that a small, but important, segment of online donors likes to make a "millennial contribution." Every nonprofit organization should make sure they offer online donors a chance to choose significant gift amounts (of $1,000 or more) either through a pledge or—as Red Cross has shown—in credit card donations. With thirteen $1,000 gifts, the American Red Cross has demonstrated that this amount seems to be comfortable and attractive to donors.

Online donors need to be coddled and cultivated like all other kinds of donors. The American Red Cross has made sure that their online donors get a personal approach. Richard Renn, Director of Development Operations at The American Red Cross National Offices states that, "All Internet donor information is sent to the local chapters across the country for a more personalized follow-up after we at national send the initial acknowledgment, which is the same for all Internet donors. Although some chapters may cultivate their donors differently, I expect that most or all high-end donors receive a special acknowledgment, along with phone calls, and other cultivation techniques."

There were two American Red Cross online gifts that qualify as major gifts according to Kathleen Kelly, in *Effective Fund-Raising Management:* one for $8,000 and another for $12,000.[1] In the case of The American Red Cross, these major gifts were made to help with an immediate need, a natural disaster. However, with a major gift made to many other nonprofit organizations, a donor may want their online

---

[1]Kathleen Kelly, *Effective Fund-Raising Management,* Lawrence Erlbaum Associates, Publishers, New Jersey, 1997, pg. 476.

major gift to help for years to come. A gift in the range of $10,000 is often seen as the minimum for an endowment and this means that many nonprofit organizations should start to offer online giving information about major gift opportunities and what a major gift and the resulting endowment could do for the donor's chosen cause.[2]

D) Think Big

If The American Red Cross experience shows that individuals will make major gifts online, then every nonprofit organization should start to think the following about online fundraising:

1. Online, a nonprofit organization could show through graphs, testimonials, and text that a major gift can make an incredible difference to the cause. How an endowment works could be very helpful to the potential online donor.
2. If it's true that the personal touch is needed with major gifts, why not utilize CUSEEME computer camera (a small camera that can attach to your computer and transmit your picture live to the internet) technology in conjunction with Internet voice software to allow individuals who want to make a major gift online to talk to and see a major-gifts or planned-giving officer about their gift opportunities. This could be the virtual face-to-face visit.
3. Use interactive programming to show prospective gift givers what their gift can do in the future.
4. Let major gift prospects—or online major givers—get access to the people they may help with email addresses. They can talk directly to the people they're going to help.
5. Give major donor prospects the chance to email financial planners, lawyers, planned giving, and major gift planners to get more information about making a large gift.

PLEDGES

WPLN, a Nashville public radio station, (**http://www.wpln.org/**), has run an online pledge campaign since 1995 as seen in Exhibit 1–1. Julianne Stankiewicz, Director of Marketing and Development, states that, "We are promoting online pledging as part of a larger campaign we conduct, which includes on-air, direct mail and telemarketing."

[2]Ibid, pg. 482.

```
┌──────────────────────────────────────────────────────────────────────────────┐
│ □                     Netscape: Join WPLN - Become a Member!              ▣▤    │
├──────────────────────────────────────────────────────────────────────────────┤
│  ⇦     ⇨     ⌂      ℝ     ▤     ⇉     🖶     🔍      ●                      Ⓝ   │
│ Back Forward Home  Reload Images Open  Print  Find   Stop                      │
├──────────────────────────────────────────────────────────────────────────────┤
│ Location: https://secure.telalink.net/wpln/genericpledge.html                  │
├──────────────────────────────────────────────────────────────────────────────┤
```

Nashville Public Radio
...Made Possible with the Support of
Listeners Like You!

Support your public radio station by becoming a member! With a contribution of $35 or more, you will receive a year's subscription to InPrint, our member magazine. To join, simply complete the information below.
Thank You!

◉ New Membership ○ Renewal ○ Additional Gift

Please fill out the information below:

Name(s) [   ]
E-mail [   ]
Daytime Phone [   ]
Evening Phone [   ]
Address [   ]
City [   ] State [   ] Zip [   ]

Select your membership level

○ $1000 ($83/mo.)
Enjoy benefits as a major supporter including

EXHIBIT 1–1   Online Pledges: WPLN

Julianne adds, "The total amount pledged online since 1995 is $11,235. We tend to average between $2500 and $3000 per week when we incorporate online pledging as part of our membership campaigns."

There are important characteristics of online donors, as revealed by WPLN supporters, that nonprofit organizations should note:

- Online donors use credit cards in 25–30% of their pledges—the same as real-life donors.
- Online donors, as in the case of WKLN donors, pledged an average of $75 per person—much higher than the average pledge outside the online environment.
- The online donor fulfilled at a 60% rate, which is approximately the same as telephone pledge fulfillment rates. The pledge fulfillment rate for online donors at the ACLU (American Civil Liberties Union) web site was also much like their telephone pledges.

Each nonprofit organization that already conducts pledging in their fundraising campaigns (especially with pledge campaigns through the telephone, TV, and radio) should think of adding the online pledge campaign to complement their other pledge fundraising. However, Julianne offers some sober perspective:

> "We have found that online pledging has significant results for us only when it is being reinforced in other ways: on the air, in print, etc. It seems to be helpful as an additional tool and an additional opportunity for those interested in using this method, but does not seem to yield results significant enough to warrant using it in replacement of other methods."

MERCHANDISE SALES

Nissan has launched a Web site that sells an "Internet-only car." It is for sale only on the Net and has features solely available to purchasers who surf to buy their automobiles.

If commercial organizations are getting this committed to selling merchandise online, then nonprofit organizations must do the same. Of course, there are nonprofit organizations that are already selling products online to raise money, increase their public profile, and improve the donor relationship. However, more nonprofit organizations need to make their merchandise sales as efficient as possible through a medium that allows cheaper advertising to reach potential consumers, a low-cost point of sale, and attractive presentation of merchandise.

The Rainforest Action Network (RAN) (**www.ran.org/ran/**) seen in Exhibit 1–2 has discovered that its Web site is a good place to sell merchandise. Mark Westlund, Media Director at RAN, states that, "The site has been a great place to get rid of extra stock. If we had to get rid of stock in the real world, it could have entailed sending out a mailing with a more expensive color reproduction of the T-shirts or phoning supporters—both cost money. Instead, we used the relatively free method of showing our beautiful T-shirts online."

Rainforest Action Network quickly ran through its overstock of approximately 800 T-shirts through online sales. It has also had recent success selling 1998 calendars on its Web site, with approximately 700 sales during the holiday season.

Many nonprofit organizations have begun to offer their expertise to the private sector to raise additional revenue. Without a doubt, this kind of product should be advertised online. The business community is already offering, and finding, professional services online; the charitable sector should be there as well.

The Family Service Association of Metropolitan Toronto offers its counseling services to the commercial sector through its Employee Assistance Program. That kind of service could, and should, be offered online because commercial companies are already scouring the Internet for human resource assistance.

St. Stephan's, a church-based charity in Toronto, has excellent conflict mediation skills that it is now offering to the private sector: selling its mediation skills to

Rainforest Calendar: Celebrate biodiversity year-round!

We're back with another beautiful, full-color rainforest calendar, just in time for the holidays! It's got photographs of rainforest canopies and landscapes, each one a framable work of art-and lots of animals, from the malachite butterfly to the jaguar.

You'll see breathtaking scenes of nature's power-from the awesome splendor of La Hacha falls in Venezuela, to the terrible beauty of Costa Rica's erupting Mt. Arenal volcano.

Enjoy rainforest beauty month by month- and buy extra copies to share with friends! They're a bargain at $10.99 each. And the proceeds go to benefit Rainforest Action Network. Last year's calendars sold out early. Be sure to get yours today!

Order yours here! (**Netscape required**)

| Top of Page | Search | Join | Email RAN | Homepage |

EXHIBIT 1–2   Selling Merchandise on the Web: Rainforest Action Network

solve tough landlord/tenant impasses. With the housing sector heavily represented online, those services should also be offered in cyberspace.

Not every nonprofit is flying by the seat of its pants, offering online merchandise without tracking results nor having a solid marketing plan in place. There are some nonprofits that are making more careful plans to sell a wide range of products online.

Ducks Unlimited (**www.ducks.ca**), an environmental protection organization, is a good example. Ducks Unlimited has hired staff who are responsible for marketing products online. They have crafted a plan that has introduced a wide range of products with excellent tracking programs in an attempt to see what products will be most profitable online.

In addition, they have laid the groundwork for future merchandise sales by building a site that is attracting a large number of visitors (many of them are regulars). Ducks Unlimited has made it part of its plan to create a lot of traffic on its site before its merchandise sales are launched. It wants to guarantee good sales results to solidify its supplier relationships. Now that it receives approximately 42,000 visitors a week, it is ready to launch a wide range of Web site products, including the following:

• A home furnishing section where online visitors can see a range of home furnishing products that, when purchased, give Ducks Unlimited a sales commission. There are links to various suppliers with more information.

- Well-known naturalist artists, like Robert Bateman, sell their products through the site.
- A sportswear company sells its product on the site, with a commission arrangement much like the home furnishing section.
- An affinity MasterCard and affinity phone card are offered online.
- An AT&T offer for the home phone is coming soon.

To make sure that it will be able to take care of future sales, three full-time staff are getting the site ready. They are confident that some of those 42,000 weekly visitors will become online merchandise consumers.

Not only does the merchandise order have to be processed; the merchandise must be delivered to the customer's doorstep. Today's consumers are very comfortable buying high-end products from specialty mail-order catalogs like L.L. Bean or Oxfam's Bridgehead, and they expect their product to be delivered within 5 to 7 working days.

How can nonprofit organizations meet this expectation when they can barely get their tax receipts to donors? How can they afford to deliver products? The answer is for nonprofit organizations to find creative partnerships with courier companies.

A socially responsible multinational company, The Body Shop, is now selling T-shirts online in Canada (**www.thebodyshop.ca**) to raise money for its social change campaigns. Individuals can order T-shirts, which will be delivered within one to seven days to anyone's doorstep for $4. Even much larger packages that include their hair care and toiletry products are still delivered anywhere in Canada for $4. That was a price leveraged by The Body Shop with a national courier company.

Courier companies want to be involved in this new medium, and nonprofit organizations should aggressively solicit their partnership—perhaps by putting the courier's logo on their site in return for a cheaper delivery rate.

A lot of online consumerism is impulsive (just like charitable giving online and off), and the faster you can get the product to their door, the better the chance they will be back again.

ONLINE AUCTIONS

The nonprofit community has made auctions a part of their fund-raising repertoire. Many special events have included an auction as part of the event's agenda.

Now the Internet provides an opportunity for nonprofit organizations to raise money through online auctions. However, along with opportunity comes risk. This is a new medium and with less accumulated experience amongst nonprofits on exactly how to be successful with online auctions, they should turn to an experienced online auctioneer, like Brian Erman, the self-described, "owner, webmaster, and janitor" at **www.keybuy.com**. He's been running online auctions for over three years, and he's only failed to sell an item once or twice after tens of thousands of sales.

Brian Erman was generous enough to provide advice to nonprofit organizations contemplating an online auction, either through a service like his, or on their own. Here's his seasoned advice:

1. The first thing any nonprofit organization needs to do is decide what items they're going to sell and then visit an index site like **www.bidfind.com** to see what auction site might be most appropriate for the nonprofit's auction items.

2. Once a nonprofit has found an auction site that looks like it would be the best place to attract buyers for their items, then they need to contact the owner or the managers of the auction site.

3. The nonprofit needs find out if the auction site will reduce their sales commission for the nonprofit organization. Commission fees range from 2.5% with **www.keybuy.com** to 5% for **www.ebuy.com**; the former offers a 50% reduction in commission fees and that is what every nonprofit should fight for as a minimum reduction.

4. A number of auction sites also charge a listing fee. Every nonprofit organization should ask for the listing fee to be waived for their items. Often a listing fee is a minimum fee (e.g. 10 cents) that helps to reduce the number of items that are posted with outrageously high beginning bids. Online auction sites that charge listing fees are trying to ensure that only serious online sellers post items.

5. Every nonprofit organization should be prepared to provide the following for each auction item:

   a) A short, one paragraph description of the auction item. The description should include the brand or specifications of the item (especially for computer goods). This is important. For example, if a nonprofit organization is selling a computer, then the make of each component is vital in getting the item sold. Some organizations provide a link to a manufacturer's web site from the description of the item, but this is not recommended as it drives people out of the auction web page and many won't come back to buy. Every nonprofit should include important brand/make information in the description of the item.

   b) A picture should almost always been included. It boosts sales and the final price.

   c) It is often effective to include a hypertext link from a description of the auction item to the nonprofit's home page.

   d) The nonprofit should include a hypertext link to a list of other auction items that the organization has for sale.

   e) A one sentence explanation of the mission and mandate of the nonprofit organization, included in the description of the auction item, is also important.

    f) To receive a reduction in commission or listing fee, most online auction houses need a letter, on the nonprofit's letterhead, asking for the fee reduction. In addition, a brief explanation of the nonprofit organization's work is helpful.

    g) Many online auction houses will shy away from more controversial advocacy nonprofits, since showing favor to a group representing one side or another may upset some of their repeat customers.

    h) Studies by **www.keybuy.com** have shown that online bidders spend an average of $80. However, the value of the item will naturally dictate the final bid—if a $1,200 antique is offered, the final bid will be higher than a $12 computer part.

6. Nonprofit organizations need to think carefully about a starting price for their online auction items. Starting every item at $1 is likely to be a successful strategy for online auctioneering. Online donors are afraid to make the first bid. They are wary of bidding too high for an item with an initial high bid amount because other online bidders will ridicule their bid. Others might say that the bid is too high and this person is being cheated. By starting at $1, individuals are not afraid to begin bidding and as experience has shown, once people make that first bid they're hooked.

7. Furthermore, people are even more hooked into the bidding process online when they get an email notice telling them they've been outbid. That means every nonprofit organization should make sure that the online auction house they're going to use, or their own system, includes an email outbid system that tells bidders if they've made the highest bid or not.

8. Nonprofit organizations should think carefully about how long they'd like to offer their items for. A seven-day bid period is often the most effective. Not always, but usually. The **www.keybuy.com** service offers a three-day, five-day, seven-day and fourteen-day auction period to choose from.

9. It is important for nonprofit organizations to understand standard activity during that seven-day bid period. Usually almost all of the activity is on the first day and the last day of the seven day bid period. If a nonprofit organization is thinking about bumping up the bidding, they may want to state that the bidding might be cut off at any time during the seven-day period if a high enough bid is received. This termination threat may be enough to get bidders to be active before the last day of bidding and help drive up the selling price.

10. If a nonprofit is going to use an online auction house, they need to make sure the auction has been around for at least one year.

    There are other online strategies that can help a nonprofit's online auction sales improve. The first is the use of free classified ads online, at websites such as **www.recycler.com**, **www.pennysaver.com** and **www.classified2000.com**. The pennysaver.com site offers free ads that give a nonprofit one week of advertising for 15 words or less, for sale of items for $50 or less. Nonprofit organizations can place free ads, or paid ads if they like, and help drive traffic to their auction items.

When a nonprofit organization is contemplating whether they should approach an online auction house to sell their items, or create their own online presence, it is important to remember that online auction houses have three important strengths:

1. Online auction houses draw an incredible number of visitors to their sites because of immense paid advertising. Brian Erman estimates his web site spent nearly $50,000 in paid advertising in their first year of business and since then they've spent tens of thousands of dollars a year. His online business has analyzed the best places to advertise and without a doubt, the major search engines are the place to advertise. Banners on search engines like AltaVista, Yahoo, etc. bring in over 90% of the visitors to his online auction house. It can cost upwards of $10,000 a month for keyword banner ads on the major search engines. Nonprofit organizations should approach these search engines and negotiate a reduced rate (or donated banner space) when they are running their online auction.

2. Outside of banner ads on the major search engines, Brian has found the web services that guarantee a top 10 listing in all the major search engines are the next best investment to drive traffic to the auction items. One good example is Houddini Web Sign Posts at **http://www.websignposts.com/index.html**. These services charge anywhere from $500 to $1,000 to ensure that an organization's web site appears in the top 10 listings for the major search engines.

3. After a number of years in business, online auction houses have created large databases of auction customers. The **www.keybuy.com** service has over 5,000 regular customers on their database and they've collected extensive information on who their auction buyers are, what they like, how much they spend. With extensive systems in place to track customers, most online auction houses can track bogus bidders and block them out of the bidding process.

Brian Erman is surprised by the inconsistent effort of nonprofit organizations who come to him to sell items online. It is his experience that a nonprofit will approach him with a number of items to sell. After selling all of the items and making an excellent return, the nonprofit organizations will not come back to him.

He believes there two reasons for this:

- There has to be some commitment on the part of the nonprofit organization because they're responsible for delivering the product to the winning bidder. There is a human resource and monetary expense of running the back-end, and many nonprofit organizations may not be prepared for that responsibility.
- The nonprofit organization has to wait for the money to come in from the bidder. The fulfillment rate is usually around 80%. Twenty percent of the time, a win-

ning bidder will not pay for their item and the nonprofit has to go through the process of auctioning the item again.

Nonprofit organizations have an opportunity to make a lot of money through online auctions—possibly consistent income. Brian is sure that nonprofit organizations can make thousands of dollars a month if they are willing to invest and plan for their online auctions.

If a nonprofit organization starts from the assumption that every item they post will sell and that they can sell their items for many times the price they bought it for, then a plan may begin to form:

- Many nonprofit organizations have sophisticated structures in place that acquire donated items which are then sold to discount stores. For example, the Canadian Diabetes Association runs a program called the Community Collection Crew. The program is run by a number of paid staff who distribute flyers to, and then call homeowners, asking them if they have household items they would like to donate to the organization. The Community Collection Crew have drivers who'll pick up the items and then take them to a commercial discount retailer, Variety Village, that pays a bulk rate for the used goods. For some provincial divisions of the Canadian Diabetes Association, the income from this program is vital to the survival of the organization. There is no reason why a concerted effort could not be made to collect and sell items on the Internet—in lieu of, or as an adjunct to, bulk used-goods sales to commercial retailers.
- Many collection programs build a database of past customers who've given goods to a particular nonprofit and they receive a call when a used-goods drive is happening. This kind of database could be used for collecting goods for Internet auctions.

Online auction houses make the most amount of sense for nonprofit organizations when they are selling standard, non-unique items. If a nonprofit is selling items that are one-of-a-kind on the Net, then they might want to create their own online auction site.

One of the best examples comes from the Ottawa Children's Aid Foundation. Volunteers created an engaging site in the spring of 1996 that gave the online community the opportunity to bid and, if lucky, buy a celebrity "doodle." They used the Internet to find the celebrity painters. They found the email addresses of 1,200 celebrities and sent them an email explaining the good work of the organization and how they could help.

The next thing they knew, scores of original doodles by the likes of Bill Cosby, John Travolta, and Cindy Crawford came through the door, as well as Steve Martin, whose handiwork can be seen in Exhibit 1–3.

Steve Martin

To see a large reproduction of Steve Martin's S t a r D o o l e F o r K i d s, simply click on the picture.

Includes autographed photo

I'd like to [Make a Bid]

The current bid is $130 Canadian

I'd like to go back to the StarDoodle home page

EXHIBIT 1–3   Online Doodle Auction: Champions for Children Foundation

---

They scanned in the artwork for the world to see at **www.stardoodle.com** and potential bidders began to come. Online bidders went at it for four weeks—fighting for favorites by Sir Edmund Hilary and Robert Bateman. The online auction led up to a live gala auction, with Internet bidders allowed to bid during the live gala and their bids read out as the people in their seats raised their hands to bid.

In one case, a supporter in Switzerland could not stay up for the event because a six-hour time difference between Ottawa and Geneva meant that he would be bidding at 3:00 A.M. local time. To guarantee his bid, he bid $300 for one doodle that had a previous highest bid of $100. His cyberspace bid beat all "live" competitors.

From a nearly free "virtual" auction site, the Ottawa Children's Aid Foundation (now The Champions for Children Foundation) raised a total of $1,800 online, out of a total of $9,600 raised.

Paul Nattrall, of the Champions for Children Foundation, notes that, "Our auction was more exciting with our online bidders. The people at the tables liked to compete with their online brethren and competition at any auction can only help raise more money for any good cause. Now that we've got one under our belts we're doing it again."

The stardoodle site has a new set of celebrity doodles. It went online November 2, 1996, and in three weeks had 21,225 visitors in comparison to the first auction, when there were 5,000 visitors over four weeks. Paul Nattrall explains, "More people know about our site now. The search engines have found us, we go to local malls and tell people about the Web site, and we make sure every medium of communication we use—radio, Internet, and all printed material—mentions the Web site. And to build up demand for our third auction, we're creating a *coming soon* section, which will highlight celebrity art waiting in the wings."

Now, in 1998, the organization has decided it is not enough to hope people come to the site so they have implemented a marketing strategy to help improve online auction sales:

- An important part of that strategy includes a 19-year-old volunteer who is Net savvy. The Champions for Children Foundation pays for the Net access fees for the volunteer. In return, he's expected to: monitor online chat groups, news groups, and web sites that have fans of particular celebrities who have submitted a doodle to the organization for auction. The volunteer can whip up excitement with Elton John fans at the numerous Elton John web sites like at **http://pages.prodigy.net/gagne1/ejpage.htm.** by posting news of the doodle for sale. There has been a significant increase in traffic since the volunteer began his outreach program.
- In addition, another part of a more concerted plan has been to pull off old doodles and keep the offered doodles up for a shorter time—keeping everything fresh and exciting.
- They've set a goal of $2,000 a month in sales. Right now, there are selling approximately $1,500 a month.
- A nonprofit staff person has to be responsible for raising a set goal from the online auction. By taking responsibility in the budgeting process, there will be a managerial and staff incentive to make the online auction meet revenue expectations.
- If an outside consultant or firm is managing the auction site it might make some sense for the nonprofit organization to pay a commission-based fee for auction sales.
- They have set more ambitious goals for obtaining doodles and getting them online, with a current spring 1998 plan to get 300 new doodles.
- Tracking more carefully to see which kinds of celebrities sell best and pursuing more celebrities in similar areas and marketing to parts of the Net interested in those sectors, (e.g., music, sports etc.)
- They have implemented a quicker bidding process. It is vital for online bidders to feel the process is both fair and exciting. If a bidder has to wait months before they can win the doodle, they could lose interest or feel the process was unfair. Now the bidding goes on for 7 to 10 days.
- To heighten excitement and to give the bidders a chance to get quicker consumer gratification, the organization has created a "fast track" process in which bidders are given the chance to bid a particular amount that will shorten the time for anyone else to make a higher bid.
- The organization has come to understand that it can make sense to sell something at a lower price then the nonprofit wanted. They have also come to understand that the longer you wait to get a better price, the more disgruntled bidders can be-

come—and disgruntled online customers are immersed in a medium that can allow them to announce, far and wide, their displeasure with an online auction.

- The organization has come to understand that bidders need to have quick and easy access to the organization to register a complaint or get more information. A telephone number and email should be available to all bidders.

Paul Nattrall can see a pattern of increasing online purchasing power, "We expect the percentage of dollars raised this time on the Internet to equal the 'real world' bidders and probably pass them by the third auction."

What Other Nonprofits Are Raising through Online Auctions

Nick Allen, director of the Internet Services Group at Mal Warwick & Associates, has done some excellent research on what other nonprofits are making through their online auctions. In the March 1998 issue of *Successful Direct Mail and Telephone Fundraising*, Nick mentions three examples:

1. Oxfam America auctioned off 228 items—paraphernalia from the computer game, Riven. They received 400 bids and grossed $27,000.
2. Operation USA conducted an Internet auction made up of air tickets and travel items, in conjunction with a dinner event in September of 1997. The combined event grossed $145,000.
3. The UCLA Athletic Fund conducted a 30 item auction (both live auction and Internet auction)—mainly consisting of athletic items signed by the university's athletes.

ONLINE LOTTERIES

Sue Schneider, editor of Interactive Gaming News (**www.rtgonline.com**) is a veteran observer of the online gambling scene, as well as spending twelve years as a staff member of a youth services nonprofit organization.

She believes "It's just a matter of time until governments in North America, Australia and other jurisdictions allow nonprofit organizations to raise money through online gambling." Why? Because a number of charitable online gambling operations are setting up their companies on offshore locations, like the Caribbean, Gibraltar, Finland, and Lichtenstein (Internet casinos are bound by the laws of their host country) and are now beginning to raise a large percentage of their profit from North American and Australian players. However, they still give a percentage of profits to charitable organizations that exist outside of the countries where the majority of players come from.

It is probably true that politicians in North America and Australia will soon get wise to the fact that their constituents are conducting charitable gambling outside of their jurisidictions. These governments are already aggressive charitable fundraisers through other methods of gambling, and they'll want their citizens doing charitable gambling on online web sites which benefit charities from North America or Australia.

New technologies are becoming more important to gambling. In Canada, bingo halls are being linked by satellite through the Satellite Bingo Network **http://www.satellitebingo.com.** A central studio broadcasts the game to whoever pays to hook up to the game. This is a purely commercial venture, but nonprofit organizations could be offering the same kind of gambling service. It is also important to note that indigenous groups in North America are moving to online gambling services.

It is up to nonprofit organizations to keep up in the online charitable gaming environment.

The International Red Cross and Crescent's Online Lottery

The International Red Cross has been running an online lottery, Plus Lotto, since April of 1997. Dwight Mihalicz, Director, Revenue Generation Department, International Federation of Red Cross and Red Crescent Societies in Geneva, states that the site "is a qualified success."

It is the qualifications to their success that could prove very helpful to other nonprofit organizations who are contemplating an online lottery. The International Red Cross first decided to enter into a partnership with a commercial organization, the International Lottery in Liechtenstein Foundation (InterLotto). Together, they operate the Plus Lotto as seen in Exhibit 1–4, authorized by the Liechtenstein Government.

Finding a partner can be the first important step. A commercial partner should already have experience in online lotteries. The technical demands would be too great for a nonprofit organization to do it on their own. In the Red Cross's case, InterLotto runs the Web site lottery and sends them 25% of the gross revenue.

Other nonprofit organizations should remember the following when beginning an online lottery:

• It is vital to enter into a contractual agreement with a commercial partner that gives the nonprofit organization joint ownership of the registered lottery players. For the International Red Cross and Crescent this has proven to be lucrative. Over 100,000 people have registered as Plus lottery buyers and they can be approached in the future with other fundraising and marketing opportunities.

EXHIBIT 1–4   An Online Lottery That is a "Qualified Success" www.pluslotto.com

- The nonprofit group should understand the legal issues involved with an online lottery. Since there are no national borders online, citizens from around the world can come and purchase an online lottery ticket. For the International Red Cross and Crescent, they came to understand that while it is legal for world citizens to visit the Plus Lotto site, housed in Liechtenstein, and buy a lottery ticket, it is not so simple to advertise or push the lottery "on the ground" in nation states. The International Red Cross and Crescent has learned there needs to be concerted research and lobbying with Red Cross and Crescent National Offices to get agreement from them, and their respective government bodies, to allow "on the ground" marketing of the online lottery. In North America, responsibility for gambling is a decentralized process with states and provinces holding the decision making power. In many other countries, national governments hold that responsibility. The International Red Cross and Crescent has been working hard to get national governments to allow them to market the online lottery "on the ground" in their countries. After a year of work, Dwight Mihalicz says "they are on the verge of success."

- There is still a huge resistance to giving credit card information online through the Plus Lotto site. There are many times more people who come to the lottery Web site and don't leave their credit card information. But every nonprofit organization who enters into this kind of fundraising endeavor should understand that new security protocols are being developed and slowly, but surely, people are using their credit cards more often online.

- Online lotteries are more successful if the need presented is immediate and urgent. With Plus Lotto, there is a weekly draw. Dwight Mihalicz feels that "many lottery buyers may decide to miss one week's draw and they'll buy a ticket in a few weeks." The information about the nonprofit organization needs to be continually updated to be urgent and immediate. That way, buyers may be spurred to buy a ticket when they visit a site and read about an urgent emergency somewhere in the world.

- Nonprofit organizations need to understand that these online lottery ticket buyers are just that—lottery ticket buyers first and supporters second. Dwight Mihalicz hasn't noticed an increase in lottery sales when there is a high profile world emergency. Instead, lottery ticket sales are consistent from week to week and indicate that the registered lottery ticket buyers are feeding their gambling need first and charity second. This is in contrast to the American Red Cross experience with their online credit card donors. Their donations increase when there is a disaster. For example, when the Grand Forks flooding happened in the spring of 1997, the first weekend of the disaster spurred the highest online donation total ever for The American Red Cross: $18,000. Without a time specific contest, the International Red Cross feels it has lost some of the attractiveness to their lottery. To offer online lottery buyers with a one-of-a-kind lottery opportunity, instead of the pedestrian weekly draw, the International Red Cross and Crescent has created Millions 2000, a one-time lottery to be drawn at the dawning of the new millennium. The organization has set itself a goal of $1 billion dollars with over 4 billion tickets available for sale. The site and lottery was launched on April 15th of 1998 and the first month of sales and visits are very good.

- There is a proliferation of online gambling sites and this increased competition will make charitable online lotteries more challenging. Dwight Mihalicz is sure that "increased competition has lowered our results somewhat. We've made over $1 million dollars from our online lottery in its first 12 months. That's lower than we had budgeted, but we believe our lottery will reach its full potential—$1 million per month—with more hard work and an evolving online market."

Nonprofit organizations understand there will be some human resource demands on staff. Dwight is quick to outline three areas for staff to prepare:

- There will be negative press. Some journalists will use sensationalist stories to indicate that the charity may be lowering its standards by entering into a

medium that is unproven and still dangerous to the charitable consumer. Staff will need to counter this negative media.
• Commercial gambling sites that offer games of chance outside of lotteries will be approaching nonprofit organizations to enter into partnerships. Gambling sites that offer more than lotteries are the most profitable gambling sites and nonprofit organizations could make good money with a partnership, but every nonprofit will have to carefully chose any partnerships.
• Hire a commercial online marketing firm that can conduct the time-intensive task of telling the whole Internet about the nonprofit organization's lottery. This job cannot be done effectively by nonprofit staff.
• There is considerable legal work and lobbying to get governments and a nonprofit's offices (on a state, local, and national level) to agree with and then help with the marketing of the online lottery.

Though there isn't North American charitable gambling happening online right now, Sue Schneider states that "There's a lot of interest in online gaming from the charitable sector. I'm getting calls every week from nonprofit organizations wondering how they get into online gambling. My best advice is for them is to become knowledgeable about gaming regulations in their political jurisdictions and begin to read up as much as they can on trade issues." Sue adds that online gaming operators indicate that 50-80% of their online gamers are North Americans, while Scandinavians and Australians make up another significant chunk of online games players.

Sue emphasizes that nonprofit organizations need to make sure that their online games of chance are fair and they pay out. There are a number of gaming sites that have not paid out on time and have been put out of business through negative word of mouth.

Outside of the International Red Cross and Crescent example, there are a few other interesting examples of online charitable gaming that nonprofits should watch carefully:

1. There is a Finnish gaming site at **www.paf.fi**. The name "PAF" is short of Ålands Penningautomatförening which directly translated means "The Åland Islands' Slot Machine Association." PAF is an association under public law with the purpose of acquiring funds for the benefit of social welfare on the Åland Islands by offering gaming entertainment to the public. 100% of the net profit which PAF generates is distributed to a variety of charitable organizations and causes on the Åland Islands. PAF operates under the supervision of the government of Åland.

   The members of PAF are nonprofit organizations and foundations on the Åland Islands which represent the societies for social welfare and activities, culture and sports. The eight member associations of PAF are:

   • The Society for Social Welfare
   • The Red Cross
   • The Save the Children Fund

- The Sea Rescue Association
- The Martha Association
- The Disability Association
- The Youth Association
- The Association for Sports (Åland divisions)

Each year a council with a representative from each of the member associations, a representative from the government and a representative from PAF decide to which organizations and causes the funds should be distributed.

2. There is a Gibraltar-based online gaming site at **www.casares.com** with the tag line that states "bet4abetterworld." Legally registered in Gibraltar, this gaming site distributes 20% of its gross revenue to The New World Foundation, an international, nonprofit foundation that strives to create a better future for children and young people in the Third World, and improve the environment on our planet. One of The New World Foundation's current projects is the construction of a children's home in Peru.

Is this the future of North American charitable gambling? With so many North Americans doing online gambling to aid Finnish charities, how long can it be before North America provinces and states sanction their own charitable online games?

One of the best ways for a nonprofit organization to research the online gaming industry is to subscribe to Interactive Gaming News at www .rtgonline.com.

ONLINE FUND-RAISING BEHAVIOR

What kinds of gifts do online supporters give? Do they like to give large gifts? Small gifts? Merchandise purchases?

Greenpeace Canada received 74 gifts or purchases online over a set period of time. They decided to look at those online transactions over that time and uncover who was doing what online. It was determined that 35 of them were one-time donations; 21 were individuals joining the monthly donor club, Friends of the Rainbow Warrior; and 18 individuals purchased merchandise (either a T-shirt or ball cap).

One-Time Donors

The 35 donors who made one-time donations gave a total of $1,705. That works out to an average donation of $48.71 per donor—a higher average donation than a direct mail donor, a door-to-door donor, and a telephone donor.

Monthly Donor Clubs

The 21 donors who joined the monthly donor club gave a total of $297 per month, which, extended over 12 months, is $3,564. The average gift was a $14-a-month deduction. Every monthly gift would be deducted automatically from the donor's credit card.

Merchandise Donors

The 18 donors who purchased a T-shirt or ball cap gave a total of $270 dollars. The average purchase amount was $15.

How Does All of This Compare to "Real World" Donors?

Most of these online donors are first-time donors to Greenpeace Canada, and it is instructive to notice that first-time donors through direct mail give an average of $29 whereas they give $24 at the door. Online donors seem to be more generous—giving an average of $20 to $25 more per gift. Online donors who already give to Greenpeace average $8 to $9 higher per donor.

The most telling difference is in the number of online donors who decide to make a commitment to the monthly donor club in comparison to "real world" donors contacted through the mail or by door to door solicitation. Approximately 10% of all Greenpeace donors are members of the monthly donor club. However, this pales in comparison to the 28% of online donors who chose a monthly donor club over a one-time donation or a merchandise purchase.

What Can Any Nonprofit Learn from This?

The online environment is automated. It is an electronic and computer-driven medium that seems to align itself with the path of least resistance: like automatic deductions from a credit card. Exhibit 1–5 shows how almost three times as many online donors for Greenpeace Canada chose the automated, monthly donor club over any other kind of online generosity in comparison to "real world" donors.

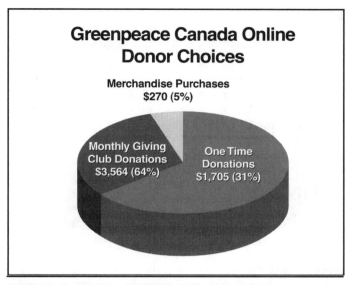

Greenpeace Canada Online Donor Choices

Merchandise Purchases
$270 (5%)

Monthly Giving Club Donations $3,564 (64%)

One Time Donations $1,705 (31%)

EXHIBIT 1–5   Greenpeace Canada: Online Donor Choices

CONCLUSION

The evidence so far, in this very new medium, shows donors and supporters are choosing to give online in a wide variety of ways: from major gifts, to automatic monthly deductions, to single small gifts through a pledge or an online credit card donation.

Nonprofit organizations need to offer their current and prospective supporters as wide a range of online giving options as they do in the "real world." Doing anything else would be ignoring the evidence in this chapter and be putting organizations in the always dangerous position of thinking and deciding for their supporters.

Appendix 1-A

THE ONLINE FUND RAISING CHECKLIST

This Online Fund Raising Checklist has been designed to remind you of the most essential fund raising issues related to your nonprofit organization's Web site.

DIRECT DONATIONS

( ) With the World Wildlife Fund USA increasing their online memberships by 270% from April of 1997 to April of 1998, are you planning to offer your on-line visitors a chance to become members directly from your web site?

( ) With the American Red Cross raising over $128,000 in online credit card donations, are you planning to offer your online visitors a chance to make a secure, credit card donation online?

LARGE GIFTS ONLINE

( ) With the American Red Cross receiving 22 online gifts totalling $49,400, are you planning to offer online visitors a chance to make a large gift on your site?

( ) Have you ensured that a $1,000 gift amount is presented to the prospective online donor?

( ) Have you included information on your Web site to show prospective major donors what an endowment could do for your organization?

( ) Have you ensured that major online donors get a personal approach that is outside of the electronic environment?

( ) Have you used interactive programming to show prospective gift givers what their gift can do in the future? Visit web sites like **imoney.com** or **smartmoney.com** to discover the wealth management tools that could be transferred to major gift/planned gift analysis.

( ) Have you given prospective major/planned gift givers a chance to email financial planners, lawyers, or professional assistance if they have questions about larger gifts?

PLEDGES

( ) Knowing that online pledgers act much like direct mail and telephone pledgers (in regard to use of credit cards and pledge fulfillment rates) have you offered prospective online donors the option of pledging online?

( ) If your nonprofit organization already offers a pledge option in your giving campaigns, then add this online option.

( ) Make sure that the online pledge option is marketed through other mediums (TV, radio, and print).

MERCHANDISE SALES

( ) Have you investigated the possibility of selling extra stock of smaller items like calendars and T-shirts through the Net, like the Rainforest Action Network?

( ) Have you investigated the possibility of offering professional services online?

( ) Have you planned to track online sales to ensure you know which products will sell and which don't?

( ) Have you planned how to get the merchandise delivered to the online merchandise consumer? Have you investigated a sponsorship with a national courier company to lower your delivery costs?

ONLINE AUCTIONS

( ) Have you followed the wise advice of a seasoned online auction practicioner, Brian Erman, and his ten important points in operating a successful online auction through an established auction house?

( ) Have you used free classified web sites (like **www.classified2000.com**) to sell your items?

( ) Have you investigated the efficacy of an online auction house selling your items?

( ) Have you planned your online auctions to have the staff and resources to continue selling items into the future, building a buyer database?

( ) Have you investigated the efficacy of conducting your own online auctions like **www.stardoodles.com**?

( ) Have you followed the wise advice of Paul Natrall, of the Champions for Children Foundation, and his eleven important points in operating a successful online auction on your own?

ONLINE LOTTERIES

( ) If your organization is already involved with game of chance, why aren't you investigating and preparing for online games of chance to raise money since most experts agree that North America, Australia and other jurisidictions will soon allow nonprofits to raise money through online gambling.

( ) Have you followed the wise advice of a seasoned online lottery practicioner, Dwight Mihalicz of the International Red Cross, and his seven important points in operating a successful online lottery?

( ) Have you made sure that your online games of chance are fair and pay out?

( ) Have you reviewed other charitable online lotteries like **www.paf.fi** and **www.casares.com**?

( ) Have you subscribed to Interactive Gaming News at **www.rtgonline.com** to stay on top of this ever-evolving medium?

▼ 2 Who Is on the Net: Demographics

The rank of Internet users under the astrological sign of Taurus: 1

—*Harper's Index*, December 1996

In a medium still very much in its infancy, the measuring tools, the measurers, and the statistical results about the Internet are maddeningly wide ranging.

WHAT IS A NONPROFIT MANAGER TO DO?

When one needs the statistical backup to begin a TV fund-raising campaign or an advertising/awareness campaign in traditional print media, one has solid, reputable statistics that one can trust and one's superiors can believe in. The problem with the Internet is that there is no way one can completely trust a statistic regarding the Internet. As John Quarterman, a respected Internet statistician, says, "The Internet is distributed by nature. This is its strongest feature, since no single entity is in control, and its pieces run themselves, cooperating to form the network of networks that is the Internet. However, because no single entity is in control, nobody knows everything about the Internet."

He goes on to say, "Measuring it is especially hard because some parts choose to limit access to themselves to various degrees. So, instead of measurement, one has various forms of surveying and estimation."

That means that all the statistics presented in this chapter are based on estimates and conjecture. Even if they were absolutely true, growth rates change.

There is only one conclusion that can possibly be drawn from such vague data: *The Internet is getting big, and it is happening quickly.* That means a nonprofit organization has to gather data and try to make sure that it is as trustworthy as possible. Here are a few tips to follow:

- Survey a number of different statistical results on a particular area of the Net one needs to know about (e.g., the number of women online in comparison to men). Then, try to find a mean number (comparing the studies) that reflects a best estimate. The more statistical sources one can compare, the better.
- Trust university-based statisticians more than other sources. They usually care more about their research methodology and are less prone to hyperbole (i.e., they do not have commercial clients to impress) when describing the Net.
- Look for researchers who are conducting rolling studies over a number of years. Their long-range statistics will give your organization a chance to see how a chaotic medium is changing and therefore help in strategic decision making about the Net.

This chapter sets out to do three things for the nonprofit manager or decision maker. First, it will examine who is on the Internet as a whole. Second, it will take a look at who visits nonprofit Web sites. Finally, it will take a look at the demographic profile of people who are giving to nonprofit Web sites. By examining these demographic categories of people on the Internet, one will be able to get a better understanding about who is out there looking for a certain nonprofit Web site.

WHO IS ON THE NET?

Two of the most confusing statistics are "How many people are using the Internet?" and "How many Web sites are there on the Net?"

The Irresponsible Internet Statistic Generator (IISG) site (**http://www.anamorph .com/docs/stats/stats.html**) seen in Exhibit 2–1 puts the widely divergent user projections into humorous perspective.

The site begins with a quote from *Business Week* that "There are 27,000 Web sites, and this number is doubling every 53 days."[1] This statistic was created three years ago, and it is still quoted by newspapers and other media sources. *Business Week* turned out to be quoting someone at Sun Microsystems. (The figures were supposedly true on or about February 20, 1995.)

The IISG site asks, "If this information is correct, and Web growth were to continue at this rate, how many Web sites will there be in December of this year? Or two years from now?" By using the *Business Week* statistical parameters, the IISG

---

[1]Robert Orenstein, *Internet Statistics Generator at Anamorph,* 1995.

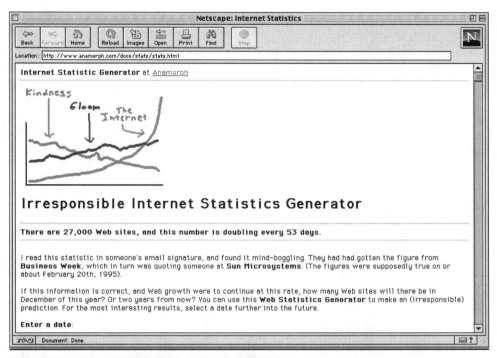

EXHIBIT 2–1   Internet Statistic Generator at *Anamorph*

came up with a figure, as of July 1, 1998, of 251,473,458,316 sites on the World Wide Web (this represents 41.91 Web sites per person on the planet)!

How could this statistic possibly be true? Of course, as the generated number proves, it is impossible for Web growth to continue at this rate. A more responsible figure, which has been widely quoted, is that the number of people that have access to the Internet is doubling every year (as opposed to Internet account holders), starting with 13.5 million Internet potential users as of October 1994. This figure comes from John S. Quarterman at Matrix Information and Directory Services (MIDS), and this growth rate has been accurate for some time now.

Using the Statistics Generator (based on the John S. Quarterman projections), to figure out how many people will have access to the Internet on July 1, 1998, the Generator said that there would be 176,952,246 people who have access to the Internet (this represents 2.95% of the world's population) on that date.

Matrix Information and Directory Services is an organization that gathers Internet statistics and is much more responsible in its presentation of data. They hem and haw and say things like "We do not claim great accuracy for the estimates reported herein." This is not too much different than the statistical washing of hands that many fund raisers and accountants do when they make projections in their areas of expertise.

Matrix Information and Directory Services's terms are well-defined: By Internet users in the statistic above, they mean anyone who can use Internet services such as ftp and the Web. Exhibit 2–2 shows the MIDS Web site (**http://www4 .mids.org/index.html**) and use some of their statistics (one has to pay for a more complete set of data from them) to compare the ones used in this book.

Nonprofit organizations cultivate a special relationship with their members and with the general public. They need to know as much as possible about the composition, behavior, and attitudes of the Internet community.

WHO IS ON THE NET RIGHT NOW?

No one disputes the Internet's tremendous growth and potential, but when one decides to put a nonprofit organization on the Internet, is one simply communicating to 70 million young, white, male computer nerds? The statistics show a different story.

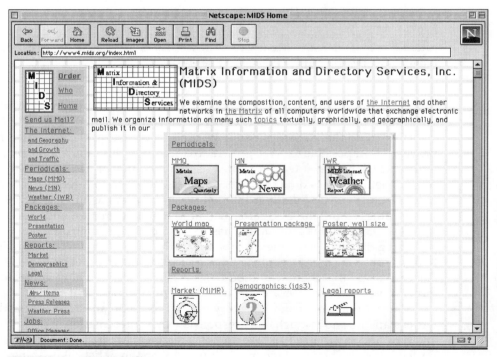

EXHIBIT 2–2   MIDS Web Site

If one listens to the mainstream media, the image of the young, male computer geek is predominant, but if one gets beyond the headlines and digs around in reputable statistics, one finds a more balanced group of Internet users.

Are Internet users the type of people who will support a nonprofit organization? Do they have money to donate? The answer is yes. According to a FIND/SVP Survey published in the June 1995 edition of the U.S. magazine *Internet World*, the average household income of a wired family was $66,700 compared to $42,400 for a nonwired family.

Six months later, a January 1996 survey showed income levels dropping slightly, but the findings still showed an affluent citizenry online, with the average income of an online European family up a little to US$56,000, compared to the U.S. average of US$64,700, and Canada with an average US$59,000.

A November 1996 study by the Georgia Institute of Technology's Graphics, Visualization, and Usability Center (GVU) (a survey with over 59,400 unique responses were collected from over 15,000 unique respondents) indicated that the mean average household income is US$60,800 for all world users. The distribution of income levels was as follows: less than $29K: 18.8%, $30 to $50K: 23.0%, over $50K: 41.1%.

It is the GVU studies that are the most trustworthy about the Internet. This chapter will take a closer look at their findings about who is really using the Internet.

The Georgia Institute of Technology's Graphics, Visualization and Usability Center study is often called the GVU's WWW User Survey, and its homepage can be seen in Exhibit 2–3. The Survey is an excellent example of a trusted, academic rolling study that pioneered the field of Web-based surveying when it was first conducted in January of 1994. Since then, GVU's Surveys have been conducted every six months, providing one of the oldest sets of data on World Wide Web (WWW) and Internet demographics and usage. The findings under each category are taken from GVU's eighth survey (**http://www.cc.gatech.edu/gvu/user_surveys**). The latest survey was completed in November 1997. The following paragraphs discuss what their surveys indicate about some key areas of Internet demographics since 1994.

Age

The average age of users responding to the eighth survey is 35.7 years old. This average is slightly higher than the seventh survey average (35.2) and continues the trend of increasing average age, which has been noted since the fourth survey.

Education

The distribution of educational attainment has been virtually unchanged since the fourth survey. For the eighth survey, 46.96% of respondents have completed a col-

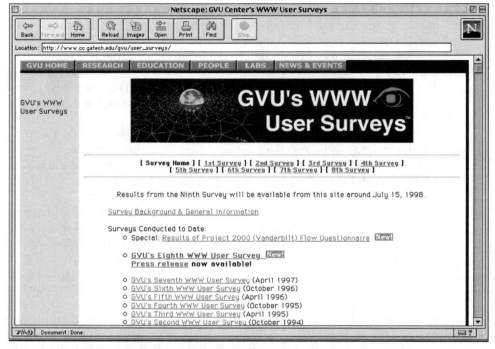

EXHIBIT 2–3   GVU's WWW User Surveys Home Page

lege or advanced degree. (This percentage was 54.24% for the seventh survey.) European respondents continue to report higher levels of educational attainment than U.S. respondents. Commercial Internet service providers are not as widespread in Europe as they are in the United States; as a result, many European users access the Web as a result of their affiliation with a university.

Household Income

The mean average household income is US$53K, which is slightly lower than the previous survey (7th—$58K).

European respondents reported a lower average income ($48.5K) than U.S. respondents ($54K). Europe has a higher percentage of users with incomes less than $19K, which is not surprising because many European users are students.

The percentages of men and women reporting incomes under $50K are very similar. Above $50K, male respondents outnumber female respondents by about 2 to 3%. As one would expect, older users report higher income levels, although there was generally little difference between the 26 to 50 group and the 50+ group.

Gender

The percentage of female respondents to the survey (38.5%) has increased from previous surveys. For the past 1½ years, the gender ratio was very consistent (fifth—31.5%, sixth—31.4%, seventh—31.3%), so an increase of 7% was quite unexpected.

What most people don't realize, however, is that as the number of online subscribers continues to increase, the fastest-growing user group is women. With total online subscribers at somewhere around 50 million by early summer 1998, around 17 million of them will be women.

What are the women who are online like versus the rest of the Net? An Interactive Publishing Alert survey of women online confirms that women who use online services tend to log on frequently and are willing to pay for it. Eighty-two percent of women who responded said they went online at least once a day. By contrast, only 54% of total online users log on daily." In addition, an America Online (AOL) survey found that "women with children log more hours online."

The best customers of the Internet Shopping Network spend about US$2,000 each year—and 30% of these customers were women. Considering that when this statistic was compiled three years ago, women made up only 10% of the total number of users, it demonstrates that women are disproportionately more engaged as online consumers and charitable donors.

Major Occupation

On average, 20.63% of respondents reported being in a computer-related field, 23.14% in education, 21.4% in professional, 11.69% in management, and 23.14% in other occupations. Compared to the previous survey, the percentage of respondents in computers decreased (30.24%), and the percentage in other occupations increased (14.73%).

European users were more likely to be in computers or education than their U.S. counterparts. Female respondents are less likely than male respondents to be in computer-related fields (20.28% female vs. 34.77% male) and in management (9.1% female vs. 13.32% male). Women are more likely to be in education and other occupations. Professional occupations were equal for men and women.

Most Important Issues Facing the Internet

The order of the top two responses has changed from the past two surveys. Currently, the issue that respondents say is most important is privacy (30.49%), followed by censorship (24.18%), and navigation (16.65%).

Among European respondents, navigation and censorship were equally most important, with the next most important being privacy. Among women, privacy was the most important issue. For men, censorship is most important, with privacy a close second.

Primary Place of Access

As with past surveys, the majority of respondents report that they primarily access the Web from home (65.17% eighth vs. 60.38% seventh vs. 63.6% sixth). In Europe, however, only 28.93% (40.10% seventh, 36.7% sixth) report having their primary access from home (59.49% report having it primarily from work). Across all age groups, most access the Web primarily from home, but that is especially true for users over age 50 (84.51%).

Novices clearly are accessing the Web from home (85.96%), whereas experts access the Web both from work (53.36%) and from home (42.22%). There are no observable gender differences.

Race

The majority of respondents identified themselves as "Caucasian/White" (88% eighth vs. 89.35% seventh and 88.1% sixth) which is nearly identical to previous surveys. Of those aged 19 to 25, 5.33% identified themselves as "Asian," with 93.81% of the older users reporting being "Caucasian/White."

Community Building

As with the sixth and seventh surveys, almost half (45.47% eighth vs. 45.06% seventh vs. 46.1% sixth) of the respondents felt more connected to people who share their interests since coming online. Only 2.29% report feeling less connected, although more than a quarter of the respondents (28.45%) state that they do not know. The other 23.79% report feeling equally connected since going online. This provides some evidence for the claim that the Internet is more than just an information resource; rather, it is building new communities based on common interests.

European respondents feel more connected overall than their U.S. counterparts. Younger respondents also feel more connected than older respondents. Gender has little effect on the feeling of connectedness.

Willingness to Pay for Information

Results from the eighth survey are very similar to the seventh survey. Almost half of the respondents cited being able to access the content on other sites as the main reason (41.11%). Next in line, people feel that they are already paying to access the Web via connectivity charges, so why should they pay to access specific sites (33.66%). Another popular reason is that it costs too much to access (8.02%). Only 1.18% state that they would pay regardless.

Years on Internet

Results from this category were used to split respondents into categories of Novice, Intermediate, and Expert users, which were used to analyze other data from this survey. Novices were evenly split—half started on the Internet in the past 6 months and half in the past 6 to 12 months. Most experts (as we have defined them) have been on the Internet for 4 to 6 years (72.33%), with the rest being on for 7 years or more.

The continued migration of users to the Internet is still seen in the eighth survey, which indicates that 36.62% of the users have gone online in the past year. This percentage is higher than for the previous survey (25.34%), but is similar to results from the sixth survey (36.11%). About 7% of respondents have been on the Internet over 7 years, compared to 10% in the seventh survey and 7.14% in the sixth survey.

Respondents from the United States are more likely to have started on the Internet within the past year, whereas respondents from Europe are more likely to have been on for 1 to 3 years.

Female users still are flocking to the Internet, with 42.64% having gone online in the past year, compared to 32.86% for males. Men are more likely than women to have been on the Internet for greater than 4 years.

Use of the Internet by the 50+ age group has increased over the previous survey, with 52.65% having gone online in the past year compared to 33.72% in the seventh survey, 48.26% in the sixth survey, and 55.86% in the fifth survey. The 26 to 50 group have the largest percentage of people on the internet for 7+ years, while the 19 to 25 group have the largest percentage on the Internet for 1 to 6 years.

How Often Do People Use the Web Instead of Watching TV?

Only 12% of respondents report never using the Web instead of watching TV. Large numbers of respondents, though, report doing this on a weekly or even daily basis. Twenty-nine percent use the Web more than once a day instead of watching TV.

What Do People Look For and Purchase on the WWW?

"Other Services" has now risen to the top of the list of products sought after and purchased on the Web. For choices do occur in this question, respondents seek information about hardware and software over $50 (61% and 58%, respectively) and about software under $50 (57%). These are the same top three as in the last survey. However, travel and books/magazines have surpassed hardware under $50 in terms of the percentage of respondents looking for information about these items. For items actually purchased over the Web, books/magazines are the most common (30%), followed by software under $50 (30%) and travel (26%). Overall, respondents seek information on the Web about various items a lot more often than they actually make purchases. The items that are purchased most frequently are not the same items that respondents seek information about most frequently.

How Much Have People Spent in the Past Six Months?

The largest category of respondents has spent less than US$50 on the Web (34%); the next largest category has spent $100 to $500 (24%). Sixteen percent of respondents have spent over $500 on the Web in the last 6 months. These figures are consistent with the previous survey.

Are People Comfortable with Sending Credit Card Information over the WWW?

On issues related to providing credit card information through the Web, there is no clear consensus among respondents. Respondents are divided on whether it is riskier to use a credit card on the Web or to use it over the phone. Being a well-known vendor makes a difference to many respondents (48%). Forty-five percent of respondents say that having to give credit card information is not the main reason they do not shop on the Web, but another 36% say that it is the main reason.

SURVEYS CONDUCTED OFFLINE

It may be useful to look at surveys conducted outside of the Internet, in order to understand how people online and off view the world.

For example, one can look at *Wired* magazine's December 1997 poll, "The Digital Citizen," to understand some of the politics of Netizens and how they feel about the idea of community. *Wired* is a slick commercial magazine, which often treats the Internet as a potential utopian free market environment.

In the *Wired*/Merrill Lynch Forum Digital Citizen Survey, 1,444 Americans were polled about technology and society. The respondents were divided into four groups: Superconnected, Connected, Semiconnected, and Unconnected (all to reflect their levels of Internet connectivity).

This survey reveals that the most connected citizens are knowledgeable, tolerant, civic minded, and radically committed to change. Connected citizens are twice as likely to know the Chief Justice of the Supreme Court of the United States. Seventy-nine percent of these connected citizens were able to name the Speaker of the House of Representatives (Newt Gingrich), while only 49% of unconnected Americans could do so. The two connected groups felt that diversity was an asset in the workplace 80% of the time, whereas the two unconnected groups felt it was an asset only 49% percent of the time. The connected also believe that they can change the world (68.5%) as opposed to the unconnected (only 48%).

They are optimistic about the future. Sixty-six percent of the Superconnected and Connected groups believe that the future will be better and believe that technology is a force for good. It is also interesting to note that the most connected citizens are highly engaged in politics. More than 60% of the connected vote, much higher than the United States average.

What this poll tells us is that online citizens tend to be politically active and believe in social change. They have a libertarian streak, believing that the Internet should be policed by its online citizens. Because they vote so often and want to see positive change, it is good news for nonprofits online, which are seeking people who identify with their messages about positive social change.

WHO IS VISITING NONPROFIT WEB SITES?

Some nonprofits are conducting online surveys from their Web sites in order to understand who is visiting them. One good example is the Arthritis Canada Web site. Arthritis Canada claims that it gets 13,000 visits to its Web site every week.

Of those who visit the site, some 67% are female and 33% male. The average age of the visitor is 45 years. These visitors are educated as follows: 39% college, 33% university, and 28% secondary school. The visitors have had arthritis for just under 10 years, and 89% said that they were collecting information from the site for their own personal use. It seems clear that in the case of this Web site, people who suffer from arthritis are flocking to the site. They are also predominantly women. As yet, it is not known whether there have been any online donations made to Arthritis Canada.

Another organization that has extensively examined the visitors to its Web site is World Vision. Larry Short, its Internet Program Manager, recently set out their extensive measuring tools for visitors to the site. They have a number of ways to try and understand their visitors, including a survey, a guestbook, a child sponsorship area, an appeals section (also for donations), and a feedback mechanism (see Exhibit 2–4).

WHO LIKES THE SITE?

How can a nonprofit organization know if its web site is a success with online visitors? What benchmarks are there out there for a well received Web site? World Vision USA bravely puts forward the results from 1,423 respondents who sent back an answer when asked to "Please give us an overall rating for this site."

Many nonprofit managers are being confronted by board members, citizen supporters and staff asking them to prove whether their site is being well received. Now a manager in charge of the Internet can use the World Vision results as a benchmark, something to measure their results by.

Hits

It's proving to be a challenge for nonprofit organizations to tell their staff, board members, or corporate supporters exactly how many people are visiting their site. Just what does a hit represent? How many pages will each visitor ask for? Again, Larry Short and World Vision offer their "hit" analysis since May of 1997 until April of 1998 (See Exhibit 2–5).

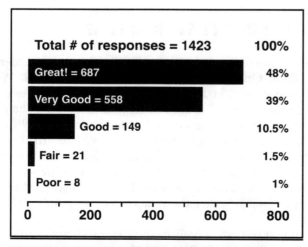

EXHIBIT 2–4   Overall Rating of a Web Site: World Vision

Larry Short states, "Changes in statistical software beginning Feb. 1, 1998 decreased our apparent number of 'hits.' The old software included a graphics request on the server as a 'hit,' and the new software only counts page requests. Thus the 'hits:visits' ratio for the last three months, as well as the total, may be skewed."

It is important to note that with statistical software that counts both graphics and pages as separate hits, World Vision had an average of 13 to 16 hits or information requests for a page or a graphic for every visitor to the site. Now, with the advent of more accurate statistical software in February of 1998, World Vision is receiving approximately four to nine hits per visitor to the site. Every nonprofit organization should try to remember these ratios for their own web sites.

Now, let us move from the statistics of Web site visits to demographics. This chapter has previously looked at demographic information from studies that are not specifically gathered from nonprofit Web sites. Once again, World Vision has compiled the demographic information from its web site from April of 1997 until April of 1998 (see Exhibit 2–6. Data was collected 4/25/97 to 4/30/98).

Month	Total Hits	Estimated Visits	Hits:Visits Ratio
April '97	* 10,000	500	20:1
May '97	79,546	5,983	13:1
June '97	109,320	8,220	13:1
July '97	147,343	11,067	13:1
Aug '97	159,681	12,276	13:1
Sept '97	182,100	11,220	16:1
Oct '97	264,430	19,499	14:1
Nov '97	347,880	25,380	14:1
Dec '97	299,832	18,693	16:1
Jan '98	354,392	22,289	16:1
Feb '98	211,904	24.080	9:1
Mar '98	** 124,866	31,242	4:1
Apr '98	** 94, 018	24,742	4:1
Total	**2,385,312**	**215,191**	**11:1**

* Partial month (five days); hits and visits estimated

** Changes in statistical software beginning Feb. 1, 1998 decreased our apparent number of "hits". The old software included a graphics request on the server as a "hit", and the new software only counts page requests. Thus, the "Hits:Visits" ratio for the last 3 months, as well as the total, may be skewed.

EXHIBIT 2–5　Hit Analysis: World Vision

Demographic	Subtotal #	Subtotal %	Total #	Total %
Female	707	47.0%		
Male	671	44.6%		
No Response	125	8.30%	1,503	100%
Single	696	46.30%		
Married	607	40.40%		
Divorced	70	4.70%		
Widowed	6	0.40%		
No Response	124	8.30%	1,503	100%
17 and under	192	12.80%		
18 to 25	381	25.30%		
26 to 34	301	20.00%		
35 to 44	276	18.40%		
45 to 54	193	12.80%		
55 to 64	38	2.50%		
65 and over	10	0.70%		
No response	112	7.50%	1,503	100%
$15,000 or less	365	24.30%		
$15,000 - $29,999	185	12.30%		
$30,000 - $44,999	174	11.60%		
$45,000 - $59,999	117	7.80%		
$60,000 - $74,999	48	3.20%		
$75,000 - $99,999	75	5.00%		
$100,000 or more	37	2.50%		
Not a wage earner	30	2.00%		
Less than $15,000	14	0.90%		
$15 - $30,000	21	1.40%		
$30 - $45,000	15	1.00%		
$45 - $60,000	20	1.30%		
No response	402	26.70%	1,503	100%

* These categories (in gray) were established only between April 25 and May 30, 1997. The categories were then rewritten to correspond with those in white.

EXHIBIT 2–6   World Vision U.S. Guestbook Demographics

Three items stand out in this demographic study done by World Vision USA:

• Though the Internet is still used by more men than women, this nonprofit web site was visited and used by more women (47%) than men (44.6%). This may mean that more women visit nonprofit sites in general. Other nonprofit sites should take that possibility into account when constructing their own online presence. The Arthritis Society Canada statistics also confirm a majority of online users of their site are women not men.

- Though individuals under 35 years old made up the majority of visitors to the World Vision site (56.1%), the number of visitors who were 35 years and older was still significant (over 34%). The number of Internet users who are 35 and older is growing faster than those under 35 (who were early adopters) and nonprofit organizations should be aware that the majority of their visitors in just the next few years will probably be older than 35.
- The majority of visitors to the World Vision web site were lower income earners though the average income of Internet users in the GVU Survey is quite high. It may be that nonprofit sites like World Vision (with a high profile with students through its 30 hour Famine program) attract a disproportionate number of lower income earners who are students or recent graduates.

WHO IS MAKING ONLINE DONATIONS TO NONPROFIT WEB SITES?

Many nonprofit managers are wondering if the Internet is a world where money does not exist—a place where only information transfers here and there. However, it is clear that people are starting to give online (as outlined in Chapter One). Just who are these donors?

This is a large body of potential supporters one wants to begin cultivating online right now. Until now, there has been very little data about online nonprofit donors. However, for the purposes of this book, Greenpeace Canada, World Wildlife Fund, and World Vision have kindly provided data about their online donors.

Greenpeace Canada's Online Donations

First, one can look at one of the few studies of online donors compiled by Greenpeace Canada. (See Exhibit 2-7.)

At first glance, the data seems to point to the fact that online donors are considerably younger, well educated (but not as well educated in further education) and quite a bit more affluent. For nonprofit organizations, this is an interesting demographic group that has been the most difficult to reach with traditional fundraising media like direct mail, the telephone, and door-to-door donors. This young, well-educated and very affluent group who like to give online could be the future of fundraising for nonprofits in the next millennium.

	ONLINE	DIRECT MAIL
AGE:		
<35	65%	18%
35–44	21%	29%
45–54	14%	15%
55+	0%	33%
EDUCATION:		
University	52%	68%
Technical/Community College	17%	17%
High School or Less	31%	13%
FAMILY INCOME:		
<$35,000	10%	32%
$35,000–$50,000	29%	22%
$50,000–$80,000	41%	17%
$80,000+	20%	17%
GENDER:		
Male	68%	40%
Female	32%	60%

EXHIBIT 2–7   Greenpeace Online Donor Demographics vs. Direct Mail Donor Demographics

Further Findings

Greenpeace Canada wanted to know more about what these early online donors thought about making a gift online. So they asked the following three questions and received the corresponding results:

1. Do you have any concerns about online transactions?
     Yes (45%) No (55%)
2. Have you ever made an online donation or purchase with another nonprofit organization?
     Yes (14%) No (86%)
3. Will you make online donations your preferred way to help nonprofit organizations in the future? Why or why not?
     Yes (48%) No (34%) Don't Know (18%)

It would seem that the donors to Greenpeace are "virgin" online donors—making a gift to that organization their first online gift. This is important for nonprofits to remember. Unlike the other forms of fundraising, these donors are not sharing their online giving attention with any other nonprofit, and every nonprofit should try to keep the undivided attention of their online donor with excellent relationship building.

Also, these donors are cautious about their online giving. Almost half of them have security concerns about giving online, yet many gave simply because they trusted Greenpeace. One survey respondent stated, "I wouldn't trust most commercial credit card opportunities online, but I trust a nonprofit like Greenpeace and accept their statement that their online form is secure." Every nonprofit should understand that while many online users are wary of using their credit card online, they are willing to give a nonprofit the benefit of the doubt.

Finally, a majority of Greenpeace donors indicated that they would make online giving a preferred way to help Greenpeace and other organizations in the future. This cautious optimism for future online donations needs to be nurtured by every nonprofit organization.

To further define the behavior of their online donors, Greenpeace Canada asked them, "What other nonprofit web sites have you visited?" The online donors tended to use the Internet to visit other environment-related Web sites that included:

- Alberta Environmental Network
- Green Party
- Sierra Club
- WCWC
- PETA
- Canadian Parks and Wilderness
- WWF Canada
- Panda

Nonprofit organizations need to understand that they share the Internet with a wide variety of other like-minded organizations and online users are bound to see all of the Net as their resource. For that reason, it may be in the interest of a nonprofit organization to give links to like-minded sites, although there is the possibility that the online visitor may travel to another site and make an online donation there.

A final question asked the Greenpeace Online donors was whether they would like to receive future publications from Greenpeace in an electronic format, like email? They replied:

Yes (94%) No (3%) No answer (3%)

That answer should tell every nonprofit organization that they should begin to investigate how to take the relationship developed from fundraising techniques with other media (like direct mail, face-to-face, or the phone) and begin an online relationship that includes publications, correspondence, and yes, future online solicitations.

CONCLUSION

It is difficult to get exact statistics about the Internet, but this chapter has tried to direct the nonprofit manager to some respected and trustworthy statistical sources. The chapter has also been able to do a rare examination of demographic results from a number of nonprofit web sites.

As the chapter outlined at the beginning, all the statistics presented in this chapter are based on estimates and conjecture. And even if they were absolutely true, the Net is constantly changing from day to day. But there are a number of general conclusions one can draw from the statistics in this chapter:

1. Online users are younger than in more traditional media.
2. Online users to nonprofit sites tend to be women.
3. Online users tend to be more affluent but not better educated than donors giving through traditional media like direct mail.
4. Online donors tend to be men and not women. Perhaps men, as early adopters, have come first to feeling comfortable in making an online credit card donation.
5. Online donors tend to be younger and more affluent than donors giving through more traditional media, like direct mail, but surprisingly, they are less educated.

There is at least one conclusion to be drawn from these demographics: these online "Netizens" are a demographic strata that more traditional fundraising media have had a hard time attracting. Since they are such a valuable group of donors for the future of all nonprofits, one needs to take a careful look at Net statistics, draw accurate conclusions, and then make projections as to how to reach these potential donors and supporters.

Appendix 2-A

THE ONLINE DEMOGRAPHICS CHECKLIST

This Online Demographics Checklist has been designed to remind you of the most important demographics issues related to your nonprofit organization's Web site.

SURVEYS

Have you tried to follow the following tips to find the most trustworthy online statistics?

( ) Survey a number of different statistical results on a particular area of the Net one needs to know about (like the number of woman online in comparison to men). Then try to find a mean number (comparing the studies) that reflects a best estimate. The more statistical sources one can compare, the better.

( ) Trust university-based statisticians more than other sources. They usually care more about their research methodology and are less prone to hyperbole (i.e., they don't have commercial clients to impress) when describing the Net.

( ) Look for researchers who are conducting rolling studies over a number of years. Their long-range statistics will give your organization a chance to see how a chaotic medium is changing and help in a strategic decision making about the Net.

( ) Have you bookmarked The Georgia Institute of Technology's Graphics, Visualization and Usability Center study—often called the GVU's WWW User Survey? It's a good example of a university-based, rolling study.

NONPROFIT ONLINE DEMOGRAPHICS

( ) With nonprofit online demographics showing that online users are younger than in more traditional media, have you made Internet content and strategy decisions to take the age factor into account?

( ) With nonprofit online demographics showing that online users tend to be women not men, have you made Internet content and strategy decisions to take that gender factor into account?

( ) With nonprofit online demographics showing that online users tend to be more affluent, but not better educated, than donors to more traditional media like direct mail, have you made Internet content and strategy decisions to take those factors into account?

( ) With nonprofit online demographics showing that online donors tend to be men and not women, have you made Internet content and strategy decisions to take those factors into account?

3 ▼ Seeing Is Believing: How People Read Online

During a day in the life of a nonprofit organization's supporter or donor, he experiences the world with the aid of his senses. He sees, feels, smells, tastes, and hears his surroundings, filtering the stimuli to find meaning and relevance. Online, his expectations to find stimulation are similar, but his experience is radically different from the real world.

Imagine a supporter attempting to cross a busy street on his way to a special event put on by an organization. He checks the streetlight and looks right, then left. He listens for the sound of traffic, of screeching brakes or honking horns. Depending on what he perceives, he places a cautious or a confident foot off of the curb. He crosses the street and safely continues on his way to the special event.

Now, imagine that journey with only a single sense to guide him. Imagine that he cannot hear or feel, but only see. Then imagine that his range of vision is severely limited to what is directly in front of him. With that single vista before him, his reliance on the streetlight increases dramatically.

This is what it is like in the online world, where, through the window of a computer screen, a Web traveler experiences a multidimensional universe with a single sense. Stripped of the collective power of their senses, Web site visitors can feel confused and unsure. Because what they see is determined by someone else, their dependence on visual cues, or online street signs, becomes much stronger than in a "real world" environment.

In addition, it is more difficult to read online than in traditional media. Light coming from computer screens, varying monitor sizes, color palettes, and resolutions all conspire to play havoc with one's eyes. Therefore, when people read online, they are most engaged when that reading is made easy for them.

LEARNING FROM GOOD DIRECT MAIL WRITING

Nonprofit organizations have always had some guidance in making their printed materials easier to read. There are a wide range of resources that organizations can rely on. However, when one looks for studies of how people read online, there is little that is useful. That is good and bad for nonprofits who are creating Web sites—bad because the organizations are not completely sure that what they are doing online is comprehensible to visitors.

However, it is good that there are excellent and relevant studies about how people read printed material.[1] Throughout the book, *Type and Layout*, sets out nine golden rules for direct mail writing that a nonprofit organization can also apply to its online writing:

1. Elegant serif faces are comprehended by more readers than sans serif faces.
2. The use of high-chroma color, such as hot red or process red—especially in headline text—will increase comprehension.
3. People begin reading from the top left and move down to the bottom right. This gravity is at work on screen as well. Therefore, headlines and important information should be at the top left.
4. Text color should be black.
5. Text in high-intensity colors is difficult to read.
6. The higher the percentage of colored background tint beyond 10%, the less comprehensible the text.
7. Black text on a white background is the most legible.
8. Any reverse-out text is much less legible than no reverse out text.
9. Totally justified-setting text is much more legible than ragged-right or -left text.

BEYOND THE RULES OF THE WRITTEN PAGE

With the preceding list as a rough guide, every nonprofit organization needs to make sure it highlights its logo with placement and design, combined with a single compelling image. That logo will have a much greater impact than a dozen bright buttons and flashing icons. It is important for every nonprofit Web designer to make ample use of negative space instead of crowding together columns of text and banks of images. Using negative space makes good Web sites eminently more legible. The Ploughshares Fund page seen in Exhibit 3–1 provides crisp narrative imagery to augment concise text. Just as dark text set against pastel and off white shades reduces eyestrain, brightly colored or heavily patterned backgrounds can make the online experience unpleasant or even painful.

[1]Colin Wheidon, *Type and Layout: How Typography and Design Can Get Your Message Across*, Strathmoor Press, 1984.

THE PLOUGHSHARES FUND

SUPPORTING EFFORTS TO BUILD GLOBAL SECURITY IN THE NUCLEAR AGE

**BAN
LAND
MINES**

**PREVENT
ARMED
CONFLICT**

**RESTRAIN
THE WEAPONS
TRADE**

**CUT
PENTAGON
WASTE**

**CLEAN UP OUR
RADIOACTIVE
ENVIRONMENT**

**FIGHT NUCLEAR
TERRORISM AND
PROLIFERATION**

GRANTS + SUPPORT US + FREE NEWSLETTER + ABOUT US + SEARCH

EXHIBIT 3–1   Use of Whitespace: The Ploughshares Fund

Iconography is one of the great tools of the Web and it is discussed in more detail in Chapter Four. Readers are drawn to illustrations, and photographs help to narrate a message online just as they do in print and on television. They add impact and meaning to a page. Online, however, readers look to images to provide more than information. They rely on graphical elements to guide them in their journey. Therefore, although the temptation to use a wide variety of colorful buttons and blinking icons may be strong, it is important to remember that images online can serve a second, vital function. Exhibit 3–2 is an example of an elegant and inexpensive approach to a nonprofit organization's home page.

With print, we move through a linear progression from the top of a page to the bottom. We can see where we are going and where we have been. Online, the exact dimensions of a reader's screen represent an enclosed universe. Web site visitors cannot know that important information is available just below the perimeter of their screen unless a nonprofit organization tells them. That becomes very important to the reader because when a nonprofit creates the front page (or home page) for its site, it is working with a canvas that is much longer than it is wide. Every nonprofit organization should think that it is writing on an electronic page (the computer screen) that is an average of 10 to 11 inches wide and 7 or 8 inches long.

Founded in 1994 and based in New York, Action Without Borders is a nonprofit organization that promotes the sharing of ideas, information and resources to help build a world where all people can live free, dignified and productive lives.

Action Without Borders, formerly called the Contact Center Network, is a 501(c)(3) nonprofit organization.

To date, AWB has been funded by donations from friends and supporters, and by grants and in-kind contributions from Aladdin Knowledge Systems, Inc., the AT&T Foundation, the Markle Foundation, and the David and Lucille Packard Foundation

Who works here   In the News   What people are saying about us

EXHIBIT 3–2   Iconography: Action Without Borders

This means that they must make sure that there are words at the top of the home page that keep the visitor attentive and intrigued enough that they will wait for the whole site to download. If possible, a nonprofit should try to put everything on its home page on the first screen the visitor sees, because the more text that must be scrolled down, the better chance a nonprofit has of the online visitor's hitting the *Back* button and getting out of its site.

Sun Microsystems, one of the largest Internet-related computer companies in the world, has written a Guide to Web Style. In it, they state:

Scrolling the browser window allows a reader to advance in the text with less loss of mental "context" than does following a link. This advantage lasts up to about four screens full of text. After that, there is a tendency for people to lose their context, and get frustrated with the mechanism of scrolling, and their inability to keep track of what's else-where on the page.[2]

Therefore, every nonprofit should do its best to write text that does not demand a lot of scrolling for the online reader.

Successful Web sites respect the online reader's greater need for clarity of design and layout. They begin with a home page that fits, whenever possible, onto a single, nonscrolling screen and that uses iconography to help tell a story. They use recognizable visual metaphors as virtual streetlights to guide the reader safely from one page to the next. Exhibit 3–3 provides a combination of direct, concise descriptions with helpful iconography for the National Film Board of Canada.

Why is it important to create a concise, single-screen front page? Not only will a nonprofit begin to lose visitors by having a home page that demands a lot of scrolling (as mentioned earlier), but it will lose people if its first page does not come up quickly.

When someone decides to visit a nonprofit's Web site, he or she is probably sitting at a computer in his or her office or at home, connected by modem through an Internet account, using browser software (like Microsoft's Explorer or Netscape's Navigator), and looking at graphics, text, and perhaps audio and video.

Using a standard setup, it probably takes the average Internet visitor a minimum of 5 to 10 seconds to see a simple home page (with a few graphics and text). A research paper presented by Walt Howe and Delphi Internet Services Corporation in 1997 found that for every 10 seconds it takes for graphics to load before the page contents can be seen, a nonprofit risks losing 20% of its remaining viewers.

Therefore, every nonprofit organization will want to create its site's home page and then test it. How long does it take to download on the average machine (a Pentium computer, with a 28.8 modem with 16 RAM)? Every organization should get staff and volunteers to call up the home page on their computers and time it. Every nonprofit organization should call up its site during heavy traffic times (mid-evening, around 8:00 P.M. EST) and then during times of lighter traffic (9:00 A.M. EST) and at noon (EST) to see how long it takes for its home page to fully appear on the computer screen. It is surprising how many nonprofit organizations do not take the time to conduct this simple test.

Here are some quick and hard rules to make sure any nonprofit Web site comes up fast enough for impatient Web readers:

• Forget about putting lots of content on a main page. Keep it modest and create links to other pages behind the first.
• Keep the files as small as possible. Find ways to reduce the size of the graphics (there are tricks of the trade).

[2]See **www.sm.com/styleguide**.

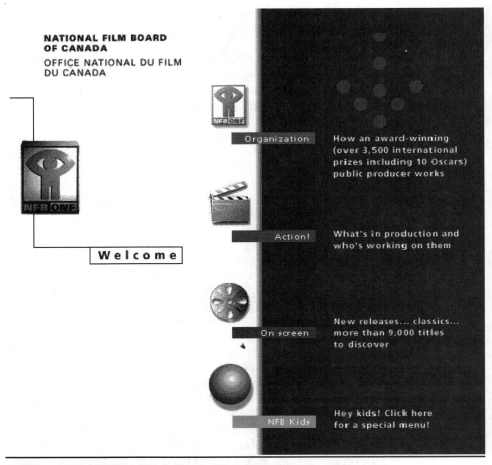

NATIONAL FILM BOARD OF CANADA
OFFICE NATIONAL DU FILM DU CANADA

Welcome

Organization — How an award-winning (over 3,500 international prizes including 10 Oscars) public producer works

Action! — What's in production and who's working on them

On screen — New releases... classics... more than 9,000 titles to discover

NFB Kids — Hey kids! Click here for a special menu!

EXHIBIT 3–3   Iconography: The National Film Board of Canada

- Always use height and width tags with graphics, which allows text to appear before the graphics finish loading.
- Do not use a resolution beyond 72 dots per inch because computer screens cannot project a picture more detailed than this.
- Use low-quality photos and pictures saved as .gif files. Don't worry—better graphics do not look any better than lower standard graphics on a Web site.
- Use GIF files for solid colors, text art, cartoons, and poster art, and use as few colors as possible.

What follows is a reminder about how to get readers to take action through a printed medium such as direct mail. In numerous studies, researchers have found that there are two points at which people throw away printed material. The first throw-away wave happens after about 20 seconds. That is the average time it takes someone to read quickly through a letter or newsletter and decide whether to continue. With a Web site, nonprofits have about 10 seconds before the first 20 percent wave decide to leave the Web site, and another 10 seconds before the next 20 percent is lost. If nonprofits follow the previous recommendations about online writing, they will keep more readers engaged on their Web site.

USE OF COLORS

There can be many colors at play on a Web site. Every nonprofit organization has the opportunity to use more colors and textures on its Web site than on its printed material. However, readers may become confused unless the use of colors follows some common sense rules.

First, always be aware that the hypertext links in a Web site can use a number of color combinations—one color for an unclicked hypertext link and another to indicate to online readers that they have used that link before. Every nonprofit needs to know how its two color choices look in relation to the color of the text and any background color chosen for its Web pages. This is already more to think about than with printed material! There are a number of Web sites where the color of the hypertext link is the same color as the background. It becomes very difficult to see the hypertext link and know whether a visitor has clicked on that link in the past.

Color and design can be used to confusing effect as a background for a nonprofit's Web site. The easiest choice is to use a simple white background, which helps the hypertext links, text, graphics, and pictures all appear clearly. However, there are strategies to use elaborate and effective backgrounds without confusing the reader. For example, the Ducks Unlimited Canada home page (**www.ducks.ca**) seen in Exhibit 3–4 has a soft, fluffy, and effective background of feathers floating across the screen. To ensure that its hypertext links and text are legible, it has sunk them in green surrounded by a large box. If the text and links were on their own in the downy background, the visitor would probably have a difficult time seeing all the information clearly and comfortably.

BUILDING A NONPROFIT WEB SITE TO BE COMPREHENSIBLE

The architecture of a site is key to its readers' experience. There are no corridors one can follow in a straight line online, only a vast number of rooms with many

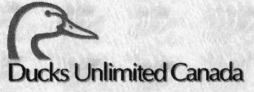

Our Mission: Ducks Unlimited Canada's mission is to conserve wetlands and associated habitats for the benefit of North America's waterfowl, which in turn provide healthy environments for wildlife and people.

Ducks Unlimited Canada

'The nation's most trusted and respected conservation organization'
Angus Reid Group, April 1995

Habitat Programs	Membership	Conservator Magazine
Buy Ducks	What's Hot	Research and Education
DU Staff and Volunteer Options		
Please Participate in Our Internet Survey		

Dial toll-free in Canada!
1-800-665-DUCK

EXHIBIT 3–4   **Effective Use of Texture: Ducks Unlimited Canada**

doors—each door leading to another room. A nonprofit should think of a house built 50 stories high, with one room on top of the other. As visitors navigate the house, learning and accessing information, they travel upward from the ground floor toward the attic, dozens of floors above. The progression is linear and seems natural at first, but online it soon becomes impractical and frustrating. If on the second floor, for example, a visitor reads an article about senior care and on the thirtieth something about housing resources, there would be no way for the visitor to get back to the information about seniors without descending 28 floors.

Now, imagine a house built like a series of rings surrounding a central courtyard. The number of rooms is the same as in the tower but in this house they are organized so that the visitors is never more than two or three doors away from any other. The visitor can easily relate an experience in one area of the structure to another. So it is with hypertext linked documents. Each leap is like going through a doorway into another room.

If a nonprofit remembers that the online world is perceived as multidimensional and that online readers have only sight to guide them, a nonprofit will become even more sensitive to the need for intelligent navigation tools within the architecture of its site. Deep in the third tier of a 100-page site, with only memory to guide visitors, they are more likely to exit a site in panic or impatience than traverse their way back up to the home page on the surface.

The National Film Board of Canada's site map (seen in Exhibit 3–5) displays a well-thought-out three-tiered hierarchy that makes navigation a breeze.

Successful nonprofit Web sites respond to their readers' unique online needs. They use site maps to provide points of reference and to encourage widespread site visitation. They group information logically, by subject, date, or theme. They use colors to delineate different sections of their sites, knowing that familiar colors will trigger associations and increase their readers' comfort levels. They are consistent in their use of navigational iconography, designing tags or labels that change color, content, or shape to indicate different areas of a Web site. A tool bar guarantees that visitors always know where they are as the navigation bar changes to reflect their place on the site.

HOW DO ONLINE READERS READ?

The fact that the Web is vast is common knowledge. It is a message that is repeated over and over to first-time users and a reality that has been proven to hard-core

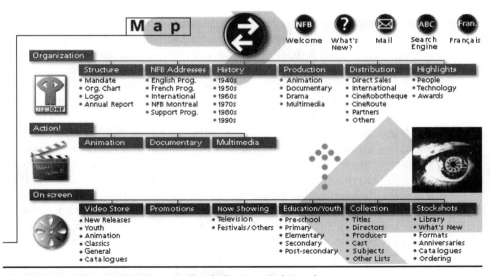

EXHIBIT 3–5   Effective Site Maps: National Film Board of Canada

Net denizens. Choice is the cornerstone of the online world and its users know this. They move, they surf, they jump from site to site with none of the commitment inherent in their experience with other media.

In a review of online studies looking at how people use the Net, it appears that there are two major types of readers inhabiting the Web: browsers and seekers. Browsers are using the Web like a recreational vehicle on a random road trip. They surf from site to site, looking for enticement. Seekers are researching, excavating with intent. Both are demanding, impatient, and promiscuous, but for different reasons. They both skim text, looking to derive as much meaning from as few words as possible. They keep one hand on the virtual doorknob, paying more attention to hyperlinked words than to any others on the page. They know that they are always just a few mouse clicks away from another experience, another opportunity to be informed, entertained, or enlightened. They assign less value to words onscreen than they do on paper. Even so, they are far less tolerant of spelling and grammatical errors than one would expect within such a disposable medium.

There is a charming irony to the fact that the more value online readers assign to what they see onscreen, the more likely they are to print it out. This is especially important for those in the nonprofit sector. Within this virtual three-dimensional world, both types of readers have a heightened awareness of the fourth dimension—time. A fast-loading site, however inane, is more likely to hold the interest of a browsing visitor than whatever might be behind the mystery of a three-minute download.

The International Development Research Centre adds value with elegant imagery but saves on download time by loading grayscale images that are then replaced by more sophisticated, full-color illustrations after the initial download of the site (see Exhibit 3–6). Respect the reader by giving your nonprofit site continuity and an activity level that keeps the attention of each reader.

Your visitors have spent a great deal of money, time, or effort to get online and expect to be repaid quickly. After all, if they wanted to wait around for information, they would take a bus to the library.

Nonprofit Web sites designed to attract and retain browsers and seekers give value in different ways. They tempt browsers with elegant images, virtual bumper stickers, quizzes, surveys, and inclusive language. They show their wares up front and offer ways to include the visitor in their cause, but they should still try to follow the rules outlined in this chapter.

Even a little giveaway can go a long way. At **www.idealist.org**, visitors are encouraged to pick up a button that, like a cyber bumper sticker, they can place with pride on their own Web sites. Seekers can be tempted best by fast-loading home pages that clearly and briefly outline the contents of the site with as few words as possible, leaving the lengthy documents within easy reach for printing out or reading online.

The Office

Research

Resources

International Development Research Centre

The International Development Research Centre is a public corporation created by the Canadian government to help communities in the developing world find solutions to social, economic, and environmental problems through research.

Johannesburg Office

The **Johannesburg Office** responds to the needs of South and Southern African countries.

EXHIBIT 3–6   Grayscale Images as Part of Gradually Appearing Images

---

MEMORY

Brent Johnston, Donor Relations Campaign Officer for the University of Toronto, has come up with some intriguing findings about human memory that can be applied to a nonprofit's Web site design. He recounts what he has discovered in a series of articles on human memory and how it can be applied to the Web: "Most individuals can't remember more than three items, numbers, or objects together. But then how do we remember telephone numbers? Humans group the numbers in three categories and remember the numbers that way. We'd put 416 together, then 345, then the last four digits.[3]

Brent continues, "So, if we understand how human memory creates categories, we can apply this to the Internet. If a nonprofit web site creates eight content icons and groups them together, it will be hard for a visitor, as they scroll down the page, to remember more than three of the icons. However, if a nonprofit decides to break up those eight icons into three distinct categories, then a visitor will have an easier time remembering those icons or content areas. For example, a

---

[3]Brent Johnston, phone interview with author, 23 April 1998.

nonprofit might create a navigation bar at the bottom of the home page with three categories: return to home page, contact us, and search. The top of the page could have three icons: Who we are, New Stuff, and Giving.[4]

Following Brent's advice, a nonprofit's home page that is constructed with the limitations of human memory could look something like Exhibit 3–7.

Most studies of online readers concentrate on the commercial world and do not look exclusively at the nonprofit sector. The author has been lucky enough to be given an inside look at the first part of an extensive study of online readers and how they relate to nonprofit Web sites. In an interview with Marc Nohr, Creative Director with Burnett Associates, one of the most respected fund-raising firms in Europe, he revealed the following findings from their study, "Charities Online New Media, New Relationships."[5] Individuals who had both given to a nonprofit organization and used the Internet over the previous 12 months were studied. Before bringing them in for a focus group study, they asked these donors/Internet users to go online and view eight charity Web sites:

- American Red Cross
- One World (an online charity)
- Greenpeace International
- Multiple Sclerosis Society of America
- The National Trust (U.K.)
- Save the Children
- Water Aid (a U.K. charity)
- Relief Net (an online charity)

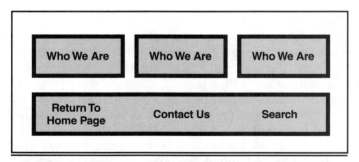

EXHIBIT 3–7   Constructing a Home Page Considering the Limitations of Human Memory

[4]Johnston, phone conversation with author.
[5]Charities Online "New Media, New Relationships" (Burnett Associates, September 1997).

When these donors/Internet users were asked who they thought would be on the Net, no one thought of charities first. Instead, they thought of commercial or personal interests. When pressed further to think about the Net and nonprofits, the participants admitted that they were not impressed by the nonprofit sites they saw. They also believed that there would be a small number of nonprofit Web sites worth visiting.

This study also helps nonprofit organizations refine the idea that there are two kinds of readers: browsers and seekers. Among nonprofit Web surfers, there appears to be four kinds of users:

- Surfers—People who move about the Web without a goal or destination in mind. It is very difficult to get their attention and keep it when they stumble across your nonprofit Web site.
- Paddlers—People who still zoom around the Web but often find focus while they are online. It is easier to get their attention and keep it once they have stumbled onto your nonprofit Web site.
- News junkies—People who look for the Web to supplement their other media outlets' information. For example, if there is an article in a newspaper on homelessness, they will search for a Web site on homelessness to get more information.
- Info seekers—People who are very specific searchers. They use the Net as a primary source of information on issues important to them, and they know how to find what they need.

The largest number of readers fell into the first category, and each category thereafter was progressively smaller as a percentage of total readers. Many findings in the study were counterintuitive. For example, the brand strength of a nonprofit organization influenced expectations on what kind of Web site its public wanted to see. For example, the American Red Cross's site was disappointing to many vistors in this study because a lot was expected from this high-profile organization. However, Water Aid, a nonprofit with a very low public profile, impressed most visitors. Paradoxically, the study participants were disappointed in Web sites that did not ask them to give directly online, but they also said they would not give if they had been given the opportunity.

A NONPROFIT ORGANIZATION'S RESPONSIBILITY TO LEGIBILITY

There are close to 50 million North Americans in the United States and Canada whose disabilities restrict their access to this new medium's sights and sounds, and they should not be left out of this newest development of the Information Age. Nonprofit organizations should construct their Web sites with this in mind.

There are online resources to help nonprofits create Web sites that are as accessible as possible. One such organization is the CPB/WGBH National Center for Accessible Media (NCAM): a research and development facility that works to make media accessible to underserved populations such as disabled persons, minority-language users, and people with low literacy skills. The NCAM is an extension of public broadcasting's groundbreaking work in media access that began 25 years ago with the creation of captioning for deaf and hard-of-hearing viewers, and has more recently resulted in the development of video description for blind and visually impaired audiences. The NCAM and its sister organizations, The Caption Center and Descriptive Video ServiceÆ (DVSÆ), make up the media access department of the WGBH Educational Foundation.

The NCAM has created a Web access symbol, shown in Exhibit 3–8. Web masters of nonprofit sites can denote that their site contains accessibility features to accommodate the needs of disabled users. The symbol should always be accompanied by its description and alt-text tag, Web Access Symbol (for people with disabilities). This image was created by Stormship Studios of Boston, Massachusetts. There is no charge to use this symbol, and it may be used in electronic or printed form. A nonprofit can simply copy it from its page at **http://www.boston.com/wgbh/pages/ncam/symbolwinner.html** and paste it into the nonprofit's Web document. To assist nonprofits in accessible Web site design, professionals in the area of assistive and accessible technology have compiled a list of hints and suggestions, which may be found at the Trace Research & Development Center (**http://www.trace.wisc.edu/world/world.html**). There is another great resource on making a nonprofit Web site more accessible at **http://www.cast.org/bobby/**.

Bobby is a graphical Web-based program designed to help Web site designers and graphic artists make their Web pages accessible by the largest number of people. It will help find design problems that prevent a Web page from being displayed correctly on different Web browsers (e.g., America Online, Netscape Navigator, Mosaic, Microsoft Explorer, Lynx) without having to individually test the page on each of those programs. In addition, Bobby performs a series of tests to determine the ways in which a Web site is inaccessible to those with disabilities such as blindness, deafness, or physical disabilities. Once a nonprofit uses Bobby, it should be sure to grab its Bobby-approved graphic to put on its site.

There is no way to guarantee that a site with either of these two symbols (Web Access & Bobby Approved) will be 100% accessible or was even designed following the guidelines. However, in the spirit of the Internet, both services leave it up to Web surfers to let the Web masters know when a site is or is not accessible, and to offer suggestions for greater accessibility.

If a nonprofit organization uses either symbol, it should do so at its own discretion, understanding the goals of the growing group of people dedicated to making the Web useful for everyone. Every nonprofit should be a part of that growing group because the largest new user group of Internet users are the late

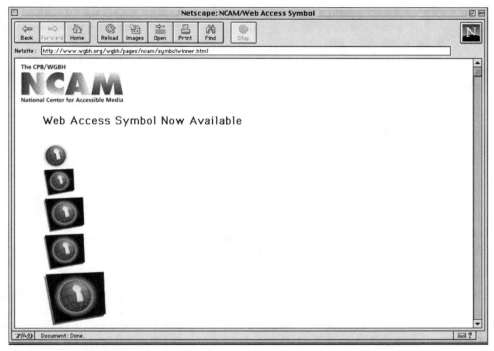

EXHIBIT 3–8   The Web Access Logo

adopters—those 50 and older—so it makes sense to make a Web site more accessible to everyone.

As a final note, here is what Julie Howell, the Web site editor of the Royal National Institute for the Blind (RNIB) in the United Kingdom, has to say:

> The advent of the World Wide Web has meant that many blind and partially sighted people are now able to access a great wealth of information which was previously unavailable to them. Some visually impaired people read Web pages with access technology, such as speech or Braille software, while others read the screen by sight.
>
> Some Web site editors do not think about accessibility when designing Web pages. As a result, much of the Web has become inaccessible to many visually impaired people. Is your Web site accessible to everybody who may want to read it? Accessible pages should not be boring pages! They can be well designed, fun, and attractive, while at the same time providing good accessibility.[6]

[6]Julie Howell, email letter to author, 17 April 1998.

Any nonprofit organization can get a good outline on how to make its Web site more accessible by visiting Julie's factsheet at **http://www.rnib.org.uk/wedo/ research/hints.htm**.

CONCLUSION

Once a nonprofit organization understands how the Net is read, then it is time to learn about writing for the Net.

Appendix 3-A

WEB READER'S CHECKLIST

This Web Reader's Checklist has been designed to remind you of the most important things for visitors to your Web site:

LOAD TIME

( ) Have you tested how long it takes for your Web site to load on to a computer screen?
( ) Have you followed the six rules that help your site get on the screen faster?
  ( ) Forget about putting lots of content on your main page. Keep it modest and create links to other pages behind the first.
  ( ) Keep the files as small as possible. Find ways to reduce the size of the graphics (there are tricks of the trade).
  ( ) Always use height and width tags with graphics, which allows text to appear before the graphics finish loading.
  ( ) Do not use a resolution beyond 72 dots per inch because computer screens cannot project a picture more detailed than this.
  ( ) Use low-quality photos and pictures saved as GIF files. Don't worry— better graphics do not look any better than lower standard graphics on a Web site.
  ( ) Use GIF files for solid colors, text art, cartoons, and poster art, and use as few colors as possible.

YOUR SERVER

( ) Have you asked other nonprofit organizations where their Web sites reside?
( ) Have you put your Web site on a powerful and proven service provider host computer?

SCROLLED TEXT

( ) Have you kept all pages of text on your Web site to four scrolled hypertext markup language (html) pages or less?

HYPERTEXT LINK COLORS

( ) Have you made sure that the colors chosen for your hypertext links (before and after they have been clicked) are legible on your Web site?

ICONS

( ) Have you used icons that are effective complements to your text?
( ) With the understanding that human memory generally allows us to remember only three icons, have you created effective categories and groupings of icons to help increase memory retention and effectiveness of numerous icons?

RULES FROM THE PRINTED WORLD

( ) Have you followed the nine golden rules, applicable to the online environment, culled from Colin Wheildon's work, on *Type and Layout,* in printed material?
    ( ) Elegant serif faces are comprehended by more readers than sans serif faces.
    ( ) The use of high-chroma color, such as hot red or process red—especially in headline text—will increase comprehension.
    ( ) People begin reading from the top left and move down to the bottom right. This gravity is at work on screen as well. Therefore, headlines and important information should be at the top left.
    ( ) Text color should be black.
    ( ) Text in high-intensity colors is difficult to read.
    ( ) The higher the percentage of colored background tint beyond 10%, the less comprehensible the text.
    ( ) Black text on a white background is the most legible.
    ( ) Any reverse-out text is much less legible than no reverse-out text.
    ( ) Totally justified-setting text is much more legible than ragged-right or -left text.

BUILDING YOUR SITE TO BE COMPREHENSIBLE

( ) Have you designed a site that takes into account that readability and effectiveness are heightened when the architecture and navigation has a flattened hierarchy?

WHO ARE YOUR READERS?

( ) Have you designed a site that takes into account four kinds of readers?
    ( ) Surfers
    ( ) Paddlers
    ( ) News junkies
    ( ) Info seekers

ACCESSIBILITY

( ) Have you designed your site to be as accessible as possible, following the rules and help outlined by:
    ( ) NCAM?
    ( ) Bobby?
    ( ) Julie Howell of the RNIB?

4 ▼ The Electronic Tablet: How People Write Online

How does a nonprofit organization write effectively for a medium that combines computer technology, text, graphics, audio, video, and a culture that is a bit idiosyncratic? How can nonprofit organizations write effectively on this new medium in a way that best fits their mission and mandate?

When a nonprofit organization is writing for the World Wide Web (WWW), the best place to start is right at the top—at the top of the computer screen. All Web pages are viewed with browsers and contain a number of standard elements that one needs to be aware of when writing for the WWW.

ELEMENTS OF A HOME PAGE

The eight elements numbered in Exhibit 4–1 represent the major features a visitor to a nonprofit site will encounter and any nonprofit needs to understand when writing for the Web.

1. The Menu Bar

This operates in the same way as a standard menu bar in any software application, providing access to the full range of options available for viewing the Web through Microsoft Explorer software. The standard menu bar has created an expectation

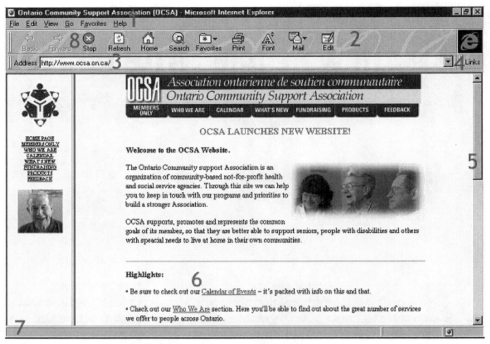

EXHIBIT 4–1   Eight Key Elements of a Web Site: OCSA

with users on the Net that they can control their environment from the top of the screen. Nonprofit organizations might think of putting their own Web site control/menu bar for content at the top of the window within the browser. It also means that visitors to a nonprofit Web site are used to using pull-down menus, and organizations should think about using this pull-down function in their sites.

2. The Button Bar or Tool Bar

Again, like the menu bar, users expect functionality and control to be found at the top of the screen, and any functionality within a nonprofit's Web site might be put at the top of the screen.

This feature is found on most browsers. The button bar or tool bar provides easy access to a range of commands also found in the menus. The button bar also means that visitors are used to hitting graphic icons to get action or results. Nonprofit organizations should try to provide graphic icons that can be clicked on to provide functionality/results/action to any visitor to their site. Note in particular the following buttons on the button bar that a visitor will probably be using a lot:

- *Back*—allows visitors to retrace their steps. This button is the left-pointing arrow on the far left of the button bar. Sometimes, it can be difficult for visitors to retrace their steps through many Web pages. For that reason alone, it is important for a nonprofit to make sure its online writing takes into account the following: What if the dog ate everything but the piece of paper the reader is holding? Can the reader contact the nonprofit organization for more information, to complain, to praise the organization, or to make a donation quickly?

To ensure that readers have all the facts they need to find out more or to take action, an organization must have contact information and a précis of their goal on almost every piece of a direct-marketing appeal. It should be no different for every page of a Web site. Every page should have a standard tool bar (or range of content options) that a visitor can act on at a moment's notice. In Exhibit 4–1, a content list (including home page) is always visible on the left-hand side of the screen for any visitor to the Ontario Community Support Association (OCSA) Web site.

- *Home*—takes a visitor quickly to a designated favorite starting page, perhaps a search engine or the home page of one's Internet service provider. This button is the one that looks like a house.

There is now a trend among some Web designers and programmers to block the ability of a visitor to their site from using the Back button to leave a site. Nothing is more frustrating to the user. Nonprofit organizations should never use this kind of programming with the Home button!

- Favorites (or Bookmarks)—provides quick access to a library of favorite Web sites. In Microsoft Explorer, this button looks like a file with an asterisk on its front. In Netscape, it is a tagged file folder on the left-hand side with "Bookmarks" written above it. A nonprofit wants visitors to bookmark its site.

Nonprofit organizations might contemplate an explanation on their home page, telling visitors to bookmark their site, and have a brief, explicit explanation of how a visitor can do that.

3. Uniform Resource Locator (URL) of Current Web Site

This displays the URL (or address) of the Web site the visitor is currently browsing. A visitor can go to a new Web site by typing in a new URL here and pressing ENTER or by going to their Bookmarks and selecting another destination. Some writing and marketing skill can help a nonprofit organization choose a more effective Web site address. A nonprofit wants to choose a Web site address or URL that is simple to remember and intuitive if possible. A good example of an intuitive

Web site address is West Park Hospital's URL: **www.westpark.org**. The organization, Stop Prisoner Rape, relies on the address of its service provider combined with its acronym to create the awkward result of **http://www.igc.apc.org/spr/**. That would be difficult for many citizens to guess at if they were looking for the Stop Prisoner Rape Web site. Therefore, URLs demand intuitive, effective writing.

4. Link to Button Bar

By clicking here, a visitor replaces the URL area with a range of buttons that are links to Web sites that the visitor has been to recently.

5. Scroll Bar

This allows the visitor to move up and down the current Web page. There is sometimes a scroll bar along the bottom of the screen as well. If no scroll bars are visible, then what the visitor is looking at is the complete Web page. If scroll bars are visible, more of the page is available outside of the visitor's immediate view. A visitor can get to the rest of the page by clicking on the bar and dragging the filled-in gray portion of the bar toward the empty part of the bar.

When a nonprofit organization creates the front page, or home page, for its site, it is working with a canvas that is much longer than it is wide. The computer screen should be considered an electronic page that is an average of 10 to 11 inches wide and 7 to 8 inches long. This means that a nonprofit must make sure that there are words at the top of the home page that keep the visitor intrigued enough to wait for the whole site to download. A nonprofit should try to put everything on its home page on the first screen the visitor sees, because the more text that must be scrolled down, the better chance a nonprofit has of a visitor's hitting the BACK button and getting out of the nonprofit's site.

6. Links

This takes the visitor to new Web pages. The cursor is at a link when the usual arrow shape changes into a pointing finger. Any object can be used as a linking item, and there are different kinds of links. There are five kinds of links nonprofits will be using when they are writing on the Web.

Text-Based Links

These are almost always a different color from the standard text and are underlined. They are called *hypertext links*. The OCSA site shown in Exhibit 4–1 has blue underlined text links. Note that they change color when visited as a way of helping users remember their route around a site. The OCSA site's blue text changes to pink once a user has visited a particular link. The change of color is like Theseus laying down string in the Minotaur maze: It helps tell visitors where they have been and can sometimes help them out of a Web site's maze of information.

Both Microsoft Explorer and Netscape Navigator can be set to remember the links users have visited, and therefore help them retrace their steps (or avoid them!) at a later date. In Microsoft Explorer, users can set the colors of unvisited and visited links by selecting the View menu and clicking on Options. Then, they click the General tab and look toward the right of the screen. They will see a box showing the color of visited and unvisited links. Clicking on a color will bring up a palette from which they can make their own selection of colors to use. They can click on Apply when they are happy with their new settings.

Images

Graphics can be links to other parts of a single Web site or to other Web sites. Images can be icons, photographs, or even typography. As the cursor is run over an image with a link, the user will see the arrow change into a hand with a pointing finger.

Image Maps

Some graphics on the Web have many links embedded in a single picture. This may be subtle or obvious, as in the case of the map on the OCSA home page (**www.ocsa.on.ca**), which looks like a single picture but actually contains links to different pages of the site. Users will see their cursor change from an arrow to a hand and, if they look at the bottom frame of their browser, they will see the destination URL change as they run the cursor over the image. A user can click on different spots on an image map to go to different places on the Web site.

Blind Links

These are links that say one thing to the visitor but are actually something else. They are becoming more common on the Web because they help bring more visitors to a Web site. For example, a link might say something like "click here for a free picture." When a visitor clicks on it, there is no picture but instead a link to a Web site. Moreover, the Web site the visitor has clicked on has no free picture. This devious strategy helps increase volume of visitors incredibly for Web masters who employ these tactics. Nonprofit organizations should avoid blind links. Getting more visitors to a Web site is not worth the cost of angering a small minority who will spread news of the organization's online deceit.

Links in Writing

Look at the example of the OCSA, a nonprofit agency that provides service to seniors and individuals with developmental disabilities (Exhibit 4–1). The OCSA site is composed of many different screens, or *pages,* in Web terminology. Each page contains many different elements, including text, graphics, and animation. Each page is connected to other pages by links, and these links join connected topics rather than following the purely linear progression of a book. Nonprofits should think of the links as an index that does not appear at the end of the book but instead is spread out across the site and embedded into every page.

Any Web page can have as many links as the writer wants, so that a visitor to the Web pages can skip around to related material quickly and efficiently. Exhibit 4–2 is an example of a working link on the OCSA home page. Notice that most links are underlined text or a graphic. When the mouse arrow passes over the link, users can see that the arrow becomes a hand, which means that they can click their left mouse button and they will immediately go to the page *hyperlinked* to that underlining or graphic.

Following are some style rules nonprofit organizations should remember with hypertext links.

- *Write about the nonprofit's subject as if there were no links in the text.* At the Sunnybrook Health Science Centre Site seen in Exhibit 4–3, the home page states: "These pages are provided by Sunnybrook Research Computing. You can see personal home pages of some Sunnybrook Research Computing users and statistics of our server use." The design of the page is excellent, but this kind of writing overexplains. Just by "seeing" the hypertext link (the underlined text) the visitor understands they can go to personal home pages by clicking on the hypertext link. They do not need to be told, "You can see . . ."

  It would be more effective to write: "Our Sunnybrook Research Computing team works hard to bring you this Web site and they keep track of how often the site gets visited." This kind Web writing is more intuitive for the reader.

EXHIBIT 4–2   Links to the OCSA Web Site

EXHIBIT 4–3   Wrong Use of Hyperlinks: Sunnybrook Health Science Center

- *Try to underline more than one word as a hypertext link.* The original one word hypertext link, *here*, is probably too short to stand on its own as a link. While using one word as a hypertext link might make sense, it can also be easily missed. When reading a computer screen, it is easy to miss one word (and therefore an important link), so nonprofit Web writers should be careful about using just one word as a hypertext link.
- *Make hypertext links fit comfortably into a sentence or statement.* There is good Web writing on the Toronto West Park Hospital Web site seen in Exhibit 4–4 (**www .westpark.org**). An example of that good Web writing can be found on the page that talks about volunteer opportunities (**http://www.westpark.org/foundation/ volunteer.html**). The sentences read as they would on paper:

  - You may be interested in a "front line" activity, such as working in the Gift Shop (first hypertext link), being a volunteer buddy or lay pastoral visitor, or escorting clients to recreational events or appointments in and outside of the hospital.

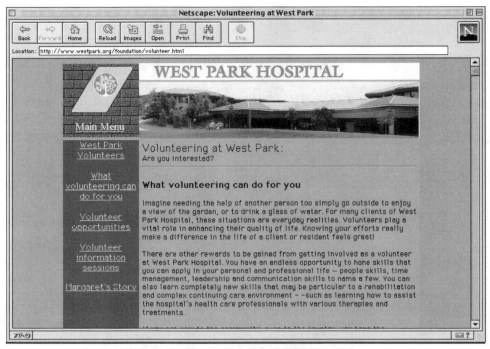

EXHIBIT 4–4   Correct Use of Hypertext Links: West Park Hospital

- Or perhaps a "behind the scenes" activity like helping to stock the shelves in the <u>library</u> (second hypertext link), or participating on a special event committee would be more appealing to you.

A poor Web writer might have written the same two paragraphs as follows:

- You may be interested in a "front line" activity, such as working in the Gift Shop. Click <u>here</u> to see our Gift Shop. (first hypertext link), being a volunteer buddy or lay pastoral visitor, or escorting clients to recreational events or appointments in and outside of the hospital.
- Or perhaps a "behind the scenes" activity like helping to stock the shelves in the library. Check out our cool library by clicking <u>here.</u> (second hypertext link), or participating on a special event committee would be more appealing to you.

The additional sentences asking the visitor to "click here" are superfluous. The hypertext links integrated into the first two paragraph examples keep the text short and flowing smoothly. The final two sample paragraphs are awkward and self-aware of their online nature.

7. Status Bar

The status bar gives visitors a live indication of progress while they are downloading a Web site. It can be very helpful. When visitors first type in a URL, the text on the left of the status bar informs them of progress in finding the Web site they are looking for. Then, when the Web site is found, the same text gives them an indication of what part of the Web site is currently being downloaded. Meanwhile, a bar to the right of the status bar indicates their progress toward completing the download of the current page. If movement along that bar is slow, they might want to stop trying for the moment and come back when traffic is a little lighter. When a Web page has finished loading, the status bar will often say DONE.

The status bar is also a place where a Web site writer can put some text. In Exhibit 4–5 the Vancouver General Hospital has put some text in its status bar area to give more information to each visitor to its home page. The text—"Vancouver Hospital, together with the University of British Columbia is a member of COUTH (Council of University Teaching Hospitals)"—scrolls across the screen from left to right. Every nonprofit organization can place important text in the scroll bar on its Web site and take advantage of this often underutilized area. The site changed in early 1998, and this scroll bar text has been eliminated.

8. Stop

Online users simply click on the STOP symbol across the button or tool bar if they want to stop trying to download a nonprofit's Web site. In Microsoft Explorer, they will notice the STOP symbol is a stoplight; in Netscape, it is a stop sign. Every nonprofit organization should follow the rules of writing for a Web site in this chapter. It will help to prevent visitors from hitting the STOP button and exiting their site.

A WEB WRITER'S PREPARATION

Before a nonprofit organization can get down to writing for its Web site, a number of vital tasks must be completed.

- *Gather the content.* Every nonprofit should ensure that there is collaboration between all of the departments in the organization who will need to provide infor-

EXHIBIT 4–5   Vancouver Hospital Scroll Bar Message

mation. In one sample case, West Park Hospital, the Web design team made sure seven important groups were involved in gathering the material: the Assessment Center, the Clinical Evaluation and Research Unit unit, Employee Services, Foundation and Public Relations, Information Technology, and Volunteer Services. Each group was told what information it needed to provide.

- *Define categories and placement of content.* All of the content is spread out on a table and all of the departments try to answer the following questions:

  - How are the donors, supporters, and visitors to the site going to make sense of the material?
  - What does the nonprofit want them to see first on the home page?
  - What categories should there be?
  - What is the focus within each information category?
  - Should the online representation of the organization mirror your real world presence?
  - What information will remain static and what will change?

- *Determine whether a tree structure, branch structure, or dynamic changing structure is most appropriate.* Once a nonprofit has decided on the main categories, then it must decide on subcategories and how they all link to one another. After finishing these vital tasks, the first Web writing exercise can be undertaken—creating the Web flowchart.

FLOWCHART/SITE MAP

When a nonprofit writes for print, its information is laid out in a linear format. One paragraph leads to one another, and though a reader can skip from page to page in any order, a structure has been created that goes in sequence from page one to two and so on. When writing for the Web, the relatively simple structure of linear print is replaced by a nonlinear format that is a maze of interlocking decisions and directions. A key aid to write more effectively through this maze is the Web flowchart or site map. An example of the first flowchart proposed for the West Park Hospital site is shown in Exhibit 4–6.

A Web flowchart/site map has several functions:

- It gives readers the freedom to create their own learning and interactive experience. Lines with arrows drawn from one content area to another makes it possible for West Park Hospital to show the visitor content areas the organization believes are linked together thematically (e.g., information on the foundation is linked to a secure credit card donation form).

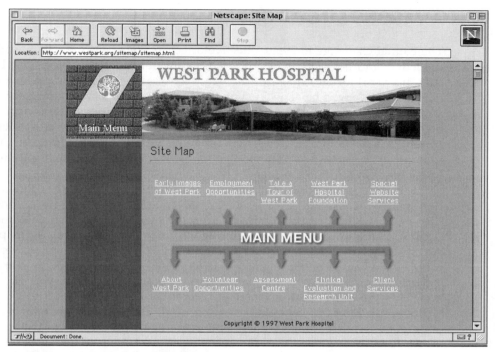

EXHIBIT 4–6   Site Map: West Park Hospital

- Flowcharts/site maps are the literal expression of lateral and vertical thinking. By creating a visual representation of its Web site, a nonprofit can link the content areas that will stimulate visitors to give, read, remember, or get involved with the institution.
- A flowchart/site map can help a nonprofit see the future effects of revisions. Continuity is an enormous issue with a Web site, and one change on one Web page can cut off whole sections. A good Web site is intricately woven together. A flowchart/site map can often help to plan for revision effects in the future.
- A flowchart/site map can often help a nonprofit organization with very little Web experience understand and participate more fully in the Web creation process.
- A flowchart/site map can often show an organization what parts of the site are more important than others, and the work can be planned in order to build the most important sections first.
- A flowchart/site map can often become the user map on the Web site itself. The map can have hypertext links, and a visitor can interact with the site from the map itself.

LONG VERSUS SHORT COPY

The eternal challenge to create effective direct-response writing has moved from the letters and newsletters of nonprofit organizations to their Web sites. Longer copy, not short forms, is most effective for Web sites for one important reason: Visitors are people who have decided on their own to come to an organization's site.

When writing printed materials, nonprofit organizations often assume that people who read their promotional materials will be a horizontal cross-section of society. When a nonprofit writes for a broader audience (like the Internet), it tends to write less because it is assumed that longer text will bore readers and they will lose interest in the Web message.

The same assumptions nonprofit organizations have about the limited attention span of readers of their printed material—that less is better—are as wrong online as in the real world. With the Web, visitors have decided to come to a nonprofit organization's Web site through more self-selection than in the printed world. They have often found the nonprofit's site through sheer will power, without seeing a banner or reading a newsletter. Long copy is not going to scare these self-selecting visitors away. Still, a nonprofit organization has to write its online copy with the unique web environment in mind.

First, the long copy should be broken up. It should not fill one long vertical page. A nonprofit does not want people scrolling down the side of the computer screen in order to get to everything they need to know. That just does not work. Too many readers will leave the Web site before finishing the text.

Instead, nonprofits need to compact their writing through the use of hypertext links. This unique ability of Web sites allows nonprofits to write in a way that can make long copy seem short. They should take their long copy and write an introductory paragraph that makes written reference to important subject areas within the text. Then, they need to make sure that each short reference within that introductory text—which should be just a few paragraphs long at the most—links to directly related text on another page.

All text must be made into chewable bits. It is pretty easy to give an online reader indigestion. In studies by Sun Microsystems of how people read text on screen, it was determined that readers act much like readers of direct mail: They "will skip over text that they consider nonessential, only reading the text of the hypertext links before they choose their next destination in your site to read more." Their studies have shown that "well-written prose with interesting links seem to attract the biggest audience."

Use hypertext links to make long text seem short. Nonprofit organizations need to use graphics as a complement to their written text. They should try to embed short text inside or around a graphic to inspire people to act or read more. On the home page of West Park Hospital, there is a picture of the facility between two bits of text. Above it is a hypertext link, "TAKE A TOUR OF WEST PARK," and a helpful sentence underneath, "If this is your first visit to West Park, join us for this short tour of our facilities." The graphic helps stimulate interest in a tour.

As seen in Exhibit 4–7, North York Branson Hospital has created a large graphic of a Greek temple on its front page. The Greek columns and a background of floating clouds may be Delphic in inspiration, but the design is also an integral part of the hospital's logo. This look would probably be out of place and too expensive on paper, but in this medium it can be inspiring. The text explaining more about the site is completely enclosed by the Greek temple graphic.

Nonprofit Web writers can also replace or combine text with an icon that is the text's visual equivalent. The Greenpeace Canada site is an excellent example of how a Web site can address many topics quickly and efficiently within one computer screen by using very short text descriptions and accompanying icons. Either the text or the icon will take the visitor to a particular topic.

Simple icons for the Greenpeace Canada site include the following:

• The writer's text, "Publications Available from Greenpeace," is accompanied by a small circular red icon with three pieces of paper (Exhibit 4–8).

EXHIBIT 4–7   North York Branson Hospital Home Page

EXHIBIT 4–8   Useful Greenpeace Canada Icon

• The text, "On-Line Survey: Tell Us What You Think!," is accompanied by a red icon with a text balloon containing a question mark (Exhibit 4–9).

Any visitor to the Greenpeace Canada site will notice most of the icons are simple and intuitive. A visitor *wants* to click on them. They stand out and look non-threatening (even a bit fun) to a visitor. Everybody likes to press red buttons, and that is what the Greenpeace site plays on. In contrast, The Toronto Hospital for Sick Children Web site, seen in Exhibit 4–10, has one long list of services and departments.

In light of the Sun Microsystems finding that visitors to a Web site do not like to scroll down the screen before losing interest, it follows that the Toronto Hospital for Sick Children should attempt to make its text listings as compact as possible on the home page, as well as find icons that can strengthen and complement the text.

Because people often make an independent choice to come to a nonprofit's site, and because demographics tell us these visitors are highly educated and highly motivated, every nonprofit needs to make sure its text is well written and does not leave out information for brevity's sake. Do not talk down to anyone. That is not to say that a nonprofit should not use playful language, because if there is any place where the skillful use of playful language is effective, it is the Web.

For example, the Comic Relief United Kingdom Web site (Exhibit 4–11) raises money on poverty issues in the United Kingdom and Africa. The text on the home page begins with the following:

Ah, you found it—not too difficult was it?
     The idea here is to spread the Comic Relief site and all it stands for around the Net—as far as it will go.
     By picking up any or all of the icons and images below and putting them on your welcome/home page, you join the first ever Net-wide charity site link up.
     In exchange for the link you provide to our site, we will credit you or your company on our "thank you very much here are our friends on the

EXHIBIT 4–9   Useful Greenpeace Canada Icon Two

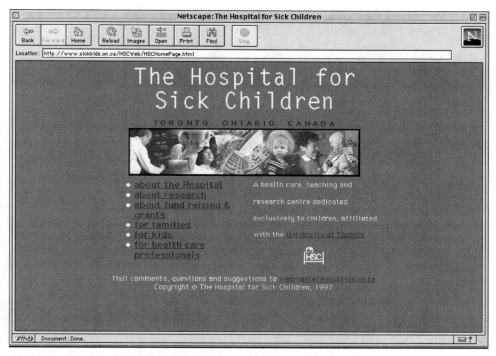

EXHIBIT 4–10   Use of Hypertext Graphics: The Hospital for Sick Children

net" page—in order to participate in this limited special offer please feel free to visit the guest book.

The introduction is breezy and self-aware, but it works. There is a culture on the Net that is very informal. Every nonprofit organization needs to try writing that works within this new online culture. Visitors to this site will notice the silly name for their thank you page. Take a look. It is a bit peculiar, but it is poking fun at some of the very long names that one will encounter in this new medium. It works. For more on the idiosyncratic culture online, please take a look at Chapter Nine.

BITE THE BULLET

Bullet points and the Net are made for each other. A nonprofit might not want to use them too often in their real world correspondence for more serious materials because they can seem gimmicky, but they are perfect for the Web. On the Web, bullets are not just quick hits: The use of hypertext links can make bullets deep information sources.

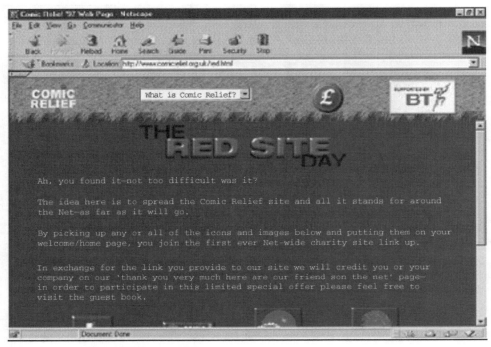

EXHIBIT 4–11   Comic Relief: Use of Humor

Exhibit 4–12 is an example from ReliefNet on the nonprofit use of bullets (there are literally hundreds of thousands examples from which to choose). ReliefNet has created three short bullet points that amount to only 13 words but with three hypertext links a depth of information behind an efficient façade.

WORDS SIGNIFYING NOTHING

Although it is a new medium, there are already a good number of overused words on the Web. It is just plain laziness when people use these words. Nonprofit organizations are as guilty as the rest of Net denizens. Good writing is the same in any medium: It takes 90% perspiration and 10% inspiration—in other words, it takes a lot of writing and rewriting until one gets it right. Good Web writing should strive for elegance and clarity. If nonprofit organizations decide to use some of the following overused words, they are achieving neither.

EXHIBIT 4–12   Bullet Point: ReliefNet

- *Cool.* This may be the most abused word on nonprofit Web sites. Cool is described in the Oxford English Dictionary as meaning (among other things) "calmly audacious." This is the meaning nonprofits are most commonly using on the Web for organizations. It cannot be hip (that is just too bizarre for a nonprofit)—but is that something any of us say about ourselves, our programs, our missions, and mandates? If a nonprofit describes its staff as experienced and professional, then it might describe its programs and services as forward thinking or the best of their kind. "Cool" is plain lazy. Nonprofits should simply avoid it and be more precise and more inspiring in their choice of words.
- *Check it out!* It could have some direct-response effect, but there are many ways to move people by simply describing something in accurate and direct terms.
- *Cutting edge.* Everything that is using the Internet is cutting edge. By using this term, a nonprofit is saying it is like all the rest.

- *Here is . . .* This is unfortunate because it usually forces the nonprofit Web writer to describe the document someone may link to instead of describing the content—and it is content that counts with nonprofit sites.
- *Hot.* Nonprofit organizations would most likely never use this word in any other medium, so they should avoid it on their Web site.
- *Neat.* Again, nonprofits studiously avoid this word in other writing. Why use it online?
- *Online.* Using this word on a Web site is redundant. Imagine if, at the top of a direct mail fund-raising appeal, a nonprofit wrote: "Smallville Hospital's Annual Campaign Using the Mail."
- *Under construction.* Web sites are organic and constantly changing places. If a nonprofit thinks it has a site that is useful enough to the public—launch it. It should not tell visitors it is not ready by putting up an *under construction* symbol and text. The online community understands the fluid nature of the Web and will understand a nonprofit telling them "Here's what we have so far." People know there is more to come.
- *About.* It is often used on the Net to begin a bullet. It is superfluous. A good example of its misuse can be found with the Toronto Hospital for Sick Children Web site. There are three bullets at the top of the home page:

  - *About the Hospital*
  - *About research*
  - *About fund raising & grants*

  It would mean exactly the same and be much cleaner if it read:

  - *The Hospital*
  - *Research*
  - *Fund raising & grants*

Every nonprofit organization needs to remember that the underlining that represents the hypertext link implies there will be more *about* each topic once a visitor clicks on each of them.

That does bring up one important linking issue: Does a nonprofit provide a direct link to the topic or does it provide an intermediary or indirect page between the first hypertext link and the content affiliated with it? For example, The Toronto Hospital for Sick Children takes someone who clicks on the hypertext link "about research" to an introductory paragraph on its Research Institute with text listings after the paragraph that provides a wide range of information on the Institute's current and past work.

However, a nonprofit may not want to provide this kind of link from the original hypertext link. The Toronto Hospital for Sick Children could have decided to place the welcome letter from the Research Institute as the direct hypertext link (which would be a more personal introduction), or an announcement about a major breakthrough at the Research Institute could have been at the other end of the direct link.

The original text link has brought the visitor to what is sometimes called a *smorgasbord* Web page where everything is laid out and one can pick and choose where to go. It is perplexing to see the proliferation of "abouts" across the Net. The author decided to see if there was a reason this word was used so often. An answer came from Gordon A. Tait, PhD, the Web master for the Toronto Hospital for Sick Children. He responded, "My rationale for the 'about' is that it is somewhat similar to the function of the 'About . . .' dialog boxes which accompany every piece of software. The difference is that you can continue to explore in greater depth. By using 'about' we're using an existing software convention which has been around (at least for Macs) since 1984."[1]

He is right. Any online browser can see "about" being used everywhere in software products. For example, if one asks for help in Microsoft's Word 97, he or she will see an "About Microsoft Word" option.

Nonprofit writers for the Web should not be restricted by the language of computer programmers. Nonprofits need to motivate people—inspire them—and they are simply not going to do it without leaving some of this 1980s computer programming language behind. This may be heresy to some people, but nonprofit organizations need to make Web writing into effective writing.

Take a look at what the Alzheimer Society of Canada Web site (see Exhibit 4–13) tries to accomplish with an intermediary destination, or what is called a *delayed* link. When visitors click on the Alzheimer Canada text and icon, they expect to be transported to a home page that outlines all of the main content areas of the site. As they are being transported to the main page, they make a quick five-second stop at an intermediary page that flashes a quote from renowned neurologist Dr. Oliver Sacks:

> People do not consist of memory alone. People have feeling, drive, will and moral being.

It is an inspiring interlude before the visitor is dropped off at the standard home page. This example should remind every nonprofit organization that hypertext links can be used creatively. Every nonprofit's link strategies can affect the excitement level, impulsiveness, attention span, and so much more for their Web site visitor.

QUALITY CONTROL

Word processing computer programs have made it easier to check for spelling and grammar mistakes, but, unfortunately, the web tools have a way to go to get these features. Web authors use programs that craft their Web sites in a language called HTML, or hypertext markup language. These HTML editors for the most part do

---

[1]Gordon Tait, email correspondence with the author 10 November 1997.

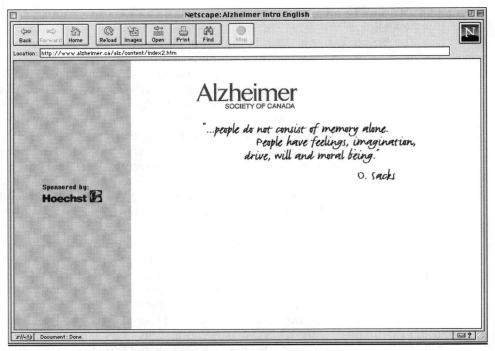

EXHIBIT 4–13   Alzheimer's Canada Delayed Link

not have grammar- and spell-checking abilities, so Web site writers should spell check their writing in a word processing program and then convert it to HTML.

Hypertext links are a vital part of Web writing, so the Web writer needs to make sure every link is working. If they are not linked, it is as if there are missing pages from a book or newsletter—extremely frustrating for a visiting reader.

Nonprofits want visitors to interact with their site. In the real world, every nonprofit wants to motivate people through a sense of urgency—a feeling of right now, right away, no time to lose. With the Net, it is even more urgent. Web site visitors believe that the Net is the most up-to-date and immediate medium. A nonprofit's online language has to communicate that urgency. To help do that, nonprofits need to update their sites as often as possible.

It is important to remember that a nonprofit can test written material (different voices, themes, and content) more cheaply online. In the real world, it is through expensive trial and error that a nonprofit finds what works and what does not. Online, nonprofits can test their messages cheaply and often. With the proper software, nonprofits can accurately track how many visitors interact with their individual Web pages. These numbers can tell a nonprofit how different written messages are being accepted or rejected by the visiting public.

COPYRIGHT AND NETIQUETTE

When writing for printed material, nonprofit organizations are careful about publishing copyrighted material. It should be no different on their Web site. It is much easier to reproduce materials online. Nonprofits can go to another site, make a few keystrokes to capture whole documents, and then put them on their sites within minutes.

Instead of reproducing someone's Web material on their site, a nonprofit might want to provide a link from its own site to the other Web document. However, every organization should be aware that just because material exists online does not mean the author wants the document to be a public resource. Before a nonprofit creates a hypertext link to a document, ask for permission from the author of the information.

The Vancouver General Hospital Emergency Room Web site decided to use the music from the television show *ER* when a visitor first came to the site. The music has since disappeared, and it can only be assumed that permission was not acquired for the music.

The Internet is a technical marvel when it comes to capturing material (text, audio, or graphics) from another source and publishing it at very little up-front cost. However, if a nonprofit organization publishes copyrighted material on its Web site without permission, the costs arising from litigation can make online publishing prohibitively expensive.

Web publishing is still a fledgling industry, and the legal principles governing it are evolving. Because creating Web sites combines work from many media, the Web site writer must understand which resources are free and which are copyrighted. As a general rule of thumb, unless something is explicitly stated as being free, then a nonprofit organization should ask for permission to use any text, graphic, photo, or other multimedia material.

Nonprofits should remember to protect themselves. They need to make sure that their copyright is found on every page of their Web site, like the North York Branson Hospital site, which states "Copyright 1997 North York Branson Hospital" at the bottom of each page.

BETTER STORYTELLING

The Web writer needs to be an expert in combining writing that can be read and heard, as well as seen. It is a mulitmedia discipline that can lead to very effective storytelling. Take a look at what the Alzheimer Society of Canada has done (Exhibit 4–14).

Under the heading *News and Stories*, we are introduced to Molly Blake, age 67, who has Alzheimers Disease. We are then given a hypertext link: <u>This is her story.</u> It is simple and intriguing, you want to click on the link and see more about her story. The picture under the text reinforces the story.

The hypertext link <u>This is her story</u> leads to a second Web page, which continues to tell her story in a few descriptive paragraphs that make excellent use of hypertext links. Molly's story has nothing superfluous in its use of hypertext links. The collage of photographs is an excellent companion to the text and keeps the visitor scrolling down the side of the screen to see everything. This is effective storytelling through a wonderful integration of different media sources.

In the future, the Web writer could take the multimedia approach even further. Imagine what it would be like to hear from the family through audio or see home movies with video. The Web site visitors who can experience such an advanced multimedia approach are in the minority for the moment, but as almost every

EXHIBIT 4–14   Storytelling: Alzheimer.ca

home computer today becomes audio and video enabled, nonprofit writers will be forced to present more complicated and persuasive storytelling in the future.

CONCLUSION

A German philosopher, Walter Benjamin, once said of writing that "good prose has three steps: an architectonic stage when it is built, a musical stage when it is composed, and a textile one when it is woven." In a Web environment, that is more true than he could have imagined.

Good Web writing is built on an architecture that is founded on a framework designed through a flowchart/site map that takes into account the unique qualities of hyperlinks. It is then composed on a stage that should take into account overused Net words; excellent use of bullets; and well-written, short prose with interesting links.

Finally, it is woven in a multimedia writing environment that takes into account the persuasive synergy of text, hyperlinks, audio, video, animation, and stunning colors. It is truly a tactile writing environment. Any nonprofit Web writer who takes all of this into account will be effective in this new medium in a way that best accomplishes his or her organization's mission and mandate.

Appendix 4-A

WEB WRITER'S CHECKLIST

This Web Writer's Checklist has been designed to remind you of the most important issues when writing for a Web site.

THE BROWSER: A WEB WRITER'S TABLET

( ) Have you reviewed the eight major browser elements, and do you understand how they work so that you can be a more effective Web writer?

( ) Have your registered a domain name that makes it easier for online users to find you?

( ) Have you kept all pages of text on your Web site to four scrolled HTML pages or less?

( ) Have you made sure that the colors chosen for your hypertext links (before and after they have been clicked) are legible on your Web site?

( ) Have you explored the possibility of using image maps?

( ) Have you followed the three rules of creating more effective hypertext links?
    ( ) Write about your subject as if there were no links in the text.
    ( ) Try to underline more than one word as a hypertext link.
    ( ) Make your hypertext links fit comfortably into a sentence or statement.

PREPARING TO WRITE ON THE WEB

Preparation is more important on the Web than in all of our other work. The costs of making changes in programming can ruin your budget. That is why you should make sure you:

( ) Ensure the collaboration of every part of your organization when gathering materials.

( ) Spread all of the content out on a table and have all of your departments try to answer the following questions:
    ( ) How are the donors, supporters, and visitors to your site going to make sense of your material?
    ( ) What do you want them to see first on the home page?
    ( ) What categories should there be?
    ( ) What is the focus within each information category?
    ( ) Should the online representation of your organization mirror your real world presence? What information will remain and what will change?
    ( ) Have you decided whether a tree structure, branch structure, or dynamic changing structure is the most appropriate structure for your Web site?

FLOWCHARTS

( ) Have you created a flowchart of your Web site?

LONG VERSUS SHORT COPY

( ) Have you used hypertext links to make long text seem short, remembering that well-written prose with interesting links seem to attract the biggest audience?

ICONS

( ) Have you used icons that are effective complements to your text?

PLAYFUL LANGUAGE

( ) The Web is a place where language can be more playful than in your other written material. Have you found appropriate places on your Web site where the language is fun yet effective?

BITE THE BULLET

( ) Bullets are very effective when used in conjunction with hypertext links. Have you made good use of bullets on your Web site?

WORDS SIGNIFYING NOTHING

( ) Have you used or overused the following words or phrases on your Web site?
    ( ) Cool
    ( ) Check it out!
    ( ) Cutting edge
    ( ) Here is . . .
    ( ) Hot
    ( ) Neat
    ( ) Online
    ( ) Under construction
    ( ) About

QUALITY CONTROL

( ) Because many software programs that create Web sites do not have a spell-checking ability, make sure you have spell checked all documents before they are sent online and even after they have been put up. Have you done that?

COPYRIGHT

( ) Because it is so easy to capture information online and publish it on your Web site, make sure you have checked that all of the material on your Web site does not infringe on anyone's copyright. Have you checked?

MISCELLANEOUS

( ) Have you included an explanation on your home page on how a visitor can bookmark your site?

( ) Have you made sure you are not using blind links or creating programming that will block users from using the BACK button to leave your site?

▼ 5 The Reply Device

> *Wilt thou know a Man . . . by stringing together bedrolls of what thou namest Facts?*
>
> Thomas Carlyle, Scottish essayist and historian

For nonprofit organizations, there is no other way to grow a grassroots movement, raise money effectively, or improve a relationship with a member or supporter than by gathering information through a reply device.

A reply device is called a number of things, from *response coupon* to *form* to *donation coupon,* but they all function the same way. They are pieces of paper, usually with the name and address of the prospective donor, that asks them to choose their gift amount and enclose their payment along with the coupon in a return envelope.

Numerous studies, and the experience of direct-response practitioners, has led to several inescapable facts: If you give prospective or past supporters a reply device to fill out, you will increase the money you make in fundraising, you will get more people to act, and you will collect more information about them. Is this true of the online environment for nonprofit organizations?

There are no definitive online studies to tell a nonprofit organization how donors use response devices on the Internet. However, it could be argued that if they are going to try and get people to respond financially online, they need to take what they have learned about reply devices in the real world, review what other nonprofits are doing online, and draw up some guidelines to help all nonprofit organizations make a better online reply device.

THE BASICS OF THE REPLY DEVICE

In the online world, as in the real world, a nonprofit organization should make a reply device as simple, direct, and persuasive as possible. It needs to be what many reply device designers call *transparent*—meaning that a prospective supporter or Web site visitor needs to see beyond the graphics and words on the Web site reply device and see their needs being met. An online reply device can be transparent only if a nonprofit organization begins with the basics.

An online reply device must make effective use of the following elements:

- *Space.* Without the printing costs, there is no need to restrict the size of a reply device to a mere 8½" by 3½". An online reply device can make use of space more effectively, making it easier to read.
- *Larger font sizes.* Following on the point about space, an online reply device should use larger font sizes, making it easier to read. Too many direct mail reply devices have too much information crammed on too little paper to save print costs. This does not have to happen online.
- *The yes and the affirmative statement.* Studies have shown that offering a supporter or prospective supporter the chance to check off, and agree with, an affirmative statement at the top of the reply device increases direct mail fund-raising results. Nonprofit organizations should not forget to use it online.
- *Only one or two decisions on the first screen.* In direct mail fund raising, a nonprofit organization should not give a lot of decisions on the first part of a reply device. This is also true of online reply devices. An organization needs to keep the first screen simple, perhaps only giving donors the chance to check off a box in agreement and decide on their gift amount.
- *White boxes.* In direct mail fund raising, nonprofit organizations get a better response when the inside of any check-off box is white. The online environment, with its ability to provide fancy graphics for virtually the same price as simple graphics, can sometimes lead to overkill on background color and design. Every nonprofit organization should make sure its online designer is not given the artistic freedom to fill in any boxes with heavy colors or graphics-heavy designs. Doing that will lower response online as surely as it does on paper.

THE AFFIRMATIVE STATEMENT

The first thing a visitor to any online reply device should be attracted to is the affirmative statement.

Visitors need the opportunity to agree with the organization, cause, or mission, and then physically demonstrate that agreement by clicking their mouse beside the statement. UNICEF's online reply, as seen in Exhibit 5–1, device does just that.

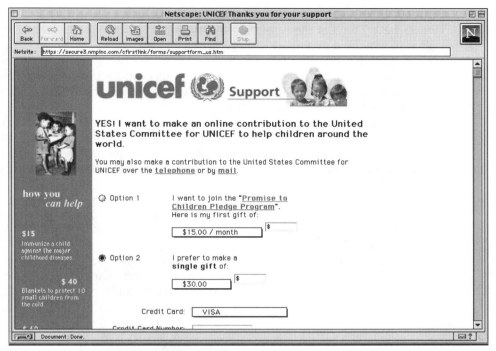

EXHIBIT 5–1   The Affirmative Statement: UNICEF

Size does matter in this case. A nonprofit organization should make sure that the font size of its affirmative statement is at least one or two points higher than the text that follows. It will help response rates.

THE GIFT ARRAY

When a nonprofit organization asks a prospective donor to make a gift, offering the donor an array of gift amounts will increase the response rate and amount of money an organization will make through its reply device.

Of course, when donors are asked what they think of these gift arrays, they almost universally state that they dislike them. Donors find it condescending that an organization would outline an array of possible gift amounts. To them, it is presumptuous. It probably is, but it works. Every nonprofit organization should use a gift array in its online reply device. Whether an organization begins the list of possible gift amounts from the lowest amount to the highest or the other way around, they both work. A nonprofit should test its online gift array to see what works best. The best place to draw inspiration from is a direct mail reply device. What works there may work online.

St. Jude Children's Research Hospital uses the same gift array in its online reply device as in its direct mail program. For its online reply device, St Jude gives the donor one gift array to choose from, whether the donor is making a single gift, memorial gift, or monthly deduction.

St. Jude's gift array begins with $10. By clicking on that amount, a gift array appears, giving one amount lower than $16 and four amounts higher. Prospective donors can simply choose a gift amount with their mouse. Another option is included for donors to type in their own gift amount if they choose to give an amount that is not listed.

It is common practice for many nonprofit organizations to highlight one gift above others. The amount can coincide with a premium. A nonprofit organization may be celebrating a 50th anniversary and would like to highlight $50 as a preferred gift amount.

Online, there are many possibilities to bring attention to one particular gift amount. With a bit of programming help, one particular gift amount could be made to glow when passed over by the mouse, or it could be made to flash off and on. The possibilities are limited only by one's imagination in this new medium.

Where the Gift Goes

Giving donors the chance to direct their money to a specific program can be added incentive for donors who like more choice. The online environment is an opportunity to use simple programming that allows donors to choose where their gift will go. If a nonprofit organization can accept directed gifts, then they should add this functionality to their online reply device.

The American Red Cross reply device, as seen in Exhibit 5–2, gives the donor the chance to make a gift to either the Disaster Relief Fund, the International Relief Fund, or local community services. Jane Pratt, Internet Service Manager for the American Red Cross, wanted "to make sure we provided enough giving options online that we could cover the wide range of donor needs."[1]

This flexibility paid off for the organization and the people it helps. In the spring of 1997, when pictures and stories of the flood disaster in Grand Forks, Nebraska, began reaching the American public, the ability of donors to give locally through the online environment meant that donors could feel their dollars were going directly to Grand Forks. They raised approximately $11,000 in the first weekend of the disaster.

[1]Jane Pratt, email letter to author, 20 March 1998.

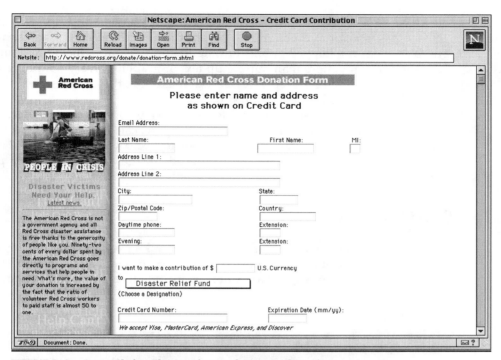

EXHIBIT 5–2   Donor Choice: The American Red Cross Reply Device

What Their Gift Can Do

In direct mail fund raising, it is often effective when a nonprofit organization out-lines exactly what each gift amount could accomplish. It is no different online, and no nonprofit organization should forget to outline what a donor's gift can accom-plish.

There is no reason why a nonprofit organization cannot take this a bit further in an online environment—allowing a prospective donor to click and choose which actions he or she would like to fund. The more interactive the giving op-tions, the more empowered donors feel, and the more money they will give.

PICTURES

A photograph can often help show donors who their gift will help and therefore make a direct mail appeal more profitable. However, most fund-raising practitioners have experienced the frustration of having a photograph (especially if four-color) that is just too much money to print in their fund-raising material. That problem does not happen online. Putting up a photograph, including four-color, does not cost any more than putting up text or graphics. Every nonprofit organization can use them on a reply device (but make sure they are designed in a way that allows them to be loaded quickly).

The West Park Hospital has made sure every prospective online donor is reminded, by a picture, of who their gift will help. As can be seen in Exhibit 5–3, the close-up of Gord Terry shows the online visitor exactly who West Park Hospital helps. Nonprofit organizations should take advantage of the low costs of putting photographs online and use them on their online reply device.

INTERACTIVITY

A review of direct mail authors indicates general agreement that response rates tend to rise with interactive opportunities for respondents. Whether surveys, sending a postcard, or signing a petition are included, response percentage and/or

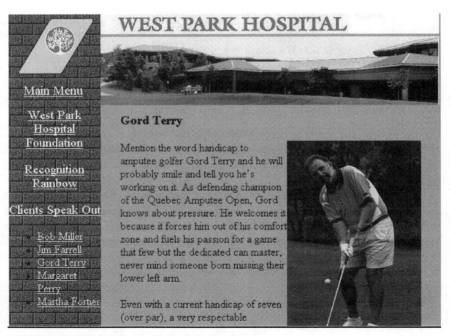

EXHIBIT 5–3   West Park Hospital's use of a picture

the dollars raised are most often higher. The online opportunities for interactivity on a response device should not missed.

The Christian Coalition has taken the step of asking online visitors to fill out an online survey as a preliminary step before join the Coalition. They ask for standard information like name and address, but then move to collecting voting district numbers and the name of the visitor's local church and denomination. Surveys are always a challenge in direct mail fund raising. There is the cost of printing the surveys. Often, there is information a nonprofit would like to capture but cannot because of the pressures of keeping the survey as short as possible in order to keep costs down.

Online surveys can be much longer because there is no extra printing cost. In addition, filling out online surveys is easier for the visitor. There is no searching for a pen or cursing an unsharpened pencil. Instead, the keyboard is right there—and much of the survey can use the click of a mouse to answer questions.

Online donors are very rigorous survey participants. When Greenpeace Canada looked back at 18 months of online donations, they noticed that 100% of all online donors had included their telephone numbers along with other donor information. Most nonprofits cannot expect that kind of response to their surveys and reply devices, but the online environment holds great promise for collecting information on a donor.

To help increase the percentage of survey recipients who fill out a survey, the real world will often send an incentive. A $5 bill might be included by commercial organizations with a survey—knowing that a number of participants will respond because of that $5. That kind of strategy is problematic for nonprofit organizations whose donors do not want to see limited resources used to increase survey response percentages, but there are a number of strategies that a nonprofit can use online.

The United Nations Children's Fund (UNICEF) has shown initiative by offering a screensaver to those online visitors who fill out an extensive survey. The survey takes approximately five minutes. The survey covers a number of areas, including the following:

- Standard demographics (gender, age, job, etc.)
- The respondent's email address.
- Fund-raising information such as "Who do you give to" and "How much?"
- Asking online visitors if they would accept UNICEF's having online corporate sponsors in the future
- Asking online visitors if they would be interested in receiving monthly email to learn about UNICEF programs
- Asking online visitors if they would be willing to purchase UNICEF cards and merchandise online?

In reviewing the UNICEF survey, the lesson for nonprofit organizations is to make sure an online survey captures the standard information an organization would ask in any real world survey in addition to data on the survey respondent's attitudes to the online environment.

There are numerous Web sites for nonprofit organizations that give visitors the option of sending a fax to pressure a company or politician on a particular issue. However, no one has put that action opportunity directly on the reply device. Why not have an action button at the bottom of the reply device? There is no better time to get online visitors to take action on behalf of a nonprofit's cause than after they have made a gift. Every nonprofit should think of offering an action option after the donation information on an online reply device.

Imagine a donor has sent a nonprofit an online gift to save the rainforest and the organization bounces back an automated thank you that also allows the donor to instantly fax a company guilty of rainforest destruction. The two opportunities to make a difference—giving and activism—need to be meshed more seamlessly (or *transparent*, as mentioned earlier) online so that giving and acting reinforce one another and improve fund-raising results.

PREMIUMS

Offering an appropriate gift for the donor's gift can help response rates and the total dollars raised in a direct mail fund-raising reply device. It is no different in the online world. The National Rifle Association has decided to offer a free mousepad emblazoned with its logo when anyone makes an online merchandise order of $25 or more. Similarly, WPLN, the Nashville Public Radio station, offered a mousepad to donors who made online pledges.

Greg Pope, WPLN's former Development Director, said two years ago when they introduced this cyber-premium, that he was sure that "online fundraising is bound to be more successful if you offer premiums that coincide with the online environment."[2]

Just the very fact that prospective donors are using computers in this medium to reach a nonprofit makes computer-related premiums a commonsense approach. That is not to say the premiums an organization has developed and offered real world donors and members should not be adopted in online fund raising, but there should be extra effort to add online-focused premiums. Perhaps a nonprofit could offer software or hardware as a premium that comes from a corporate sponsor. Or they could offer a screensaver, as UNICEF did, or downloadable games and educational tools for parents and their children.

[2]Greg Pope, email letter to author, 13 March 1996.

CONTACT INFORMATION

There is an old adage in direct-response fund raising that needs repeating with on-line reply devices: If the dog eats every piece of the direct mail package, except the reply device, prospective donors can still contact you and send in their gift. The online reply device needs to have all the giving options and contact information for the prospective supporter. A nonprofit needs to ask the following questions:

- What if they want to mail in the gift? (Nonprofits must provide their mailing address.)
- What if they want to fax in their gift? (Nonprofits must provide their fax number.)
- What if they want to telephone their gift? (Nonprofits must provide a phone number and a toll-free 800 number if one is available.)
- What if they want to email in their gift? (Make sure there is an email address where they can send inquiries or their intention to give online and perhaps indicate whether they would like an office phone call to confirm the legitimacy of the solicitation.)

Greenpeace Canada outlines a number of giving options on an intermediary Web page, seen in Exhibit 5–4, that appears before the donor makes an actual gift. They are given four options in making a gift. Greenpeace has only missed offering its fax number, which is a problem if someone prefers to print off the donation page and fax in his or her gift.

The American Civil Liberties Union (ACLU) gives online respondents the explicit option to either print off the form and mail it or send it directly online (see Exhibit 5–5). The ACLU should add a fax option. If they had a 800 number, that should be added.

FEAR OF GIVING ONLINE

The biggest impediment to getting an online reply device to bring in money is persuading prospective donors that online donations are safe to make. Every nonprofit organization needs to make them feel as comfortable as possible—that their credit card is not going to be intercepted by a hacker. It is important to note that this consumer fear is not based on real online fraud, but instead the perception that it is a dangerous giving environment.

Start with the reality. Amazon.com, the staggeringly successful online bookstore, has over 1.5 million customers using their credit cards online and they have never had one single case of online fraud.

However, it is not just reality that influences potential donors, but donor perceptions. Perceptions are an important part of what can be called *current giving cul-*

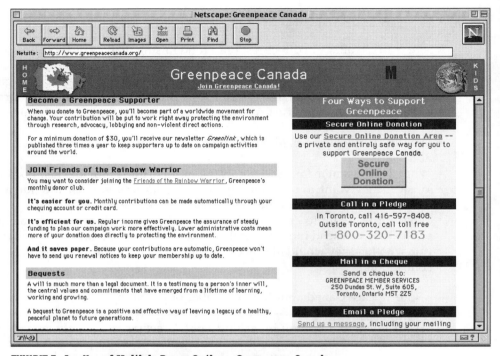

EXHIBIT 5–4   Use of Multiple Donor Options: Greenpeace Canada

---

ture. That culture relies on the giving media (e.g., direct mail, door to door, telephone, special events,) that citizens are comfortable using to make their gift. Fifteen years ago, most donors to a nonprofit organization would not make a gift by giving their credit card number over the phone. Giving culture has changed enough that many more donors will give their credit card numbers by mail or telephone today. It is an important way to give.

Fifteen years ago, if prospective donors had been asked the reasons that they did not want to give their credit card number over the phone, their response would have been many of same reasons people will not give their credit card numbers via the Net:

- It's not safe. Somebody will steal my number and use it.
- How can I trust that it is really a legitimate organization asking for and accepting my donation?
- If I don't use this method for paying for anything else, such as bills or consumer goods purchases, then why use it for giving to a charity.

```
┌─────────────────────────────────────────────────────────────────────┐
│ □   Netscape:ACLU Freedom Network: Join the ACLU               回 ▤   │
│ ┌──┐┌──┐┌──┐ ┌──┐┌──┐ ┌──┐┌──┐┌──┐ ●                          ┌──┐   │
│ │⇦ ││⇨ ││🏠│ │🔄││🖼 │ │📄││🖨 ││🔍│ Stop                        │ N │   │
│ Back Forward Home  Reload Images Open Print Find                └──┘   │
│ Netsite: https://www.newmedium.com/aclulink/forms/join.html           │
│ ┌───────────────────────────────────────────────────────────────┐▲   │
│ │  (none)    First:        Last:                                  │    │
│ │  Address: ┌───────────────────────────────┐                    │    │
│ │  Address: ┌───────────────────────────────┐                    │    │
│ │  City: ┌──────┐  State: (none)  Zip: ┌────┐  Country: │United States│ │
│ │  Home Phone: ┌─────┐  Work Phone: ┌─────┐                       │    │
│ │  E-Mail: ┌──────────────────────────────┐                      │    │
│ │  Payment Options                                                │    │
│ │  ◉  I would like to charge my contribution.                     │    │
│ │  ○  I'm printing this page and enclosing a check to:            │    │
│ │        ACLU                                                     │    │
│ │        125 Broad Street, 18th Floor                             │    │
│ │        New York, New York 10004-2400                            │    │
│ │  ○  Please bill me at the address entered above.                │    │
│ │  Card Type: │ VISA │  Credit Card Number: ┌───────────┐         │    │
│ │  Expiration Date (MMYY): ┌────┐                                 │    │
│ │              [ Join the ACLU ] [ Clear this form ]              │▼   │
│ └───────────────────────────────────────────────────────────────┘    │
│                                                                ✉ ?    │
└─────────────────────────────────────────────────────────────────────┘
```

EXHIBIT 5–5   Use of Multiple Donation Options: ACLU

Nonprofit organizations today need to create an online reply device that makes prospective donors as comfortable as possible and helps them change their own giving culture. There are a number of strategies a nonprofit organization can use to do this on their online reply device.

Find a reputable online security company to help secure the transfer of the credit card information and explicitly explain that relationship to the prospective donor. The American Heart Association, on its donation page that precedes the reply device, has explained its security arrangement seen in Exhibit 5–6.

The statement is direct and earnest. It attempts to make the prospective donors feel they are in a safe environment and that the nonprofit organization has shown due diligence in making the Web site safe for online donations.

Online surveys indicate that online consumers (including charitable givers) feel much safer about online transactions when the name of a respected financial institution (e.g., Citibank) or a credit card company (e.g., VISA or American Express) puts its name to an online security system.

When these kinds of companies are ready to introduce security systems that nonprofit organizations can afford, every nonprofit organization should be quick

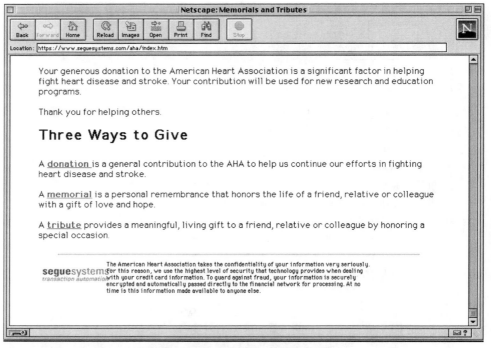

EXHIBIT 5–6   Securing Online Donations: American Heart Association

to use their systems. Most importantly, the nonprofits must slap up the financial institution's names on the online reply device to reassure prospective online supporters that giving online is so safe that the institutions that protect the real world's financial activity are backing this medium as well.

Currently, when a prospective donor makes a transaction through browsers like Explorer or Netscape (see Chapter Six for a more detailed explanation of security), there are standard security statements and icons that appear to reassure the prospective donor.

However, the text and icons are very low key, and it is probably in the best interests of nonprofit organizations to add their own additional icons and text to reassure donors.

To begin, every nonprofit organization should include some large graphic like a lock, much larger than the current ones used by browsers. When a visitor is contemplating a gift online, every nonprofit organization should add their own words of assurance, perhaps even using a guarantee like Amazon.com offers its online customers (see Chapter Six for more).

METHOD OF PAYMENT AND TYPE OF GIFT

The online environment is more amenable to the credit card as a method of payment. In a study of online donors to Greenpeace Canada (see more in Chapter Two), all gifts were made using a credit card. In an automated environment like the Net, donors will be predisposed to use plastic, not the paper of a check. This medium can be instantaneous and can take advantage of the impulsive nature of charitable giving through the credit card. Make sure you include a credit card giving option.

Monthly Deduction Gifts

Evidence seems to point to an online donor proclivity to join through a monthly deduction gift. Greenpeace Canada, in a study of its online donors, found that 28% of donors decide to join a monthly giving program in which automatic deductions are made to their credit card. When the 12-month value of those monthly donors was calculated, this 28% of all online donors made up 63% of all the revenues raised online.

This is reason enough for nonprofit organizations to carefully consider introducing, and perhaps emphasizing, a monthly deduction gift on their online reply device. Greenpeace Canada's successful form, seen in Exhibit 5–7, can help any nonprofit have a good idea of what it needs to do with its reply device to get monthly deduction donations. Nonprofit organizations with monthly sponsorship programs, such as World Vision, Christian Children's Fund, and Foster Parent's Plan should think seriously about introducing, and emphasizing, a monthly giving option via credit card on their online reply devices.

In Memory Gifts

The opportunity of offering a gift in memory of, or in honor of, someone is an opportunity that should not be missed on an online reply device. For Amnesty International in the United States, it became a request they couldn't deny. Malgorzata Garlicka, Acting Director of Direct Response, Amnesty International USA, states, "We received a number of email requests from supporters who asked us to offer a gift in memory or honour option online. We created the online giving option and immediately received a number of gifts."[3]

[3]Malgorzata Garlicka, email letter to author, 3 April 1998.

EXHIBIT 5–7   Monthly Deductions: Greenpeace

In direct mail fund raising, in memoriam gifts can take up considerable space on a nonprofit organization's reply device, and most nonprofits can afford only a reply coupon that includes a single gift option. It is common that the year-end mailing is the only opportunity for a prospective donor to make a gift in honor or in memoriam. Again, space is often the issue. It is important to remember that the online reply device does not have the publishing restrictions to do with space. Every nonprofit organization can afford to put up online reply devices that give donors a number of giving options: a single donation, a monthly giving program, and gifts in honor or in memoriam.

The American Cancer Society has given a prospective online donor all of these giving options—including gifts in memory or in honor of someone (see Exhibit 5–8). The American Cancer Society's Memorial Gift Request Form has the space to gather the information vital to this kind of gift:

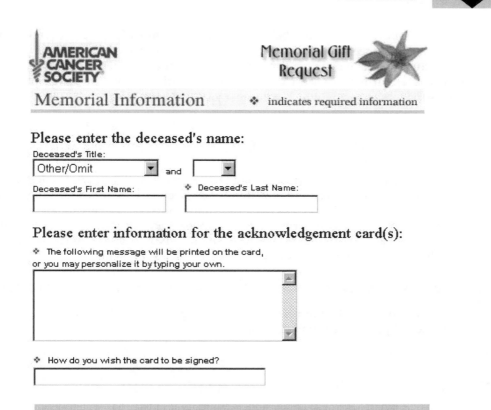

EXHIBIT 5–8   American Cancer Society: Memorial Gifts

- Captures information from the gift giver
- Captures the gift card information, including who it is to be sent to, and space asking the donor "How would you like the card to be signed?"

    This is a lot of information to be gathered, but in direct mail fund raising, space and budget constraints often preclude this kind of gift opportunity from being offered. Every nonprofit organization should try it online.

VOLUNTEERS

Online visitors not only want to make a gift, they may also want to volunteer. Every nonprofit organization should make sure their online reply device gives visitors the opportunity to offer their time. Ducks Unlimited Canada gives the visitor the chance to agree to an affirmative statement and a check-off box to volunteer. It is a picture perfect way to get a response in the best possible way. If it's possible to take it a step further, every organization should outline the volunteer options, with online visitors choosing which volunteer jobs they would like.

THERE IS HELP IF YOU NEED IT

Because this is a new medium and online visitors are still uncomfortable with responding, every nonprofit organization needs to make sure that they put up a reassuring message, telling visitors that the nonprofit is ready to accept any call, fax, or email if something goes wrong in their online response (which can happen often enough with a medium that is still in its infancy). Nonprofits should remind visitors that they are ready to help. UNICEF has such a statement:

> **Call or email us for inquiries about making a contribution online or for technical problems related to this form.**

YOUR REPLY DEVICE COVERS THE GLOBE

The Internet spans the globe. Your reply device can be seen anywhere from Australia to South Africa to Hong Kong. You might have prospective donors who would like to make a gift in their local currency. If an organization cannot manage this currency option, then it should indicate that "all donations will be taken in U.S. funds." UNICEF has decided to put the following statement and policy in place for online donations:

> ***Please feel free to mail in your check or money order in any convertible currency.**

EMPOWERING THE ONLINE DONOR

Every donor wants as much control over his or her donation as possible. For that reason, it makes sense to allow prospective donors to change their responses at any time. Donors will want to unclick one box and click another; a nonprofit needs to give them that option. A prospective donor may fill out the whole reply device and then want to start from scratch again. For that reason, every reply device should have a button at the bottom of the form that allows them to clear the form and start again. The Rainforest Action Network has such a function on its reply device:

Join RAN! Clear Form

Nothing can be more frustrating for prospective online donors than clicking on a box on a reply device and then deciding to choose another box only to find out that they cannot remove the first choice and then choose another, or find out that more than one choice is not possible. Every nonprofit organization needs to test its online reply device so that prospective donors can choose exactly want they want to send back.

BEFORE THE REPLY DEVICE

In direct mail fund raising, the reply device is often accompanied by a letter that improves the storytelling and makes the overall appeal more persuasive. A fundraising letter can be constructed in any number of ways, but one reliable standard goes as follows:

- Use a persuasive and succinct lead that grabs the prospective donor's attention.
- Detail a direct and moving problem.
- Present the nonprofit organization as the solution to the problem.
- Finish with the solicitation that asks for money in order for the nonprofit organization (or solution) to solve the problem.

The home page can be the lead. The first place a visitor sees on a nonprofit organization's Web site is the home page. This is a nonprofit's first chance to get the attention of the visitor. At a minimum, the opportunity to give should be in a prominent place on the first page. If a nonprofit follows the logic of the lead, then the opportunity to give could use persuasive language or be highlighted in some way.

The American Heart Association Web site makes sure that visitors get to see their chance to give on that first screen. Many nonprofit organizations have buried their online giving opportunities behind the home page. Can any organization afford to do that? The American Cancer Society has included the equivalent of a fund-raising letter to complement its online reply device. When visitors click their mouse on "giving," they are taken to an interim page, which is actually an online fundraising appeal. It begins with the lead: "Hope, Progress, Answers" above an effective picture of a researcher. The text moves through a thorough explanation of how a gift will help solve the problems presented by cancer, locally and nationally. After reading this interim pitch, a prospective donor can then click on the gift graphic or text and move to the online reply device.

This interim page has helped set up and strengthen the solicitation. No non-profit organization would think of sending a lone reply device in direct mail fundraising, but they do online. The American Cancer Society has kept the letter and reply device together online—an example more organizations should emulate.

AFTER THE REPLY DEVICE

In direct mail fundraising, nonprofit organizations know that the sooner they get a thank you letter and receipt to the donor, the better. The Internet gives every nonprofit organization the opportunity to send a thank you note and receipt (albeit a temporary one) seconds after receiving an online gift. What a nonprofit sends the online donor should be well thought out. After a donor makes an online gift, every nonprofit organization can automate a response. That response should do the following:

- Use the name of the donor in the reply.
- Mention the gift amount.
- Use complete sentences. Do not make it seem like a computerized receipt. Make it as personable as possible.
- Include the contact information for the nonprofit organization.
- Thank the donor.
- Ask the donor to print off the thank you and receipt as a temporary receipt.

UNICEF has created an effective online thank you (see Exhibit 5–9).

The American Red Cross has also created an excellent online thank you (see Exhibit 5–10). Unfortunately, the author attempted to print the receipt only to find the browser crashed when the print command was initiated. Nothing is more frustrating to a donor who has given online, is still a bit cautious about the medium, and wants the assurance of a paper receipt, only to have the evidence of his or her gift disappear with the crash of their browser software.

Undaunted, the author made another gift to the American Red Cross, using a different browser. The receipt bounced back, confirming the online gift, and when the print command was issued, it crashed again. A few phones calls to the American Red Cross confirmed a number of points. First, the Red Cross has shown due diligence in making sure its bounceback receipt and thank you prints through every browser and with a number of printers and operating systems. Alana Bryce, the American Red Cross's Internet Services Project Leader, worked very hard to figure

United Nations Children's Fund

DATE

Thank you, Mr. Michael Johnston. Your gift of $20,000 has been received and will help children all over the world live better lives.

      Michael Johnston
      308 Garden Avenue
      Toronto M6R 1J6
      Canada

Please print this screen if you need a receipt.

Your gift is tax deductible to the extent allowed by the law. UNICEF has not provided any goods or services in exchange for this gift.

EXHIBIT 5–9   Thank You: UNICEF

out why it was not printing. On a third try, it did print, but the problems with the first two attempts will probably never be explained, except to say that the vagaries of the Net mean any nonprofit organization should expect a few calls like this from time to time and should be as prepared as the Red Cross in helping donors find answers to the technical problems that may arise when they give online.

ONE LAST CHECK

A number of nonprofit organizations have created a reply device that bounces back to donors to show them what they have typed in and to outline what they have decided to give online. It is one last chance to review their gift.

The American Red Cross sends an excellent Gift Review form (see Exhibit 5–11). Once reviewed, the online donor can acquiesce to the gift by clicking on a process button or canceling it with another click of a button. Many fund raisers would probably say it is a bad thing to offer any extra opportunity for donors to

American Red Cross

DATE

THANK YOU!

Thank you for your donation to the American Red Cross.
Right now your donation is on its way to helping people affected
by disaster or those in your community.

Please print and retain this statement for your records. This will
serve as your receipt. Details of your transaction are listed below:

NAME, ADDRESS, AND GIVING INFORMATION FOLLOWED

Please note; no goods or services have been provided to the
donor as a receipt of this contribution.

EXHIBIT 5–10   Another Thank You: American Red Cross

hit a button and cancel a donation they have already made. They would say giving is, in large part, impulsive and this extra review page will lower total gifts sent.

In defense of the American Red Cross's strategy, it must be stated that nothing has been proven in this new fund-raising medium, but some online consumer studies show a very cautious consumer, still very worried about security. This American Red Cross confirmation page might provide some of that extra confidence in the process of online giving—and therefore improve results. As more and more individuals give online, and it becomes a part of the philanthropic mainstream, donors and nonprofit organizations alike will want to eliminate this interim gift-giving step, but until then it might make some sense to use it. To omit it may lead to frustration with this new medium.

AN EMAIL FOLLOWUP

In addition to a bounceback through the World Wide Web, a nonprofit organization may want to send an email to confirm an online donation. Amazon.com takes care of 1.5 million customers online by sending email confirmation. It works for

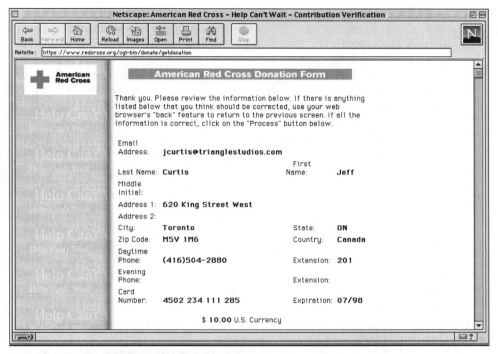

EXHIBIT 5–11   Confirmation: American Red Cross

them, they can afford to test whether it works, and nonprofit organizations should be adopting their email correspondence strategy.

There are a number of essentials in the Amazon.com email response that could be adopted by any nonprofit organization building a relationship with online donors:

- Begin with a thank you.
- Next, mention that if the customer (donor) needs to get in touch, please send an email to the attached address.
- Then, confirm customer (donor) information, including email, name and address, and telephone number.
- Give customers (donors) the opportunity to check on their own orders (gift) in the "Account Maintenance" area. A password and email need to be entered to pass into this maintenance area. Once inside, customers (donors) can examine their order (gift), change their email and password, and check on their Personal Notification Services (email services on a particular topic self-selected by the customer).

• End with the Web site address at the bottom of the email, giving the customer (donor) the chance to click on the uniform resource locator (URL) and get right back to the site.

Point four brings a very important issue to the forefront of online donor relations: self-management for donors. The online environment can allow donors to help lower the administration pressure on upkeep for donor databases by allowing donors to update their own information online.

Yale University is already offering a service called the Virtual Yale Station, in which Yale alumni can subscribe to a virtual email address. Subscribers can tell the world to send all email to their Yale address. Everything will bounce from their Yale email address and on to whatever email address is entered on their Virtual Yale Account.

However, the success of the virtual address is contingent on subscribers, who must use their password, enter the Virtual Yale Station database, and manually update their own information. Only they can change their information—no one else. Imagine nonprofits eventually having their donors updating their own donor files themselves. Any organization can only imagine the future savings in administrative costs of updating donor information! Yale has over 6,000 current subscribers to this service and every one of them is responsible for upkeep on their records. There have been no problems with security. On the accuracy side of this issue, Yale has found that the alumni are more accurate than the staff who entered email addresses in the past (to read more on data entry of email addresses, see Chapter Seven on members-only areas).

Some nonprofits are already doing it. Amnesty International USA has adopted part of the Amazon.com model. Malgorzata Garlika, Acting Director of Direct Response, states that she's "always respected Amazon.com's email sent to customers when they've made an online purchase." Not surprisingly, the same day the author made a gift to Amnesty International USA online, an email landed in his email box (see Exhibit 5–12). The email environment has immense advantages in donor correspondence because of the opportunities for automation, but therein lies the danger with this medium—the ease of duplication. When the author made an online donation to UNICEF, two emails arrived at once thanking him for his $20 gift. Every nonprofit organization needs to ensure that its email response to a donation is accurate and avoids duplicate responses.

AN EXTRA EMAIL

Amnesty International sends one email to confirm a donor's online gift. Amazon.com takes its email follow-up one step further with a second email. The first email thanks the customer for his or her purchase and outlines information mentioned above, but the second email (which came 10 hours after the first email) tells the customer:

- The customer's book has been placed in the mail.
- Customers can track the progress of their book with a reference number and by visiting the shipping part of their site.
- If customers have any questions, they can email, phone, or fax.

Imagine the effectiveness of this kind of correspondence with a donor. Every donor would love to be told that his or her receipt is in the mail just hours after making the gift. Of course, for many nonprofit organizations, it is impossible to provide that kind of donor-receipt turnaround, but the automation of the online environment might allow nonprofit organizations to send this second email at the same time they do get the donor's receipt into the mail. It is an extra chance to keep in touch with the donor and can only improve the relationship and reassure the donor about the security of making an online gift.

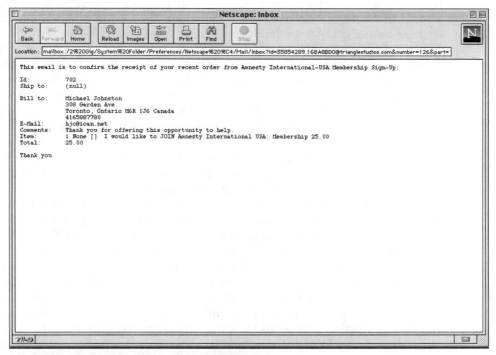

EXHIBIT 5–12   Confirmation: Amnesty International

THE FUTURE

Currently, most online reply devices for nonprofit organizations are focused on the new online donor. The reply devices are trying to attract donations for the first time—to begin a new relationship in a new medium. The opportunity exists to create online reply devices for repeat online donors.

In direct mail fund raising, nonprofit organizations often personalize a response device of a past donor—showing when he or she last made a gift, how much was given, the donor's name and address, and perhaps making mention of a particular area of work the donor has indicated, through a survey, that is of greater interest.

A number of commercial sites currently take past online customer (donor) behavior into account in their reply devices. For example, if a customer is going to make an airline ticket purchase online, he will go to the Air Canada Web site's Cyberticket Office. If the customer purchases a ticket online, the preferences of wanting a window seat by the wing, with a vegetarian meal, are built into the customer's file and are embedded into any future online ticket purchase. Name, address, and contact numbers do not have to be entered in again—they appear on the reply device. If that information needs to be updated, the customer can make his own changes immediately himself online.

Imagine a nonprofit organization offering this kind of service through the reply device of the future. Past online donors are motivated to visit a nonprofit organization's Web site and pass directly to the donor's only area. By entering their name and unique password (sent to them in the mail after making their first online gift), they have told the nonprofit organization who has come to the site to make a gift, and the personal giving information is accessed to construct a reply device unique to them.

A program area that the donor has shown a past interest in could be mentioned in a personalized *affirmative statement* at the top of the reply device. A presolicitation page could pop up before the reply device with up-to-date information on a new program area, and the gift array on the reply coupon relies on a matrix based on the donor's past online (or real world) giving history with the organization.

A highlight box on the reply device could be clicked on and the whole past giving history of the donor could be reviewed. The donor would have to choose only the gift amount with one click and everything else could be taken care of—the name, address, and credit card information—from a past gift. Imagine a future online gift made with one click of a button. It bodes well for online fund raising.

If there is one last thing to remember about online reply devices, it is this: Nonprofit organizations should not stray from the recognizable. The new online environment may look different, and it is true there are many new elements that lay outside the experience of direct mail fund raising. It is important for every nonprofit organization to apply the direct-response fundraising skills they have already acquired through the mail, phone, and TV, and apply them wisely and carefully to this new medium.

Appendix 5-A

ONLINE REPLY DEVICE CHECKLIST

This Online Reply Device Checklist has been designed to remind you of the most important elements to make your online reply device as effective as possible.

THE BASICS

( ) *Space.* Without the printing costs restricting the size of a reply device to a ubiquitous 8½″ by 3½″, any online reply device can make use of space more effectively, making it easier to read.

( ) *Larger font sizes.* Your online reply device should use larger font sizes making it easier to read.

( ) *The yes and the affirmative statement.* Studies have shown that offering a supporter or prospective supporter the chance to check off, and agree with, an affirmative statement at the top of the reply device increases direct mail fund-raising results. Do not forget to use it online.

( ) *Only one or two decisions on the first screen.* Keep the first screen simple, perhaps only giving them a chance to check off a box in agreement and the gift amount to check off.

( ) *White boxes.* Make sure you do not let an your online designer fill in any boxes with color or designs. It will lower response online as surely as it does on paper.

THE AFFIRMATIVE STATEMENT

( ) Have you started your reply device with an affirmative statement that includes the chance for prospective donors to agree by clicking their mouse on the box attached to the statement?

THE GIFT ARRAY

( ) Have you created an online gift array that relies on your best results in direct mail fund raising?

( ) Have you made effective use of online programming to highlight one particular gift amount (making it glow, flash, etc.)?

Where the Gift Goes

( ) Have you created a gift array that allows donors to choose the program toward which they can direct their online gift?

What Their Gift Can Do

( ) Have you created a gift array that also explains what each gift amount can accomplish?

PICTURES

( ) Have you taken advantage of the low cost of publishing four-color photographs on the Web by including them, if appropriate, on your online reply device?

INTERACTIVITY

( ) Have you included interactive devices online, like surveys, petitions, faxes, and emails, to increase the effectiveness of an online reply device?

PREMIUMS

( ) Have you created computer-related premiums that are appropriate and relevant to the online donor, such as the following?
 ( ) Mousepad
 ( ) Software (through possible corporate sponsorship)
 ( ) Hardware (through possible corporate sponsorship)
 ( ) Screensaver

CONTACT INFORMATION

( ) Have you followed the old adage: "If the dog eats every piece of the direct mail package except the reply device, prospective donors can still contact you and send in their gift" when designing your online reply device?

FEAR OF FLYING (OR GIVING) ONLINE

( ) If you have teamed up with a reputable online security company to protect credit card transactions on your Web site, have you explicitly explained that relationship—making reference to your partner and the steps you have taken together to protect the donor's online transaction?

( ) Have you included your own text (reassuring and focused on your donor) to supplement the cold text that is inherent in the security currently built into most current browser software?

( ) Have you offered a *guarantee* to online customers that makes them feel more secure about their transaction?

METHOD OF PAYMENT AND TYPE OF GIFT

( ) Have you made the credit card option the first and most prominent way to give online?

( ) Have you made a preauthorized (or monthly deduction) gift via credit card a highlighted method of giving on your reply device?

( ) Have you made in memoriam and in honor gift options a part of your reply device?

VOLUNTEERS

( ) Have you given prospective supporters the chance to volunteer on your reply device?

THERE IS HELP IF YOU NEED IT

( ) Have you offered a way for the donor to reach you to get help if needed?

YOUR REPLY DEVICE COVERS THE GLOBE

( ) Have you indicated the preferred currency(ies)?

EMPOWERING YOUR ONLINE DONOR

( ) Have you given prospective supporters the chance to clear their reply device and start again?

BEFORE THE REPLY DEVICE

( ) Have you included the giving option in a prominent position at the start of your home page?

( ) Have you included a Web page, after the home page link, but before the online reply device that gets a chance to act much like a fund-raising letter—setting out the problems and the solutions offering by your organization, finally making the solicitation before moving them to the reply device to make their gift?

AFTER THE REPLY DEVICE AND ONE LAST CHECK

( ) After prospective donors have filled out their online reply device, do you send them a document (a *Gift Review form*) that acts as one last check to make sure the information they have typed in is correct?

( ) Have you designed a bounceback for any online gift that:
    ( ) Uses the name of the donor?
    ( ) Mentions the gift amount?
    ( ) Uses complete sentences and avoids the look of a computerized receipt?
    ( ) Includes contact information?
    ( ) Has the logo of the organization prominent on the page?
    ( ) Thanks the donor?
    ( ) Informs donors that they can print off the bounceback as a temporary receipt?

( ) Have you tested your bounceback form to make sure it can be successfully printed by any browser, operating system, and printer?

EMAIL FOLLOWUP AND AN EXTRA EMAIL

( ) Have you created an email followup to an online donor's gift that:
    ( ) Begins with a thank you?
    ( ) Next mentions that if the customer (donor) needs to get in touch, please send an email to the attached address?
    ( ) Confirms customer (donor) information, by listing their email address, name, address, and telephone number?
    ( ) Gives customers (donors) the opportunity to check on their own orders (gifts) in the "Account Maintenance" area? A password and email must be entered to pass into this maintenance area. Once inside, customers (donors) can examine their order (gift), change their email and password and check on their Personal Notification Services (email services on a particular topic self-selected by the customer).
    ( ) Ends with the web site address at the bottom of the email, giving the customer (donor) the chance to click on the URL and get right back to the site?
( ) Have you made sure that your email response does not send multiple thank yous?
( ) Have you created a second email followup to the reply device that informs the donor that:
    ( ) The customer's book has been placed in the mail?
    ( ) Customers can track the progress of their book with a reference number and by visiting the shipping part of their site?
    ( ) If customers have any questions, they can email, phone, or fax?

THE FUTURE

( ) Are you planning to integrate donor information to personalize your online reply device?

6 ▼ Security: Safeguarding Your Homestead on the Electronic Frontier

A large white, red, and black Nazi flag flies in front of an ominous gray background of Swastikas. Under the flag is an embarrassing litany of naked photos, nasty comments, and shocking statements.

Imagine a fundraising manager of a nonprofit organization who has fought long and hard to create an effective and persuasive Internet site. Using precious budget dollars and limited human resources, the fundraising manager has crafted a meticulous site designed to clearly communicate the organization's mission and mandate and, hopefully, collect its first online donations.

One sunny afternoon, the fundraising manager types in the Web site address and up pops the above shocking description. Imagine his or her anger, and imagine what the board of directors are going to say—or worse, the press and the organization's loyal supporters!

That kind of tampering happened to the U.S. Department of Justice in 1996. Its Web site was broken into and altered into an embarrassing antithesis of what the Department of Justice stands for. If the above can happen, then how can nonprofits raise money safely and effectively online?

This chapter attempts to do two things: give nonprofit managers critical advice in keeping all aspects of their site safe (and therefore fundraising aspects), as well as give nonprofit managers both an explanation and advice on the specific aspects of taking online donations.

CAN A NONPROFIT ORGANIZATION PROTECT ITS WEB SITE FROM HACKERS?

It seems that every few months one hears of another hacker breaking into the Pentagon or the White House, despite the efforts of whole departments of computer security experts working to keep these places secure. If such sophisticated and security-conscious organizations can be broken into so regularly, then how can a small, underresourced nonprofit organization hope to protect itself from virtual vandals?

As this chapter will explain, the risk of sabotage to a nonprofit organization's Web site is not nearly as high as one might be led to believe by media stories of high profile break-ins. The steps one can take to ensure reasonable security for one's homestead on the electronic frontier are not daunting—just plain old-fashioned common sense.

IS A NONPROFIT WEB SITE AT RISK?

The first step in understanding the threat of online vandalism is to look at the risk of attack. The Pentagon and the White House are big targets for anyone trying to make a political statement. Lots of politically motivated actions are directed at government institutions, but they are also sometimes directed at nonprofit organizations, especially those involved with social issues that challenge our values, such as abortion, human rights, religious beliefs, or gun control.

One might expect that these organizations would feel somewhat cautious about setting themselves up on the Internet, where they could be easy targets for groups opposed to their activities.

In an effort to assess the risk, a survey was conducted of nonprofit organizations associated with controversial social issues who have been running Web sites on the Net. They were asked what their experience of online vandalism has been and what steps they have taken to protect themselves.

The survey covered a number of organizations who deal with issues that foster strong emotions: Planned Parenthood, Operation Rescue, the American Civil Liberties Union (ACLU), the National Rifle Association (NRA), ACT UP, and the Christian Coalition. None of these organizations have had any experience of their Web sites being tampered with.

When questioned about their security concerns, and what steps they have taken to protect their Web sites, all of the organizations admitted not having given much thought or effort to this issue. Rhonda Mackey of Operation Rescue stated that they had had no problems with the security of their national Web site. "We take care of our Web site internally through a volunteer and he hasn't really thought long and hard about security issues."[1]

For Planned Parenthood, John Magge says that "security is an issue that our external service provider takes care of. We rely on them to keep our site safe from individuals who want to enter the site and alter information."[2] At present, there still seems to be very little concern about security issues for nonprofit Web sites. Most nonprofits can expect, with good reason, that their site will be safe from hacker tampering because they do not present much of a public target.

Despite the media attention given to computer hackers, this sort of activity is not widespread. The chances of an organization's becoming the target of a malicious hacker are very very slim—and even more so if the organization does not focus on publicly controversial issues. The standard security measures that a professional Internet service provider (ISP) provides should be more than sufficient to keep an organization's Web site safe from virtual vandals. There are still a few simple steps one should consider taking to make a web site as secure as possible.

WHAT A NONPROFIT ORGANIZATION CAN DO TO HELP MAKE ITS ENTIRE WEB SITE SECURE

Public awareness of security issues on the Internet is very low, and there is a tendency for nonprofit managers to leave security concerns entirely to the computer experts, whether internal or external, that they depend on for other computer-related matters.

There are a couple of extra steps an organization can take to make sure it is safer on the Net. Although nonprofit managers may not fully understand all of the following points, they need to make sure this list is handed over to their internal technical staff or external supplier in charge of their Internet material.

Review Security Information on the Internet

There are lots of good resources on the Internet that can help a nonprofit's technical staff if they are taking internal responsibility for their own Web site. If they are relying on an external ISP, they can make sure they are keeping up to date with these resources:

[1]Rhonda Mackey, telephone conversation with author, 20 September 1996.
[2]John Magge, telephone conversation with author, 19 September 1996.

- World Wide Security FAQ (**http://www-genome.wi.mit.edu**) (**WWW/faqs/www-security-faq.html**)
- The Computer Incident Advisory Capability security site seen in Exhibit 6–1. (**http://ciac.llnl.gov**)
- The Computer Emergency Response Team (CERT) advisories (**http://www.cert .org**)
- NT security issues (**http://www.somarsoft.com**)

It is always important to "know thine enemy," and one can bet that the hackers are reading the preceding sites—so a nonprofit better too!

Check Up on the Web Site Regularly

Every nonprofit organization should have procedures in place and someone responsible for looking though the Web site to make sure material is not tampered with. Some sites become too large to check every Web site page (the Planned Par-

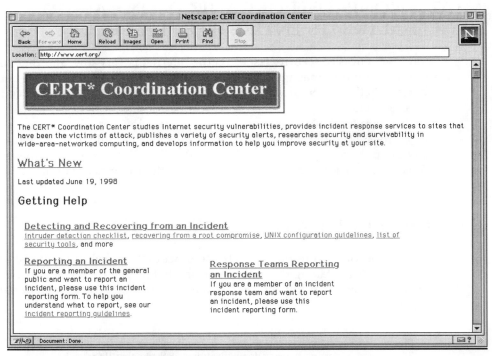

EXHIBIT 6–1   Security Information on the Internet: CERT

enthood US site has over 1,400 files). Most organizations should do spot checks on different pages (always including the home page) and rely on email from friendly visitors to warn them that something is wrong.

Protect Passwords

Probably the most important way to protect online information from tampering is by limiting the number of people who have access to Internet passwords. The more people who have password access to Web site material, the greater chance there is of someone getting unwarranted access to that password and thereby gaining free access to all of an organization's online material. Many computer industry watchers believe that passwords to the U.S. Department of Justice site were handed over to hackers, who then proceeded to alter that site.

How do nonprofits protect their passwords? John Magge of Planned Parenthood says, "I'm the only person who knows the password that gives access to the files for their national Web site. We don't even give our service provider the password. If I were to unexpectedly disappear, a senior information officer with our organization has access to the password, but that is the only other person."[3]

There's no doubt, the less people who know your passwords, the less chance there is of sabotage.

Choose an Internet Service Provider Carefully

Nonprofit organizations must make sure that the ISP they choose to house their Web site has a good reputation for security. They should ask other organizations who use their prospective ISP about the security measures that are used by the ISP to protect its clients.

Recently, a nonprofit organization in Toronto acquired an Internet account with a local ISP to house its Web site. The ISP accidentally gave this new client a "skeleton key" password that gave them access to every account with the ISP. This organization could access, and alter, any file with any organization with an account with the same ISP. When the organization pointed out the dangerous oversight, the ISP was skeptical and refused to believe the organization had been given this kind of access. After a week of pestering, the ISP recognized its error and the "skeleton key" password was taken away.

This frightening story should remind every nonprofit organization of the need to make sure its ISP takes security issues seriously. The ability to secure sensitive information can separate the wheat from the chaff when it comes to different ISPs. Therefore, nonprofit organizations need to be very careful when choosing an ISP

---

[3]Magge, telephone conversation with author.

that will be responsible for encrypting sensitive information. Victoria Boyd-Bell, a senior consultant with Triangle Studios, a multi-media firm that has helped a number of nonprofit organizations set up secure donation forms, provides the following practical list of "to do's" when a nonprofit is looking to set up a secure area within their site:

- Choose a reputable ISP by ensuring that they have been in business for at least two years
- Check other nonprofit organizations that use the ISP for secure transactions for references. Don't assume that because a reputable nonprofit organization or commercial company is listed as a client of the ISP that they are happy. It may be that they're unhappy with the ISP but got locked into a long-term contract they can't get out of easily. This happens often in a medium that many nonprofits are still unsure about.
- Check with the Better Business Bureau if a nonprofit is still unsure about the ISP's reputation around security issues and service provision.
- Some ISPs do not offer secure transaction hosting, so a nonprofit needs to ensure that they do before a nonprofit hands them their money for secure transactional ability.
- A nonprofit should ask a prospective ISP if they allow SSL or PCT encryption on the nonprofit's web site.
- A nonprofit should also ask how they will be able to pull the un-encoded information from their server to the nonprofit organization's office without compromising security.
- Be aware that that some nonprofit or community-minded ISPs will offer a very low secure rate option but the nonprofit will be bundled onto a generic secure server with all their other clients which means that:
  1. The nonprofit won't have to pay for their own certificate, but . . .
  2. The nonprofit will not have direct access to the files on that server so . . .
  3. The ISP may charge the nonprofit extra every time a nonprofit needs to change a file on the secure server

Be Wary of CGI Scripts and Java/ActiveX Applications

As nonprofit organizations take advantage of the latest Internet technologies, such as Java and Secure Credit Card transactions, their Web sites become more open to potential intruders. Many organizations start out building a Web site that contains just static pages of text and graphics and no interactivity except perhaps an address for sending an email.

Any nonprofit organization can add interactivity to its Web site by building small computer programs into its Web pages that can perform more sophisticated tasks. This can allow visitors to the site to make online donations, fill out survey and questionnaire forms, or experience multimedia animations, videos, and sound.

These programs fall into a class of helper applications that include CGI scripts, Java, and ActiveX, and they can be used to greatly enhance the quality of a site and improve the experience and response of any online visitors. However, these programs are also a potential route for hackers to gain access to an organization's Web server.

When an organization uses a credit card transaction or other types of feedback forms on its Web site, it is asking the visitor to send back some information—whether it is a name, address, or credit card number.

Less-than-honest virtual supporters can send a nonprofit Web site a command embedded in the information they send to it through their donation form. That command can allow them to dig into areas of a nonprofit's computer that the non-profit does not want them getting into. They may get in and alter information, or they may get into a confidential listing of supporters.

Fortunately, there are steps any nonprofit organization can take to prevent this kind of threat to the security of its site. For the most part, these are programming decisions to take when an organization's technical team is programming its site. Every nonprofit manager should be sure to advise them to include some "red-flag" alerts that will catch unusual and potentially dangerous use of the online forms.

Make Backup Copies of Your Website

Say a nonprofit manager has not had the chance to put these security measures in place and uncovers a screen covered in sabotaged—or destroyed material. Now what can any organization do?

Once again, John Magge from Planned Parenthood has a strategy that every nonprofit organization should prepare. He admits, "I'm a self-confessed worry wart, so I've created three extra copies of the Planned Parenthood Web site. One resides on a ZIP file, one sits on my hard drive on my computer in New York, and another was sent in the mail to the San Francisco office in case New York sinks into the ocean."

The forethought of keeping a duplicate handy is best seen in the problems a Canadian political party had when its Web site was sabotaged. The Progressive Conservative Party discovered that its site had been altered and now welcomed visitors with a burning party symbol and a peppering of quotes from liberal thinkers like Noam Chomsky that run counter to the party's firmly held right-wing views.

The party found out quickly about the tampering and called its ISP to replace the hacked site. Unfortunately, there was no duplicate ready to go. Having no replacement, the ISP could only put up an advertisement for itself until a new site could be constructed from scratch. To avoid this disaster of unpreparedness, every nonprofit organization should be a "worry wart" like John Magge of

Planned Parenthood, and keep its own archived copy of its website ready to go in case of disaster.

THE CREDIT CARD FORM

A donation form that asks for a credit card number should accept only numbers that space—not other characters. For example, if someone sent a number of letters and characters in a form that was only for a credit card number, he or she may be trying to initiate a series of command to the nonprofit's computer to penetrate past the donation form and into other parts of the system.

If numbers do not appear for a credit card field or what should be expected does not appear in any other area of a donation form, every nonprofit organization should set up a warning when that happens.

CREDIT CARD SECURITY

There are great expectations that the Internet will eventually become a place where people exchange money as freely as they swap email addresses. That day is still somewhere on the horizon, but some organizations, including nonprofit organizations, are already taking the first steps. A number of companies, like popular music stores, computer software vendors and book sellers (amazon.com) have already set up highly profitable Web sites that let Internet visitors use their credit cards to shop online.

In addition, a number of well-known nonprofit organizations have a set up transactional places on the Internet (e.g., **www.redcross.org** or **www.wwf.org**). However, there is very little data available on the subject of online donations (please see Chapters One and Two for more on online fundraising results and demographics). For the most part, nonprofit organizations aiming to find online donors and supporters through the Internet community are leaping into the great unknown.

Issues of Web site security moves to a completely different level when the subject of online credit card transactions comes up. This is due to the sensitive nature of the data being transferred, and the need to eliminate even the smallest possibility of a security gaffe.

What Are the Security Concerns?

To fully understand the security concerns around online donations, it is necessary to review what happens when someone visits a nonprofit's website. Actually, the term "visiting a website" is a misconception to begin with—because none of the people who browse a nonprofit's website on the Internet are actually contacting the real Web site data directly.

When someone types in a nonprofit's web site's URL or clicks on a link to their web site, the browser program they are using sends a request to the computer housing the nonprofit's web site. Almost always the information does not travel directly to the nonprofit's web site. It will be routed through a number of other computers, usually located in the major American cities of New York, Chicago, or Los Angeles. There is no way to control what path the request takes to reach the Web site's host computer.

When the request is received, the nonprofit's host computer looks into its file system. It finds the requested file, and sends a copy of it out over the Internet to the computer that sent the original request, where the information is displayed in the browser window. It is perhaps more accurate to think that it is a nonprofit's Web site that is doing the visiting rather than the individual who is viewing their data.

It is during the transmission process that the issues of security arise. Because a visitor's messages will pass through a number of routing computers during the transmission, there is no way that the visitor can safely guarantee that their message and the nonprofit's response will not be intercepted somewhere en route. This is a result of the way the Internet moves information. (See Exhibit 6–2.)

A secure transmission is one in which all of the data in the message has been encoded—translated into an undecipherable jumble of data that can only be unscrambled by the intended recipient of the message. That way, it doesn't matter if the visitor's message or the nonprofit's response is intercepted: the data will be protected. (See Exhibit 6–3.)

How to Set Up a Secure Donation Page

1. ISP-Provided Encrypted Pages

It is not usually necessary for a nonprofit organization to set up a completely secure and encrypted Web site. Almost all of the web pages on a nonprofit organization's web site can be completely open and accessible to anyone. Any information that is sensitive or confidential probably should not be on the Web site. Usually only one or two pages on a nonprofit organization's entire Web site will deal with the gathering of sensitive information, such as credit card or bank account numbers. It is these pages alone that need to be transmitted and received in a secure, encrypted format.

Nonprofit organizations that have their Web site housed with a local ISP will most likely be able to arrange for special security for just those few pages as a part of their Web site hosting. Most ISPs have their own secure Web servers that are able

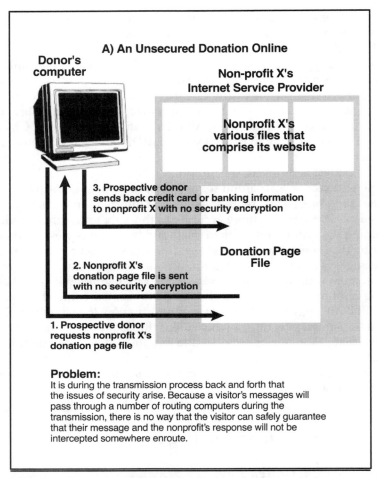

A) An Unsecured Donation Online

Donor's computer

Non-profit X's Internet Service Provider

Nonprofit X's various files that comprise its website

3. Prospective donor sends back credit card or banking information to nonprofit X with no security encryption

Donation Page File

2. Nonprofit X's donation page file is sent with no security encryption

1. Prospective donor requests nonprofit X's donation page file

Problem:
It is during the transmission process back and forth that the issues of security arise. Because a visitor's messages will pass through a number of routing computers during the transmission, there is no way that the visitor can safely guarantee that their message and the nonprofit's response will not be intercepted somewhere enroute.

EXHIBIT 6–2   An Unsecured Donation Online

to transmit and receive encrypted files and Web pages. For a small extra fee (which can be as low as $100 flat fee or a smaller fee per month), an organization can move the Web pages that deal with online donations over to the secure server. Every nonprofit organization needs to shop around for a reputable and competitively priced secure option from an ISP. It is important to note that because secure, encrypted services are relatively new, nonprofit organizations should say that their secure donation page is an opportunity for the ISP to highlight this service. This may enable the nonprofit to have these secure Web pages put into place at no or little cost to the nonprofit, since the ISP will be showcasing a new service to its commercial clients.

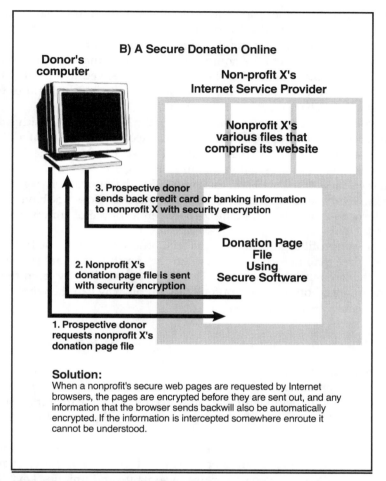

B) A Secure Donation Online

Donor's computer

Non-profit X's
Internet Service Provider

Nonprofit X's
various files that
comprise its website

3. Prospective donor
sends back credit card or banking information
to nonprofit X with security encryption

Donation Page
File
Using
Secure Software

2. Nonprofit X's
donation page file is sent
with security encryption

1. Prospective donor
requests nonprofit X's
donation page file

Solution:
When a nonprofit's secure web pages are requested by Internet browsers, the pages are encrypted before they are sent out, and any information that the browser sends backwill also be automatically encrypted. If the information is intercepted somewhere enroute it cannot be understood.

EXHIBIT 6–3   A Secure Online Donation

When these secure Web pages are requested by Internet browsers, the pages are encrypted before they are sent out, and any information that the browser sends back will also be automatically encrypted. Internet visitors will be advised by their browser programs that the pages they are looking at are protected by encryption. That simple arrangement will assure visitors to a nonprofit organization's online donation area that they can safely submit personal details and credit card or banking information. The information they submit will be encrypted while in transit across the Internet.

However, there is another aspect to Internet encryption that also needs to be considered: what happens to the information after it reaches the host computer? Once the host computer receives and decodes the information from the browser, it must pass that data then on to the nonprofit organization that owns the Web site. The donation or purchase details can be automatically saved to a local database, but far more commonly it is sent to the email address of whoever handles the on-line donations or purchases for the organization.

This is where another potential danger lies in the handling of sensitive data. If the email address of the nonprofit organization concerned is located at a different ISP than the secure web pages, then the email must travel over the Internet to reach its destination. That makes it vulnerable once again.

Only if the destination email is at the same ISP as the secure web pages will the email be completely secure. That is because the message does not have to travel over the Internet—it only has to be move between a couple of computers within the office of the ISP.

When the nonprofit organization's financial officer dials in to the ISP to check for new mail, the email messages that contain the sensitive data are sent over the regular telephone connection (which is certainly secure) directly from the email server to the financial officer's computer. Only in this way can the whole process be said to be secure. (See Exhibit 6–4.)

2. *Setting Up Security on a Nonprofit's Own Web Server*

Nonprofit organizations that run their own Web servers must go through a much more complicated process in order to provide encrypted Web pages for online do-nations or purchases. To begin with, they may need to upgrade the server software that they use, or purchase an add-on component that will provide the encryption and decryption.

Secondly, the Web server must be registered with a digital certificate service. The digital certificate service is another necessary link in the security chain that protects Internet data. Each web server uses a separate and unique "key" to both encode and decode information sent across the Internet. These keys are recorded in a central registry and referenced by a digital certificate number issued by that registry to guarantee the identity of their owner.

When sensitive data must be encrypted for transit through the Internet (or de-crypted to be shown on a browser or recorded as a transaction), the keys used for the encoding and/or decoding are confirmed by checking the digital certificate against the registry.

Digital certificates are issued by a small number of companies, the largest being Verisign. Obtaining a digital certificate can be a bit like applying for a bank loan. Typically, the certificate-issuing companies will demand a detailed back-ground check on a client before they will issue the certificate. Certificates are usu-

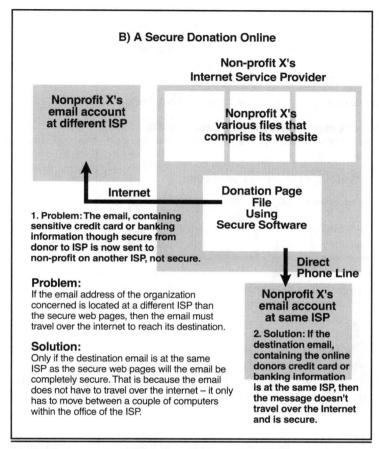

B) A Secure Donation Online

**Non-profit X's
Internet Service Provider**

**Nonprofit X's
email account
at different ISP**

**Nonprofit X's
various files that
comprise its website**

Internet

**Donation Page
File
Using
Secure Software**

1. Problem: The email, containing sensitive credit card or banking information though secure from donor to ISP is now sent to non-profit on another ISP, not secure.

**Direct
Phone Line**

Problem:
If the email address of the organization concerned is located at a different ISP than the secure web pages, then the email must travel over the internet to reach its destination.

Solution:
Only if the destination email is at the same ISP as the secure web pages will the email be completely secure. That is because the email does not have to travel over the internet – it only has to move between a couple of computers within the office of the ISP.

**Nonprofit X's
email account
at same ISP**

2. Solution: If the destination email, containing the online donors credit card or banking information is at the same ISP, then the message doesn't travel over the Internet and is secure.

EXHIBIT 6–4   Securing the Back End of an Online Donation

ally valid for one year, and must be renewed annually in order to remain in effect. This is to guard against changes in an organization's identity or status.

Admittedly, this whole process is a bit long and confusing, but it guarantees that the correct keys are in fact being used, and that only the intended organization will be able to read the data that is being submitted. The transaction will be aborted if something looks amiss.

However, a recent example shows some of the risk involved in an organization running its own secure service. (See Exhibit 6–5.) When the author recently went to make an online donation for Greenpeace International, the following popped up on the monitor:

www.greenpeace.com is a site that uses encryption to protect transmitted information. However, the digital certificate that identifies this site has expired. This may be because the certificate has actually expired, or because the date on your computer is wrong.

The certificate expires on Tuesday, January 13th, 1998.

Your computer's date is set to Friday February 27th, 1998. If this date is incorrect, then you should reset the date on your computer.

You may continue or cancel this connection.

| **Continue** | **Cancel** |

EXHIBIT 6–5   The Expiration of Greenpeace's Security Certificate

Unfortunately, when the visitor attempted to continue with an unprotected donation, it would not allow the prospective supporter to pass beyond this warning. Needless to say, any prospective supporter would be extremely discouraged to see this warning—simply because the nonprofit organization did not keep track of its security certificate.

FOR WEB SERVERS ONLY

Not many nonprofit organizations are going to run their own Web servers. This sort of setup requires a large investment in computer hardware and special telephone lines that is beyond the capacity of almost all nonprofits.

Beyond the cost, another concern that discourages many organizations from running their own Web server is the need for security. When an organization runs its own Web server, it is inviting the world to visit its computer—maybe even the whole office network of computers.

Nonprofit managers should consult with an Internet security expert to advise them on proper security setup and practices. For a start though, here are a few of the first, important steps that should be taken to keep a nonprofit office safe.

Set Up a Secure Firewall

If an organization's Web server is going to be connected into its office network, then it must be very careful to set up the firewall barrier that will keep the outside world from getting access to its office machines.

A nonprofit should always consult an Internet security expert to configure its firewall settings because of the potential havoc that could be caused in its office by an Internet intruder. If nonprofit managers are unsure about their firewall setup, or if their Web server does not absolutely *need* to be connected to their network, then the very safest solution is to disconnect it from their network.

Keep Up with Software Updates

If a nonprofit organization is running its Web site through its own computer, then it is vital that software updates that computer vendors send out are obtained. Organizations should keep in close contact with their vendors, making sure that any security software that patches up leaks in their system gets to them right away. No nonprofit manager wants to find out too late that there was a software solution that could have prevented a disastrous break-in.

Check Logs Carefully

A nonprofit manager needs to make sure the organization's own Internal web server is configured to keep track of how visitors are using the parts of a site that rely on CGI scripts. Technical staff should be monitoring for suspicious CGI use. For example, a nonprofit organization may have someone who is entering numbers or characters that are beyond what is expected with a particular form. These *out-of-range* values will result in error messages in the logs. Every organization needs to be sure these error messages are red-flagged.

When nonprofit managers see these kinds of irregularities, it could be their first warning that someone is trying to break in. Nonprofit managers must act on these seemingly innocuous beginnings.

Keep Sample Files Cleaned Out

Most Web servers come with sample programs that show a nonprofit organization how to use CGI scripts. If an organization leaves them in place after learning from them, opportunities may arise for a hacker to get into the nonprofit's system.

Hackers may attempt to enter a nonprofit organization's system by guessing what standard files or directories may exist on its system. They type in these standard names and hope to guess right. It is like a covert game of battleship that they hope to win. The best way to make sure their guessing gets them nowhere is to create a naming structure that is unique. Every nonprofit organization needs to make sure its technical staff or ISP deletes sample programs if they are not needed.

Keep Up to Date on Security Issues

This has been mentioned previously, but it is very important and especially worth restressing here. Security issues change daily on the Internet, and new potential threats are being identified regularly. Technical staff *must* strive to stay on top of what is going on in the Internet security world. In addition to the Web sites mentioned earlier, there are a number of newsgroups that focus on Internet Security issues:

- comp.security
- comp.security.announce
- comp.security.firewalls
- comp.lang.java.security

The problem of keeping up to date on every security issue is a good reason to hand over responsibility for a Web site to an ISP. It is the business of ISPs to keep up with every new security threat and solution, and many organizations would rather leave their Web sites with their ISP and avoid having to deal with a lot of extra security concerns.

CONCLUSION

This chapter has outlined some areas in which a nonprofit organization can begin to better protect its online information, including credit card numbers. However, with controversial nonprofit organizations reporting no online tampering, there is very little to worry about right now. It is more likely that most nonprofit organizations may suffer from an imported virus from the Internet or misleading information from a "bootleg" Web site put up by an unauthorized supporter.

In accepting credit card donations, a large number of nonprofit organizations have already taken the plunge in fund-raising security online. Every nonprofit organization should review the experiences of other nonprofit organizations who use secure credit card transactions (such as those mentioned throughout this book) and perhaps call or email a number of them to reconfirm that it is working. But as outlined here—it already is working. Or you can take the word of Jane Pratt, The American Red Cross Internet Service Manager. The American Red Cross has taken in over $100,000 in online donations, yet they haven't had one security problem. She emphatically states that "We haven't had one online security problem, not that I've heard about . . . and I would have, believe me! But we're on our guard constantly."

Appendix 6-A

THE ONLINE SECURITY CHECKLIST

This Online Security Checklist has been designed to remind you of the most important security issues related to your nonprofit organization's Web site.

SHOWING DUE DILIGENCE WITH ONLINE SECURITY

( ) Are you keeping up to date with online security issues by visiting the following security web sites?:
  ( ) World Wide Security FAQ—**www-genome.wi.mit.edu/WWW/faqs/ www-security-faq.html**
  ( ) The Computer Incident Advisory Capability security site—**http://ciac .llnl.gov**
  ( ) The Computer Emergency Response Team (CERT) advisories—**http:// www.cert.org**
  ( ) NT security issues **http://www.somarsoft.com**
( ) Are you checking up regularly on the Web site to see if it has been tampered with?
( ) Have you limited the number of people who have access to Internet passwords?
( ) Have you chosen an ISP wisely by checking the following issues:
  ( ) Have you checked to ensure the ISP has been in business for at least two years?
  ( ) Have you checked the references of other nonprofit clients that use their secure abilities?
  ( ) Have you made sure an ISP can offer secure transaction hosting before handing them money for this service?
  ( ) Have you asked a nonprofit or community-based ISP that is offering low secure transaction service rates whether you have direct access to make changes to your secure pages or will the ISP charge extra for any kinds of changes to secure pages?

( ) Have you made sure that your use of CGI scripts and Java/Active X applications do not compromise your security?

( ) Are you checking to make sure that the numbers returned in a credit card field or name and address fields are not, in fact, a series of commands to penetrate your systems?

( ) Have you made backup copies of your Web site and placed them a secure spot—both on-site and off-site?

CREDIT CARD SECURITY

( ) Have you made sure that only the web pages that are gathering sensitive information are using a secure, encrypted format?

( ) Have you made every effort to get your ISP to provide free or close to free secure service by presenting your donation form as a chance for the ISP to highlight this security option to their commercial customers?

( ) Have you made sure that your email address that receives sensitive credit card or banking information is secure?

( ) Have you ordered your Digital Certificate for your secure online donation/membership form?

( ) Have you made sure that your certificate is still valid and has not expired?

SETTING UP YOUR OWN SECURE WEBSERVER

If a nonprofit organization can afford to have their own Web server and would like to ensure their server is secure, they need to remember the following points:

( ) Have you set up a secure firewall?

( ) Are you keeping up with software updates on security?

( ) Are you checking your logs carefully to keep track of how visitors are using the site and to help you monitor suspicious CGI use?

( ) Are you cleaning out sample files that show how to use CGI scripts?

( ) Are you keeping up-to-date on security issues through newsgroups like:

    ( ) comp.security?

    ( ) comp.security.announce?

    ( ) comp.security.firewalls?

    ( ) comp.lang.java.security?

▼7 Members Only: Value-Added Areas for Members

member, n. One of the persons composing a society, community, or party.

membership, n. 1. State or status of being a member. 2. The collective body of members, as of a society.

Webster's Dictionary

Every nonprofit organization has a broadly defined membership. However, for a number of nonprofit organizations, membership is inextricably linked to fundraising because the size of the gift determines the level of membership.

There is no doubt that membership is important. For many nonprofit organizations, membership dues are a vital part of dollars raised. For the giving individual, it can be the symbol of his or her commitment to the cause.

Richard B. Trenbeth, in his seminal work on nonprofit membership, *The Membership Mystique,* hammered away at the idea that "it's the granting of specific benefits and privileges that distinguishes membership (as a fund-raising technique) from other forms of financial support and involvement."[1] This chapter will demonstrate how the online environment offers unique opportunities to improve membership for nonprofit organizations by providing opportunities for new, low-cost benefits and privileges.

[1]Richard P. Trenbeth, *The Membership Mystique* (The Taft Group, 1986), p. 1.

A MEMBERS-ONLY AREA

Many nonprofit organizations offer members only benefits when dues are paid. A member might receive a members-only magazine or access to a special members room at the organization's office. The same can be done online. A nonprofit organization can create a members-only area that can only be accessed by dues-paying members.

The Ontario Community Support Association (OCSA) is an organization of community-based nonprofit health and social service agencies. This organization, with over 300 member agencies, decided to create a members-only area on its Web site. As an extra benefit of membership, its members can enter a restricted area using a password and ID number. Members were sent a password and ID number in a mailing explaining the new Web site. The direct mail package included: a 120-page Internet "how to" manual; a special low-cost offer from a commercial Internet service provider (ISP) to get them connected if they were not already; an opportunity to get low-cost hardware; and the all-important password.

A nonprofit organization can be inspired by this similar offering of the Internet as an extra benefit or privilege of membership. Imagine a nonprofit organization offering all of its members a special package to get them connected to the Internet. A nonprofit could investigate a relationship with computer/Internet companies and negotiate a preferential rate for its members. This would enable more members to access the members-only area of the nonprofit's Web site.

In a members-only area, there must be an electronic gatekeeper that will only let in paying members. This can be done with some very simple programming that is explained briefly in Chapter Six.

The following is a brief outline of what OCSA members will see in their members only area. With their ID and password information in hand, they would turn on the computer and travel the electronic ether to arrive at the OCSA Web site. Right on the top of the screen, the members-only graphic seen in Exhibit 7–1 stands out.

With a click of a mouse, the member is taken to another Web page that quickly outlines the benefits for members only: "Here you can get information on upcoming events, search and reserve our library resources, and participate in ongoing discussions of importance to all OCSA members." At the bottom of this section, a button like the one seen in Exhibit 7–2 states ENTER MEMBERS ONLY.

EXHIBIT 7–1   Members Only Graphic: OCSA

EXHIBIT 7–2   Members Only Button: OCSA

With a click of a mouse, a small box springs up and asks the user for their ID and password, which they had received in the mail. With password and ID number entered, the member is transported to the member's area seen in Exhibit 7–3.

There are a number of resources in the OCSA members-only area. Members can join the listserv, or email subscription list, that discusses issues important to members. By putting the listserv within the members-only area, OCSA can better guarantee that participants on the listserv are members only. In some circumstances, friends of the organization are given access to this area.

Members can access what is available in the members-only library. The OCSA provides a wide range of resources to help health and social service agencies. A search engine gives members the ability to search the library by subject, title, or au-

EXHIBIT 7–3   Members Only Area: OCSA

thor; find out what is available to them; and then place an order to have the resource mailed to them.

A bulletin board provides members with a less controlled discussion area (compared to the listserv) where members' comments on a variety of topics can be viewed by other members. The OCSA round table is their bulletin board. Members are encouraged to post their opinions on a variety of changing topics and to read the thoughts and ideas of other members. There are currently five bulletin board topics:

- 1997 Annual Conference
- Experiences with Meal Suppliers
- Government Downloading of Services
- The OCSA Website Itself
- How to Find Good Volunteers

Publications that used to be sent by mail are now online. The OCSA Bulletin, a monthly newsletter for member agencies, is found in its entirety in the members-only area. Contact numbers for agencies, individuals, and government officials now include email addresses and Web site addresses embedded directly in the online version of the newsletter, making action on the part of members only a click of a mouse away.

A list of all known email addresses for OCSA member agencies, their staff, and OCSA staff and board members is listed. The list is in alphabetical order by agency title.

Is a password-protected area really worth it? Rebecka Torn, Manager of Communications for the Ontario Trucking Association (**www.ontruck.org**), runs a similarly protected members-only area. She replies, "The password protected area has been very well received. This area enables us to provide data exclusively for members in good standing. Several hundred members presently access the password protected area and this builds as each month passes."

She continues:

It is absolutely worth offering this on our site. It is a "value added" service we can provide members at relatively low cost. For those that do access this area, they say they greatly appreciate the information and its timeliness. The reason behind setting up the password area was so that we could share information with members that we didn't want to give away to non-dues paying industry members. The password area has become a "member service" we provide to OTA members. However, that said, we are still able to provide useful information to the community and industry at large via the public portions of the Web site.[2]

[2]Rebecka Torn, email to Michael Johnston, 12 March 1998.

She has a warning however: "Visitors to password protected areas may have higher expectations than visitors to public areas. If there is an issue building in your niche you will be expected to have something on it in your password area almost as soon as it becomes a public issue. Be prepared to devote the appropriate resources to meet this demand for the instantaneous."[3]

The OCSA asked its members what they thought about the online members-only area after they had built it. The positive answers from OCSA members indicate that they got it right, but maybe they were just a bit lucky. There is no doubt that most nonprofit organizations understand their membership up to a point. There is only so much guessing nonprofits can do about members' needs before they realize it might be good to talk to members before they build a members-only area online. Here is what members said about the OCSA password-protected areas:

- "The password doesn't bother me. However, at first when I didn't have the password, my curiosity peaked and I wanted to know what was beyond the gate."
- "I use the bulletin area, links to other sites, and the membership area. The emailing to other members is excellent, and I've used it a great deal recently."
- "I'd love to see one important addition—links to good fund-raising ideas and help."
- "If the comment area gets a lot of negative comments, that would irritate me."
- "Initially, there is a certain feeling of belonging, a sense that there is a part of the Web that isn't open to everyone. It's easy to get lost in the system, just like getting lost in a crowd at a fair."
- "Members-only areas should be actively moderated and promoted in a manner that encourages participation."

LISTENING

The best way for a nonprofit organization to foster a good relationship with its membership is to listen to their needs. In the real world, nonprofit organizations send out infrequent surveys and questionnaires. Nonprofits like to ask members, and prospective members, what kinds of benefits and privileges they would like to receive in return for their membership fees.

Often, the high costs for a mail survey or a telephone survey (and low response rates) prohibit many nonprofit organizations from listening to their members. In comparison, the costs of online surveys is low and the percentage response is usually much higher than in the real world.

Asta Thor has created a Web site (**http://www.valhallabrewing.com/**) that represents the Draught Board, a nonprofit organization that represents individuals

---

[3]Torn, email letter to author.

concerned with brewing issues. Thor's commitment to listening to his membership about online services is a model for nonprofit organizations.

In October of 1997, Asta posted a Web page that told online visitors that:

> One of the first new sections to be developed is the members only area. The section will be user ID and password protected to keep non-members out. This way more sensitive information can be discussed and protected.

In an online environment in which many users are running across aggressive, offensive behavior, nonprofit organizations can ensure a more friendly environment to discuss their issues. Thor continued:

> I've got a lot of ideas of members-only stuff to put online, but I want to get feedback from the membership first so I created a survey that listened to members on what they wanted in their area. What I wanted to do was focus their input to some extent so that I could feasibly do the work. For example, for all new members, I set up a form that asked them what they wanted for a user login name and a password and had them fill out a quick survey of questions pertaining to the direction they wanted the main web page and the members only area to go. After a period of two months, I closed down the polling and allowed them to see the results. Most of the ideas were ones I could feasibly do in the time frame and budget I had. I also allowed a comment area for people to type in their own unique ideas which I will use in future surveys.

There is a lot nonprofit organizations can learn from this experience:

- Focus their input with a survey that is not open ended.
- Make it a painless (quick survey) that asks them the direction they would like to see in the members-only area.
- Give them a deadline. A nonprofit cannot wait forever for members' answers.
- Make sure they understand that the nonprofit does not have unlimited resources and budget. With most issues around the Internet, the software to create many functions within a members-only site (e.g., chat, bulletin boards, and listservs) are relatively inexpensive. It is the staff cost of setting up and maintaining these functions that is the real expense for any nonprofit organization.
- A nonprofit needs to take some of the more intriguing ideas that cannot be accomplished immediately and get back to the membership in the future and see what they think of other members' ideas.

What did the Draught Board's members say? Overall, the members made it clear that information is paramount. They want to know more about the organization than anyone else because they think (correctly) that they are the organization. Here is what the members said in more detail:

- Ninety-two percent of respondents wanted current publications duplicated online.
- Nonprofit organizations can make online publications the first content they put in their members-only areas. However, some nonprofit organizations could lose revenue from putting their publications online. Therefore, the potential revenue gain versus losses must be carefully investigated.
- Ninety-two percent of respondents indicated that they wanted information on current and future programs and projects in their protected area. They want to know what their organization is doing.
- Nonprofit organizations can think carefully about the internal documents they could put online for members only. In direct mail fund raising and membership programs, a number of nonprofit organizations utilize what many fund raisers call the *over-the-shoulder* view with supporters. With this approach, an internal document (perhaps a strategic planning document) might be sent to members or supporters. Similarly, online members might be privy to some internal documents that give them a better idea of what the organization is doing to achieve its mission and mandate.
- Eighty-five percent of respondents indicated that they wanted to have special communications from leadership or staff. There can be no doubt that members are the most vocal advocates and critics of a nonprofit organization. They are quick to criticize when they do not have enough information to explain actions. They are almost always committed to a nonprofit organization's mission and mandate, but when they are not kept "in the loop" they can become critics.
- Nonprofit organizations may want to send extra communication to members-only areas—especially from the leadership of the organization. This is a chance to make members feel special—because they are.
- Seventy-seven percent of respondents indicated a desire for an online area outlining special membership discounts (perhaps only available online).
- Nonprofit organizations should make sure that membership discounts are outlined in the members-only area. And if there is an opportunity to offer online-only discounts for members then they should be offered. (See the Metropolitan Museum of Art's unique online membership discounts later in this chapter.)
- Sixty-two percent of respondents indicated a desire for a members-only look at the finances of the organization.
- Nonprofit organizations should include all of the financial information that appears in their Annual Report in this area—and perhaps even more if possible. With virtually free publishing costs, there is no longer any excuse not to give members as much information as you can. Nonprofits should not forget that on-

line users are the most educated (formally) and best-read generation in history (see Chapter Two). Someone once called the online user an "omnivore" for information. A nonprofit organization can never give them enough. Imagine if a nonprofit organization gave the online member a chance to see interim fund-raising results from its development office. A more fully informed donor could be spurred to make larger gifts. However, every organization will have to carefully balance fund-raising challenges (perhaps failures) versus fundraising successes when sending information online to members.

• Forty-six percent of respondents wanted to be able to check of the status of their membership. Nonprofit organizations do not currently give members the opportunity to access and manage their own membership information. If an organization were to link its supporter/member database to its members-only area, it could offer an empowering members-only service: the ability of members to access their own membership information. Exhibit 7–4 illustrates the results from the survey in graph form.

The very successful commercial site, **www.amazon.com**, allows customers to access their own information by entering their email address and a chosen password. The password-protected area gives customers the ability to:

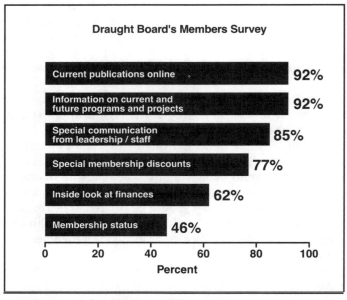

EXHIBIT 7–4   Draught Board's Member Survey

- View their own account status
- Track their orders
- See which Personal Notification Services they have signed up for
- Change their password
- Change their email address

ALUMNI ASSOCIATIONS

Universities have a very important membership—their alumni. There are a number of universities and colleges that are providing excellent members-only benefits and privileges on the Internet; one of the best is Yale University. In anticipation of providing increased Internet-related services, Yale started to collect email addresses more systematically four years ago and now over 25,000 e-mail addresses of alumni have been gathered.

To ensure the best service possible, they have had to work hard at making sure the email data was as accurate as possible. When they began entering email addresses four years ago, there were problems with data-entry staff not properly recognizing the unique qualities of email addresses. There were problems with spacing; underlining, hyphens, and underscoring; and the @ symbol. Yale University has been able to clean up the email database by "eyeballing" every email entry, testing emailings (sending out email to see which ones do not work), and sending out a mailing asking alumni to confirm or correction their email address.

With a more accurate email database, they then created three unique online services for alumni only.

The Virtual Yale Station (VYS)

Every alumnus is offered, free of charge, a permanent email alias address. The address takes the form of the alumnus' name and then the institution's unique ending: John.Doe.PC.96@aya.yale.edu. There are numerous commercial Internet service providers (ISPs) who are providing this service, so why not nonprofit organizations? Wouldn't someone who supports Greenpeace rather have an email alias that ends in supportgreenpeace.org than the peculiar and successful commercial venture hotmail.com?

Alumni register their "actual" email address through the VYS Web pages, then any email sent to their VYS account is forwarded to their actual email account.

Doug Hawthorne, Director of Information and Support Services, Yale Development Office, says, "As long as they keep their VYS address current, there will be no need to notify acquaintances that they'd left one Internet service provider for another. The alumnus may also elect to be placed in the VYS directory so that other Yalies can find the individual when they visit the AYA Web site."

To enter the Virtual Yale Station, alumni visitor is asked to enter their name and password, which has been preassigned and sent to every alumnus by snail mail (regular mail).

Imagine the possibilities for any nonprofit organization. A human rights organization might want to offer this service to members/supporters, allowing members to proudly give out their alias email as JohnDoe@stoptorture.org or an environmental group gives a supporting member the chance to hand out an email address that reads JaneDoe@savethebabyseals.org..

Class/Region Listservs—Email Discussion Groups

The Association for Yale Alumni has set up listservs for most Yale College classes, graduate and professional schools, and selected geographic regions. These listservs facilitate an exchange between classmates via email. For Yale alumni to join one of these listservs, free of charge, they simply send a message from the email account they would ordinarily use to: AYA@yale.edu. In the body of the message, the alumnus specifies his or her name, Yale affiliations, and undergraduate residential college, if appropriate, such as Doe, Jane, '95, Pierson College. As subscribers to the listserv, their email message will be broadcast to all listserv participants. They are also asked to be sure to register their actual email address with a staff member with alumni records so that they are informed of new electronic developments.

Yale University now has over 100 separate listservs with over 3,000 alumni participating on these lists. It is not only a younger generation who wants to use this new medium to keep in touch. At Yale, the graduating class of 1938 and 1940 have listservs with subscribers.

All prospective listserv participants need to be verified as actual alumni. A student volunteer manually enters participants' subscription information onto the listserv only after they have been confirmed as alumni. This process normally takes two to three days. Many listservs provide an automated subscription, but Yale wants to guarantee that every listserv participant is an alumnus. It helps keep discussions free of advertising intrusions.

There is no doubt that membership in a nonprofit organization gives an individual a chance to associate with like-minded people on issues of mutual concern. Nonprofit organizations can create listservs in their members-only area like Yale and OCSA have done. The rigor that Yale has shown in checking every subscriber is a value-added membership service that many organizations could adopt in their online environment.

Imagine health-related charities creating members-only listservs for their membership. A diabetes-related nonprofit organization could provide one listserv for parents of children with type I diabetes. Another listserv could be only for adults who were long-term survivors, and another could be for newly diagnosed adults with type II diabetes. The possibilities for bringing members together are endless through listservs with subscriptions found only in members-only areas.

The antecedents for these kinds of listservs were in the online self-help movement. One resource for any nonprofit organization learning about using their members-only area in this way can visit The Self-Help Sourcebook OnLine (**http:// www.cmhc.com/selfhelp/**). It was created by the American Self-Help Clearing-house as a guide for exploring real-life support groups and networks that are available both online and in the real world.

Online Programs

Yale University, in addition to using listservs and the VYS, has committed itself to providing distanced learning opportunities for alumni via the medium of the Internet and related technologies. These programs will attempt to provide not only an engaging educational experience but also the opportunity to do so from a distance and at the alumnus' own pace.

The inaugural effort in this new field of online programs was entitled, "Hong Kong: From Colony to Republic." It addressed the recent transition of Hong Kong back to Chinese control. Running a total of six weeks (June 26 to August 6, 1997), the AYA registered over 50 alumni and friends, 20% of whom were alumni living outside the continental United States. This strong overseas representation demonstrated how the Internet has the ability to reach distant alumni and render geographic location irrelevant. Participants included alumni from such remote locations as Port Barrow, Alaska, and a U.S. Naval destroyer in the Pacific Ocean.

At the heart of the program were six Yale panelists with considerable expertise on the subject matter who submitted essays/articles to the email mailing list. Articles were then automatically distributed to all the program participants for their review and comments. After reading the panelists' articles, participants used the mailing list to post their comments and to participate in the resulting discussion. The discussion ranged from human rights and recommendations on how the U.S. should conduct its relations with China to the nature of a particularly Hong Kong *identity*, as well as the current business climate there.

Participant response to the program was overwhelmingly positive, with many indicating that they would choose to participate in a similar online program. One anonymous participant commented that "I had only slight interest in the topic, but was very curious about how the Internet aspect would work. I thoroughly enjoyed the formal essays" and "found the comments from people in China a useful and different perspective . . ." Yale University plans to continue offering these online programs for alumni. In the end, 45 alumni signed up and each paid $50 for the six-week discussion.

Without a doubt, nonprofit organizations could offer this kind online learning opportunity by incorporating email and perhaps group software through the World Wide Web.

Imagine an environmental nonprofit organization putting together an online course on global warming that includes staff experts, outside academics, and maybe even a corporate opponent. Members/supporters could subscribe to papers posted by the expert participants and then move to stimulating discussion.

Imagine a peace and disarmament nonprofit organization getting a panel of experts on nuclear weapons issues from in-house and out-of-house, and then allowing members/supporters to subscribe to a listserv that might be called, "So you thought the Cold War was over. Think again!" Following this idea to its fruition, a nonprofit organization could host a conference online for a fraction of the cost of bringing people together for a real world conference.

UNIQUE ONLINE MEMBERSHIP LEVEL

Many nonprofit organizations have a range of membership/giving levels in which the benefits increase as the membership/donation amount increases. The Metropolitan Museum of Art in New York (**www.netmuseum.org**) is one of those organizations. It has 12 giving levels that range from $35 for a student membership to the lofty Patron's Circle starting at $7,000. However, one of those 12 membership levels is a unique Internet membership: Met Net at the fee of $50.

The Met states that "the membership category is designed for Internet users only. This kind of member needs access to the Internet, as most of the benefits are derived from being online." The Met Net membership category includes the following:

- Free admission for one to the museum and The Cloisters
- An official Metropolitan Museum of Art T-shirt
- A Metropolitan Museum of Art screensaver
- Audio-assisted guides on the Internet through selected special exhibitions and permanent installations and other special features for Met Net Members only
- Pass for one-time use of the Trustee Dining Room overlooking Central Park for Friday or Saturday dinner or weekend brunch
- Discount of 10% on all museum merchandise
- Special merchandise offers available exclusively to Met Net Members through the Internet
- Free copies of the Christmas and spring catalogs of publications and reproductions

Met Net members are sent the following in the mail: a membership card; receipt of payment; an entry pass to the Trustees' Dining Room; a museum T-shirt; and finally, instructions to access benefits online. Once each Met Net member has his or her membership account number, that number can be used as the member's online access number. That number gives the member a 10% discount with online purchases and acts as the security code for each Met Net member to access the museum screensavers, audio-assisted gallery guides, and special merchandise offers. It takes two weeks from the receipt of the member's payment for the Met to activate his or her online membership.

People are beginning join organizations through the Internet. Suzanne Gooch of the Metropolitan Opera in New York relays the fact that they have "... offered online memberships since January 21, 1998. Since that time, we have had 37 people join online. Prior to that, between August 1, 1996, and January 21, 1998, we had a form on our Web site which people could print and fax to us to become a member. One hundred eighty-five people chose to do this."[4]

Every nonprofit organization should emulate the Met and other organizations who are properly preparing for increased activity in the years to come.

ONLINE MEMBERSHIP

Asta Thor's membership findings earlier in this chapter indicated that a high percentage of online members (77%) wanted special membership discounts highlighted online. The Metropolitan Museum of Art is doing that with its Met Net membership benefits, but the Smithsonian Institution is highlighting its online membership discounts more loudly, as can be seen in Exhibit 7–5.

CHAT ROOMS AND BULLETIN BOARDS: PLACES FOR MEMBERS TO TALK

It is easy for a nonprofit organization to forget that in the late twentieth century, many individuals no longer have close connections with like-minded people in their community. The reality for many citizens is that their day-to-day life can be lonely and alienating.

Many people find membership in nonprofit organizations one of the few ways they can interact with like-minded people and feel part of something vital and inclusive. The Internet can provide nonprofit organizations with the opportunity to improve the value of their membership to bring like-minded members together through the use of chat rooms or bulletin boards online.

[4]Suzanne Gooch, email to author 18 March 1998.

EXHIBIT 7–5   The Smithsonian: Online Catalogue

The OCSA and Yale University have created listservs for alumni or members to talk to one another in private discussions. They have done so because people like to connect intellectually and emotionally through listservs.

In 1996, World Vision Australia started up a famine listserv only two weeks before its 40-Hour Famine campaign and got over 100 people to join the listserv by the time the 40-Hour Famine was done. According to John Bounia of World Vision Australia in Melbourne:

> We fully expect a few thousand people on the Famnet listserv next summer when our 40 Hour Famine campaign goes again. We like to say there will be thousands of people just like you on FamNet—hungry, but hanging out to help each other as they help hungry kids overseas. That's what I want to say next year and I'm sure I will because we'll make sure that our traditional media like our newsletter and TV/Radio adverts mention our listserv.[5]

[5]John Bouania, email letter to author, 3 March 1997.

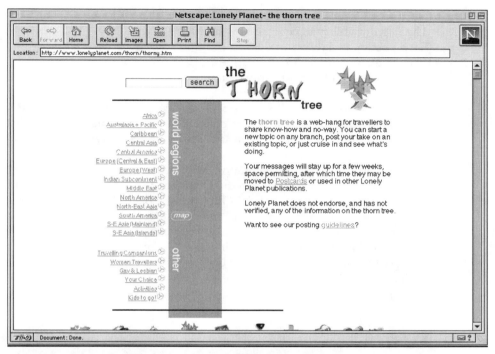

EXHIBIT 7–6   Good Use of Bulletin Boards: Lonely Planet's Thorn Tree

World Vision Australia has also started up the Global Supporter Network, a listserv that is, according to John: ". . . an electronic meeting place where you can talk to other World Vision supporters from around the nation or the world. You can chat with other people, discuss various issues relating to global poverty, share and exchange information, or coordinate with others to take some kind of action on an issue important to you."

He emphasizes that "Its success (over a thousand subscribers) comes from the fact that not only is it an interesting place to talk to like-minded people but it is a free resource for you to share your ideas and participate in helping to make the world a better place."[6]

In the area of bulletin boards, the travel company, Lonely Planet (**http://www .lonelyplanet.com**) has created a very good bulletin board, aptly named The Thorn Tree. The bulletin board (seen in Exhibit 7–6) is finely crafted and well attended. It has a number of excellent functions that any nonprofit would do well to imitate:

[6]Bouania, email letter to author.

- Number of topics on the displaying branch
- The upfront ability to create a new topic
- Each posting is date stamped.
- The poster's email address is active and at the top of the post
- At the bottom of the post is the instant ability to follow the topic or add a post.

Listservs are just a collective email service, and bulletin boards are not "of-the-moment" discussion. However, chat rooms are a whole different matter. They can give a nonprofit organization the ability to have live discussions between members.

Not every nonprofit organization has had success with online chat groups. David Smoot, Special Assistant to the Director of the Smithonian, remembers online chat sessions through America Online in the past. There were not enough participants to make it worthwhile, and those chat sessions were discontinued.

World Vision USA has created a unique chat opportunity for kids (a young membership base) to talk about famine issues. World Vision wanted a place online where participants from all over the United States (and the world) could swap stories, have fun, ask questions, share ideas, and—best of all—groan about their hunger pain!

CONCLUSION

The online environment can be a very important place for nonprofit organizations to improve the membership benefits and privileges they can offer their members and supporters. However, any organization looking to add online membership benefits should proceed cautiously and with due diligence because these kinds of services are still in their infancy.

Arthur Smith, editor at WGBH in Boston, echoes this sentiment:

> We've just turned on the 'join online' function at the end of February, 1998, as we have only recently gotten a commerce server. In about 3 weeks' time, we've gotten only 2 online memberships. Although we get a steady stream of other online member business, change of address, queries etc.
>
> We don't really have any do's and don'ts yet since we have moved into this so recently. Perhaps the only tip is not to neglect the administrative and human side of membership and member service online in favor of the technical issues. In our experience the technical stuff was relatively simple, human adaptation and other admin issues like marketing, privacy, etc. were more challenging elements of the implementation.[7]

[7]Arthur Smith, email letter to author 20 March 1998.

That is the best advice anyone contemplating online membership benefits can have: do not lose sight of the human issues in providing this new service. On the one hand, nonprofit organizations need to be sensitive to their internal management issues. On the other hand, they need to be sensitive to what members want out of their membership—a sense of belonging, of elevated status, a push out of loneliness, and a chance at sharing and learning.

Finally, if an effective members-only online area is created, a nonprofit organization has every opportunity to increase membership fees. Robert Watts, Manager of Internet Resources for the Arthritis Society of Canada, reinforces this opportunity by mentioning, "We had a donor who was so impressed with the content of our Web site that he donated to $1,500 to the Arthritis Society. The donor had previously donated $500. According to the donor, the increase in giving was a direct result of the value he saw in the Web site content."[8]

If a nonprofit organization builds real value in its members-only area online, and a member or supporter can "see" that value, there is a good opportunity to raise more money.

Case Study

LOOKING AT AN AWARD-WINNING
MEMBERSHIP NONPROFIT WEB SITE

For the last 10 years, the consulting firm Archives & Museum Informatics (AMI) has organized conferences, workshops, and seminars; published journals and monographs; and consulted for archives, museums, and cultural heritage networks worldwide (**www.archimuse.com**) on the best use of information technology. Following the April 22–24 annual Museums and the Web Conference, organized by AMI, the Museum of Contemporary Art in Chicago (**www.mcachicago.org/**) was chosen as the best membership site, as seen in Exhibit 7–7.

All organizations would do well to look at this award-winning membership site to get some excellent ideas on their own online membership offerings. This site comes highly praised from nonprofit colleagues:

- "This site is delightful to look at and easy to use. It is a model for what a museum presentation institutional site should be like."
- "The format was clear and well designed. The membership opportunities were interesting."
- ". . . appealing, stable, and informative."

[8]Robert Watts, email letter to author, 2 April 1998.

Best of the Web
Best Membership Use Site

MUSEUM OF CONTEMPORARY ART, CHICAGO
www.mcachicago.org/

Museums
and the Web
1998
A&MI

OVERVIEW
ATTEND
WORKSHOPS
SESSIONS
SPEAKERS
ONLINE
EXHIBIT
SPONSOR
BEST OF THE WEB

"[Museum of Contemporary Art, Chicago] for providing info directed to the institution's members." - **Richard Gerrard**

"This site is delightful to look at and easy to use. It is a model for what a museum presentation institutional site should be like." - **Rob Semper**

"The format was clear and well-designed. The membership opportunities were interesting." - **Erica Lynn Sebeok**

"...appealing, stable and informative." - **Cary Karp**

EXHIBIT 7–7   The Museum of Contemporary Art in Chicago: An Award Winning Membership Site

Every nonprofit organization will make a more effective online membership area by looking at the best practices of other nonprofit organizations. The Museum of Contemporary Art of Chicago is one of those rare membership sites that has actually won an award from its peers. It has to be visited!

Appendix 7-A

MEMBERSHIP ONLINE CHECKLIST

This Membership Online Checklist has been designed to remind you of the most important issues when creating benefits and privileges for your members/supporters online.

LISTENING

( ) Have you sent out a survey, in the mail or offered online, that gives members or prospective members what they would like to see in a members-only area?
( ) Does your survey:
    ( ) Focus the survey recipient and make sure it is not open-ended?
    ( ) Take only a few minutes to fill out?
    ( ) Give the survey participant a deadline?

( ) Explicitly state that answers should be given with the idea that the organization has limited resources and budget?

( ) Ask members if they are willing to pay a premium for a members-only online service?

INTRODUCING THE MEMBERS-ONLY AREA

( ) Have you sent an explanatory mail package to your members about your new online benefits?

( ) Does it include:

    ( ) A "how to" manual explaining how to use the Net and your Web site?

    ( ) A special offer from a corporate sponsor giving members a low-cost ISP connection?

    ( ) A special offer from a corporate sponsor giving members a low-cost hardware and software solution to getting online?

    ( ) A password for the member to get into your members-only area?

BENEFITS AND PRIVILEGES INSIDE THE MEMBERS-ONLY AREA

( ) Have you included the following areas of content in your members-only area in consideration of online survey results found in this chapter?

    ( ) Current publications

    ( ) Information on current and future programs and projects

    ( ) Special communications from leadership/staff

    ( ) Special membership discounts

    ( ) Inside look at finances of organization

    ( ) Ability to check membership status

( ) Have you included interactive tools that can improve communications between your organization and members and between members themselves?

( ) *Listservs.* Have you created unique email subscription lists segmented by:

    ( ) Areas of interest?

    ( ) Age?

    ( ) Graduation year?

    ( ) Year of becoming a member/supporter?

( ) Have you created LURKERS on your listservs (i.e., staff or volunteers who act as passive observers of the ongoing discussions, protecting the integrity of the discussions, keeping them focused and ready to help if asked to by the subscribers)?

( ) Have you investigated offering special listservs with a limited life span, led by in-house and out-of-house experts on one focused (and often timely) topic?

( ) Have you investigated the possibility of charging money for each participant in the special listserv?

( ) Have you investigated further Distance Education possibilities through programming beyond listservs?

( ) *Library/resources online.* Have you paralleled your real world membership information resources by:

　　( ) Creating a searchable database by subject, author, and title that allows members to find, and then order the delivery of members-only resources?

　　( ) Creating an archive of printing material in digital format to be viewed online instead of being mailed to the member?

( ) *Bulletin board.* Have you created an online bulletin board where members can post information to one another through different topic threads?

　　( ) Have you given each member the ability to sort through the discussions by date, topic, and name of member?

　　( ) Have you listed the number of topics in one discussion area posted at the top?

　　( ) Have you created the upfront ability to create a new topic?

　　( ) Have you made each posting date stamped?

　　( ) Have you ensured that the poster's email address is active and prominently displayed in the post?

　　( ) Have you included the instant ability to follow the topic or add a post at the top or bottom of any post?

( ) *Email alias service.* Have you created an email alias service in which:

　　( ) Members can route email through their virtual email address to the email of their service provider?

　　( ) Members can enter a password-protected area and administer their own email alias account?

( ) *Chat rooms.* Have you created a place:

　　( ) For live discussions?

　　( ) With a moderator?

　　( ) With in-house and out-of-house experts?

　　( ) With topics that are going to attract members' interest?

　　( ) With topics of interest to young people?

CAN YOU INCREASE DUES?

( ) Have you contemplated increasing membership dues because of the value-added addition of a members-only area online?

SELF-ADMINISTRATION

(   ) Have you created a password-protected area in the members-only section of your Web site where:
     (   ) Members can update and change their own address information?
     (   ) Members can update their own email address?
     (   ) Members can check on their giving history?

UNIQUE ONLINE MEMBERSHIP LEVEL

(   ) Have you created a membership level for Internet users only?
(   ) Have you given them unique benefits such as:
     (   ) Screensavers?
     (   ) Online discounts and offers exclusive of the Net?
     (   ) Audio/video/interactive presentations exclusive of the Net?

8 ▼ Inviting People to Action: Campaigning

Every fund raiser should think about getting supporters to act, not only to give. Studies by a number of researchers have shown that the level of involvement of donors (i.e., actions taken on behalf of the organization such as signing petitions and demonstrating) is the most crucial factor that affects their decision to give. When donors decide to get involved in activities that are associated with a nonprofit organization (e.g., sending a letter to their congressional representative or participating in a rally) they are showing their self-interest in the mission and mandate of the nonprofit organization. By acting, the donor can identify with the interests of the nonprofit.

J. R. Mixer's book, *Principles of Professional Fundraising: Useful Foundations for Successful Practice,* supports the idea that donors who take action will also give. He states that supporters "feel they are a part of the agency and their bonding extends beyond their concern for the human needs served . . . As a consequence, gifts flow readily from this involvement."[1]

The challenge for many nonprofit organizations is to find cost-effective involvement devices that can be immediately acted upon by a motivated supporter. The Internet can provide a wide range of cost-effective methods of getting a nonprofit organization's supporters more involved, and more likely to make a donation.

A nonprofit organization often needs to persuade the public, government, and other institutions to take action on its behalf. The organization may need to change

---

[1]J. R. Mixer, *Principles of Professional Fundraising: Useful Foundations for Successful Practice* (Josey-Bass Publishers, 1993).

legislation on an issue close to its supporters. For example, a health-related charity may need to galvanize public pressure against government legislation, or an environmental group may need citizens to pressure a company to change its industrial practices.

As activists, people can take to the streets to protest. Citizens can lobby government. Concerned individuals write letters and sign petitions. All campaigns have set strategies. These do not change significantly with the Internet, but understanding the best strategies about how to use a Web site might help nonprofits supplement their other campaigning activities—and hopefully their fundraising as well. This chapter outlines what campaigning features a Web site needs in order to work better toward achieving its campaign goals. An effective Web site gives a nonprofit's constituents all the tools to take action on its campaigns.

Fax servers and email writing are highly interactive strategies that can make campaigning integral to a Web site. It does not have to be expensive. These sorts of actions can be taken effectively and cheaply on any nonprofit's Web site.

BEING EXPLICIT

Take action. This is a key message that a nonprofit organization needs to send to visitors to a campaigning Web site. Although action may include giving through online donations or filling in questionnaires, there must be something more for them to do. They must be able to send faxes or emails to decision makers about the issues that matter to the nonprofit and to them. Nothing is more effective than thousands of emails landing on a decision maker's desk to make him or her sit up and listen.

For example, in 1995, the socially progressive hair and skin care retailer, The Body Shop International, ran one of the earliest organized Internet campaigns asking people to email letters to the company. The Body Shop printed the letters and delivered them to the British Foreign and Commonwealth Office. The British Company was protesting the treatment of Ogoni writer and political activist Ken Saro-Wiwa, who was languishing in a Nigerian jail. The company was asking the British government to intervene on Saro-Wiwa's behalf. On a Web site set up expressly for the purpose, The Body Shop asked for people to read, sign, and return (via email) a letter of protest.

MAKING IT PHYSICAL

The company received over 3,000 responses, which they then printed and delivered to Foreign Minister Douglas Hurd. Soon after, Ogoni leaders and a Body

Shop representative were summoned to a high-level meeting in the foreign office in London. They were told that Mr. Hurd felt obligated to act because more than 3,000 British constituents had made it clear that Saro-Wiwa's situation was unacceptable to them.

The Body Shop continues to campaign on behalf of the Ogoni people in Nigeria on its Web site, and one can still print and send letters of protest (like the one in Exhibit 8–1) from there.

The Ogoni themselves have set up a number of Web sites around the world to highlight their plight. With limited resources, the Internet is the avenue that allows them to communicate with the widest audience. Also, since most of their activists are persecuted and hunted by the Nigerian dictatorship, a Web site is something done safely outside of Nigeria by expatriate activists.

The best Ogoni site has been created by the Movement for the Survival of the Ogoni People (MOSOP) Canada (**http://www.mosopcanada.org**), an organization of Ogoni expatriates that advocates for social and environmental justice for their people. They have included a fax and letter-writing campaign on their site to help

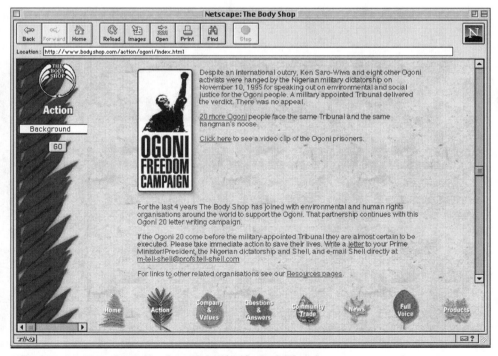

EXHIBIT 8–1   Campaign Letter from Web Site: The Body Shop

resettle Ogoni refugees in Canada. One can pressure the Canadian Foreign Minister by sending an online fax like the one in Exhibit 8–2 from their site. Once again, as stated earlier, nonprofit organizations become more effective when they allow their online protests take physical form, such as faxes or letters that can be printed off and sent in protest.

In the months following the creation of the site, six Ogoni families were resettled as refugees in Canada. These are just two examples of how effective campaigns can utilize the Internet to make positive change.

CHECKLIST OF MUSTS

There are a number of campaigning *musts* that MOSOP Canada has incorporated into its excellent Web site. If other nonprofit organizations address these areas on their web sites, they will be well on their way to having an effective online campaign. The MOSOP Canada site seen in Exhibit 8–3 will be the reference point as the chapter outlines how to create a superior campaigning Web site.

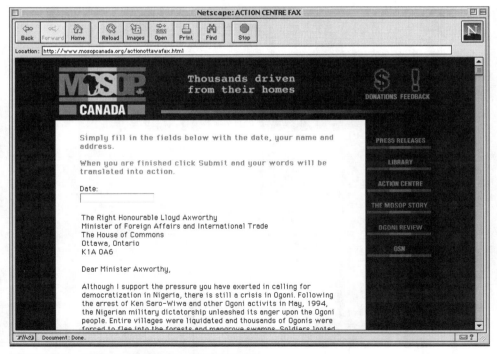

EXHIBIT 8–2   Online Fax Campaign: MOSOP Canada

EXHIBIT 8–3   MOSOP Canada

Campaigning *musts* include the following:

- Effective and accurate information about the nonprofit organization and its campaign
- A list of contact information for institutions and individuals the campaign is targeting
- A place for campaigners to exchange information
- A way for supporters to contact the nonprofit
- The ability to send faxes and emails to decision makers directly or indirectly from the Web site
- Campaign materials ready made for printing
- A way for supporters to sign up for the campaign
- An outreach system for sending campaign materials to supporters via email
- Interactive and animated elements to appeal to visitors
- Online civil disobedience

Effective and Accurate Information

First, a campaigning site must inform visitors effectively and accurately. Who is the nonprofit? What is the purpose of its campaign? What results is it aiming for?

When visitors are comfortable and confident about the information they are being presented with, they will want to take action. On the MOSOP Canada Web site, a visitor can read "The MOSOP Story" to find out about the Ogoni, their history, and what else has been published about their situation. This story of the organization allows the visitor to be briefed about the Ogoni tribe in Southern Nigeria, who have been battling nonviolently against their country's dictatorship and the oil interests that have exploited their land without recompense since the 1950s. This story has many related documents linked to it so that the visitor can see what is behind the report.

For example, in the middle of the story of the organization, there is a link to the Ogoni Bill of Rights. By clicking on the link, one can read the entire text of the group's founding document (the beginning of which can be seen in Exhibit 8–4).

EXHIBIT 8–4   Providing Good Background Information: Ogoni Bill of Rights

Also, since the MOSOP Canada Web site has a Library of background materials archived in a searchable online database, a visitor can find any sort of press release, news clipping, or report that will make them more assured about taking action in the campaign for justice for the Ogoni people.

A campaigning web site may want to supply the visitor with a FAQ (Frequently Asked Questions) document which answers common questions about the organization and what it does. This is an acceptable and familiar method for web sites to offer information to visitors. The MOSOP Story outlined above does the same thing. A good example of a simple FAQ can be found on the Canadian Center for Philanthropy's Web site.

It is important to offer supporters a place where a nonprofit can outline campaign accomplishments. This is a way of letting supporters know the results of their participation in campaigns. A good example is the Victories section of the Web site for The Rainforest Action Network. Since their Web site invites a lot of participation from visitors (there are several email and fax campaigns on the site), this keeps people interested and up-to-date in regards to the San Francisco-based environmental justice organization.

It is also important to inform supporters about upcoming events and demonstrations, which is best done through calendars. By having an online calendar available to supporters, they can be clear about what they can do to take action on the streets or in the galleries of their legislatures. MOSOP Canada has a calendar that outlines when demonstrations will take place outside of Nigerian embassies and Shell Oil stations. In this way, activists in Canada and around the world will know what is happening in their country or region.

The Rainforest Action Network Web site (Exhibit 8–5) provides an excellent list of demonstrations that can be linked to from its home page. People across the United States can find out where they can protest about rainforest devastation—from Mitsubishi offices to the headquarters of the World Bank.

Contact Information for Campaign Targets

Every nonprofit organization needs to help its supporters know their opponents. It is an important adage when campaigning. A nonprofit's supporters need to be able to contact government officials, corporate leaders, or other individuals that are the target of a campaign.

MOSOP Canada is working hard to get its supporters to pressure Nigerian government missions around the world (see Exhibit 8–6). That is why it has made a link on its Web site to a list of Nigerian Embassies and Consulates around the world, urging their supporters to advocate for justice for the Ogoni people with those officials. Once a nonprofit organization has supporters, it is good to let them know who they are trying to influence on the nonprofit's behalf. In the United

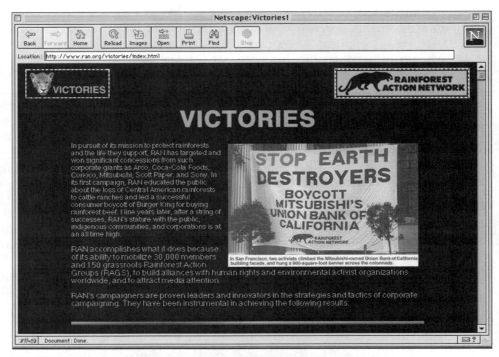

EXHIBIT 8–5   Communicating with Supporters: Rainforest Action Network

States, many organizations that are trying to get legislation passed or stopped on their behalf need to know about the elected officials who may be blocking any such action. Many organizations point their campaigners to the Vote Smart Web site (**http://www.vote-smart.org**) (Exhibit 8–7), where they can track the voting records and resumes of over 13,000 elected officials. They can also find out how to contact the officials through the Web site.

A Gathering Place for Campaigners

One of the most effective ways to campaign involves building local units of activists. National and international committees and associations need to get together to guide policy and share information. Much of the meeting among campaigners can now happen on the Internet. A Web site can facilitate these meetings, both effectively and cheaply.

There are a couple of methods that one can use to get supporters together online. The first is to create an Internet mailing list (or listserv in Net parlance), which

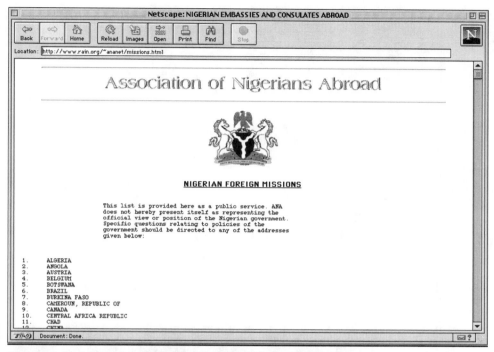

EXHIBIT 8–6   Contact Information for Campaign Targets: MOSOP Canada

can connect hundreds or even thousands of campaigners. The second is a discussion area on a nonprofit's Web site where supporters (or even opponents) can post ideas about an issue. The third way to connect campaigners is by using chat software that enables real-time discussions to happen. Finally, one can link the nonprofit organization's Web site to like-minded sites through a Web ring. The nonprofit organization must decide what sort of connections it wants to make between campaigners and the organization's staff.

Listservs

The mailing list (or listserv) is probably the most powerful tool a nonprofit has to connect campaigners. It is a place where activists can share ideas and information. There, they can plan common projects and demonstrations for their campaign. Listservs are where virtual communities are born on the Internet, as far-flung activists communicate quickly and cheaply.

MOSOP Canada does not have a meeting place on its Web site, but instead has a link to a listserv that deals with the Ogoni issue. Each listserv has a name, and the

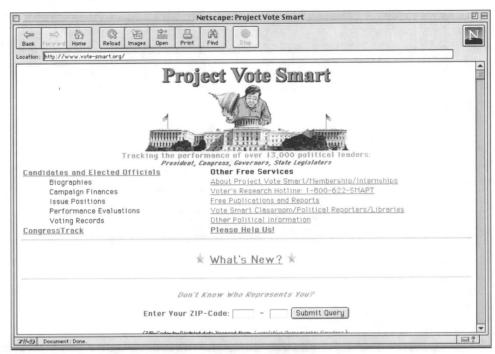

EXHIBIT 8–7   Project Vote Smart: Information about Politicians

listserv focused on the Ogoni campaign is called shell-action-nigeria. It is there that activists, journalists, and Ogonis get together to share information about what is happening to the campaign in Nigeria and around the world. It was set up by Essential Action, the Washington-based group headed by Ralph Nader.

To join the shell-action-nigeria listserv (and this should be the same for other listservs), one needs to send an email message to the owner (or coordinator) of the list. In the above case, one needs to address his or her email to shell-nigeria-action@essential.org, listproc@essential.org. One does not need to add a subject to the email. The text of the subscribing email should read:

subscribe shell-action-nigeria John Smith

That is all there is to it. When one has subscribed to a listserv, one receives an email in return that confirms the subscription and gives instructions specific about how to use that listserv. The shell-action-nigeria sends back an email confirmation like this:

From: listproc@essential.org
Date: Wed, 23 Apr 1997 08:44:53 -0400 (EDT)
Errors-To: shell-nigeria-action-owner@essential.org
Reply-To: listproc@essential.org
Sender: listproc@essential.org
To: nomad@mail.ican.net
Subject: SUBSCRIBE SHELL-NIGERIA-ACTION NOMAD@ICAN.NET
X-Listprocessor-Version: 6.0c—ListProcessor by Anastasios Kotsikonas
X-Comment: Essential Information ListProcessor

You have been added to list shell-nigeria-action@essential.org.
The system has recorded your address as

nomad@mail.ican.net

and in order for your messages to get posted (if the list accepts postings),
you will have to send them from this address, unless the list does not require subscription for posting.
    If a message is ever rejected, please contact the list's owner: shell-
nigeria-action-owner@essential.org

Your initial password is 861799492. Please change it as soon as you can by
issuing the following request to listproc@essential.org:

SET SHELL-NIGERIA-ACTION PASSWORD 861799492 new-password

WARNING: Do not use your login password;
you will be breaching security at your site.

You may change the address you are subscribed with (currently nomad@
mail.ican.net) with the following request:

SET SHELL-NIGERIA-ACTION ADDRESS 861799492 new-address

assuming that you keep the same password.

For information on this service and how to use it, send the following request in the body of a mail message to listproc@essential.org:

HELP

All requests should be addressed to HYPERLINK mailto:listproc@essential
.org(listproc@essential.org).

When one emails a message to the listserv, it is distributed to everyone who has subscribed to the mailing list. A typical message on the shell-action-nigeria mailing list may read as follows:

X-From_:shell-nigeria-action@essential.org Fri Feb 20 17:30:49 1998
Date: Fri, 20 Feb 1998 17:28:33 -0500 (EST)
Errors-To: shell-nigeria-action-owner@essential.org
Reply-To: sierra@vcn.bc.ca
Originator: shell-nigeria-action@essential.org
Sender: shell-nigeria-action@essential.org
From: Sierra Club <sierra@vcn.bc.ca>
To: Multiple recipients of list <shell-nigeria-action@essential.org>
Subject: Royal Geographic Society action . . .
X-Listprocessor-Version: 6.0c—ListProcessor by Anastasios Kotsikonas
X-Comment: To unsubscribe from this list, send the message "unsubscribe shell-nigeria-action" to
"listproc@essential.org". Leave the "Subject:" line blank.

Hi All. Shortly after the murder of the Ogoni Nine, the Royal Geographic Society ended Shell's association as a patron of the society. Can anyone help me with where this was reported and other examples of this action. Would appreciate the original post. Thanks. Take care. anon Sid

---

Sierra Club Lower Mainland Group
1672 East 10th Avenue
Vancouver, British Columbia V5N 1X5
Telephone: 604-873-8554 Fax: 604-872-0709
sierra@vcn.bc.ca http://www.sierraclub.ca/bc

This is a request for information that was posted to the shell-action-nigeria listserv. Soon enough, a response was emailed to the subscribers.

X-From_: shell-nigeria-action@essential.org Fri Feb 20 18:03:23 1998
Date: Fri, 20 Feb 1998 18:01:22 -0500 (EST)
Errors-To: shell-nigeria-action-owner@essential.org
Reply-To: marcia@essential.org
Originator: shell-nigeria-action@essential.org
Sender: shell-nigeria-action@essential.org
From: Marcia Carroll <marcia@essential.org>
To: Multiple recipients of list <shell-nigeria-action@essential.org>
Subject: Re: Royal Geographic Society action . . .

X-Listprocessor-Version: 6.0c—ListProcessor by Anastasios Kotsikonas
X-Comment: To unsubscribe from this list, send the message "unsubscribe
shell-nigeria-action" to
"listproc@essential.org". Leave the "Subject:" line blank.

Sierra Club wrote:

>Hi All. Shortly after the murder of the Ogoni Nine, the Royal Geographic
Society ended Shell's association as a patron of the society. Can anyone
help me with where this was reported and other examples of this action.
Would appreciate the original post. Thanks. Take care. anon Sid
Copyright 1996 Guardian Newspapers Limited
The Guardian (London)

January 6, 1996

SECTION: THE GUARDIAN HOME PAGE; Pg. 7
HEADLINE: ACADEMICS REJECT SHELL AS SPONSOR
BYLINE: Paul Brown Environment Correspondent

BODY:
SPONSORSHIP of the Royal Geographic Society by Shell should be
ended immediately, the annual conference of British Geographers de-
manded last night in an emergency resolution.

The vote, by 204 to 10 with 24 abstentions, follows alarm at Shell's role
in Nigeria, and particularly at the execution of the writer Ken Saro-Wiwa
and eight compatriots who had protested at the damage done to their
Ogoni homeland by oil companies.

The academics who packed the meeting at the annual conference of
the research and higher education division in Glasgow were unhappy that
the society apparently wants to hang on to its pounds 40,000-a-year sponsorship from Shell as long as possible.

Anticipating last night's vote, the ruling council had already put in
train a "major review of corporate patronage." Big business sponsorship
nets the society around pounds 160,000 a year—10 per cent of its income.
The council will have last night's vote referred to its next meeting in March.

Tim Unwin, one of three honorary secretaries of the 13,500-strong organisation, one of the most prestigious of its kind in Europe, pointed out
that Shell sponsorship over nine years had paid for many youth expedi-
tions. He described last night's meeting as unrepresentative of the membership, and said soundings would have to be taken across all the fellows.

The vote exposed renewed tensions between the organisation's academic members and non-academic fellows, who take part in activities at

the London headquarters. The two groups split in 1933 and, until an amalgamation last year, had remained separate as the society and the Institute of British Geographers.

David Gilbert, a lecturer in geography at the Royal Holloway College, London, proposing the resolution to end Shell sponsorship, said: "I believe that Shell's environmental and political record in Nigeria makes that company unfit to be the patron of any society claiming to represent practising geographers."

Shell distributed a press release which said: "We believe our most useful role is helping Nigeria overcome its economic problems and creating wealth that will give the people of Nigeria a better living standard. We will continue to try and perform this role with efficiency and integrity, and without becoming involved in politics."

As can be seen from the preceding postings, listservs are places where information is shared between campaigners.

One has three choices as to how to organize a listserv. One can make it an open listserv, which means that subscription requests and postings of information are automatically approved. This makes for a more freewheeling environment since anyone can take part. The second sort of listserv is an approved mailing list. This means that the manager of the listserv receives all subscription requests and must approve them. It also means the listserv manager can unsubscribe participants if they are not behaving properly. Finally, one can have a moderated listserv. The manager of the mailing list would approve both subscriptions and all messages posted to the group.

One must work with one's Internet service provider (ISP) to set up a listserv. Once it is set up, the nonprofit organization must make sure that someone monitors and manages it.

Discussion Area

It may be that an organization wants a place on its Web site where people post their ideas. A discussion area is one such place. It is really just one long list of thoughts about the nonprofit organization's work and campaigns. For an example of what a discussion area might look like, take a look at the roundtable area of the Hewitt and Johnston Consultants Web site seen in Exhibit 8–8. It is a simple page where people post their thoughts.

Chat Area

Chat is about real-time conversations between people on the Internet. This is not an effective method for sharing information between campaigners because it is difficult to coordinate people's schedules so that they are online at the same time.

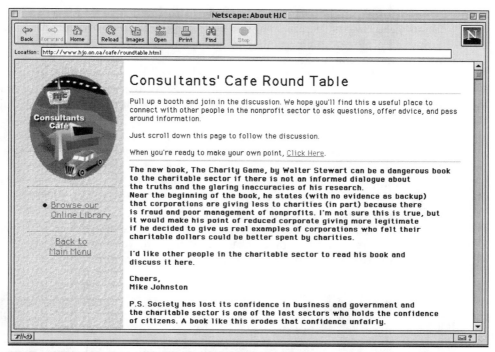

EXHIBIT 8-8   Discussion Area: Hewitt and Johnston Consulting

Generally, chat areas work only if the constituency is large, thus ensuring that some people will always be online to chat. Greenpeace International has a link to the Waveland Web site, a place where people can chat about environmental issues of concern to them. Chat areas are effective in campaigning when information needs to be shared and discussed immediately. For example, if a protest needs to be coordinated in three cities across North America the following day, then an online chat could facilitate a discussion about the action cheaply and immediately (no long distance telephone charges).

However, for most organizations, listservs or discussion areas are the most effective online environments for sharing information.

Web Rings

A Web ring is a free service offered to the Internet community by **www .webring.org.** By creating a Web ring, like-minded organizations can create a community of linked home pages that bypass the need to use search engines (or other methods) to find one's way between sites.

A simple link allows someone to go from one home page to the next home page in the ring as seen in Exhibit 8–9. It may be a cheap and effective way for a nonprofit organization to get its Web site seen by visitors who are interested in the organization's core issue.

The Web ring system has grown quickly and has some 22,000 separate rings linked together on a vast number of topics. All of the Web rings are operated by volunteer individuals across the Internet (who are initiators and/or members of specific Web rings).

Once visitors are at one of the sites in a Web ring, they can click on a "Next" or "Previous" link on that home page to go to adjacent sites in the ring, eventually bringing them to the Web site where they started in the Web ring. Of course, an organization can do this by building new links into its site, but this means that its home page must be edited to make a link to another organization. The Web ring system allows one to avoid changing the hypertext markup language (HTML) code on a home page every time someone new joins the Web ring. Instead, the "Next" or "Previous" link on a home page points to a special CGI script, in a database at **webring.org**, that directs visitors to the next (or previous) site in the ring.

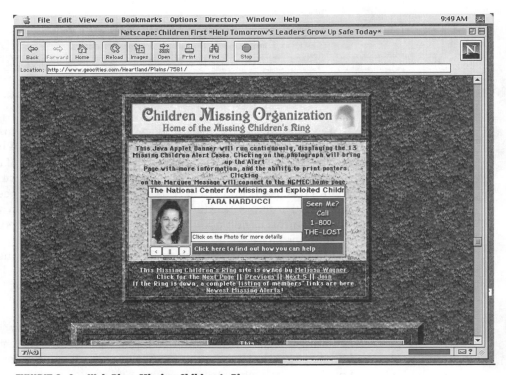

EXHIBIT 8–9   Web Ring: Missing Children's Ring

The Web ring in Exhibit 8–9 is operated by Melissa Wagner of Children Missing Organization. On her home page, one can see that it is easy get to the "Next" or "Previous" sites in the Web ring. There is also a simple way to join at any point in the ring.

One can see in the list of members that a large number of organizations concerned with missing children take part in this specific Web ring.

If organizations want to find a Web ring that is appropriate for them to join, they can visit Ring World (**http://www.webring.org/ringworld/**), the online directory of the Web ring system (see Exhibit 8–10). If they cannot find a Web ring that suits their needs, they are free to start their own.

Online Communities of Activists

There are online communities in which action-oriented campaigning groups gather. Progressive networks and progressive ISPs enable networks of campaigners to share experiences and technology, thus strengthening their work (separately and together) on a wide variety of issues.

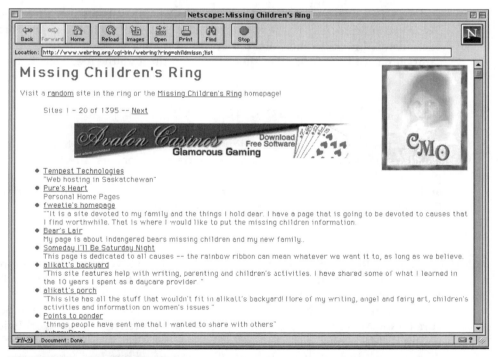

EXHIBIT 8–10   Web Ring Directory

The Institute for Global Communications (IGC) (**www.igc.org**) is an ISP that also acts as a support and gathering center for nonprofit activist agencies. They help coordinate large network of activists in EcoNet, PeaceNet, ConflictNet, WomensNet and LabourNet. They are also committed to helping get Internet technology into the developing world.

The IGC is the U.S. member of the Association for Progressive Communications (APC), a global partnership of computer networks that link activists around the world. These ISPs are support centers for activists and campaigners.

In Canada, Web Net (**www.web.net**) is the member of the APC and not only houses and assists the online needs of its nonprofit members, but also hosts specialized online conferences on a number of topics of great interest to campaigning and activist groups. These conferences are available only to members of Web Net.

How Do People Contact You?

Supporters of an online campaign need a way to contact a nonprofit organization with questions and comments. The MOSOP Canada Web site has a feedback icon displayed prominently in the top right-hand corner of its home page. This Feedback icon is linked to their email account of mailto:info@mosopcanada.org. The campaign coordinator receives the emails sent through the feedback icon.

Send Faxes and Emails from Your Web Site

In order to make an online campaign truly effective, one needs to offer supporters a chance to fax or email their messages to decision makers directly from the nonprofit's Web site. Once the nonprofit organization has discovered the fax numbers and email addresses for the targets of their campaign, they must set up a place on their Web site where people can express themselves.

Fax Servers

There are different methods for sending faxes from a Web site. The nonprofit organization must work with its ISP to set up a system for getting faxes sent from its Web site to a fax machine at the opposite end, all via the Internet.

Rainforest Action Network (RAN) has used faxes sent from its site to put pressure on the Mitsubishi Corporation to clean up its activities in the worldwide timber trade. Mark Westlund, the Media Director for RAN, says that their Web master "reports that their Web site is generating some five hundred faxes a week to the

Mitsubishi headquarters." He goes on to point out that their statistics "show that nearly 1 person in 10 who visits the site uses the Action Alert fax/email feature. This is an extremely high rate of return, especially when compared to an old-fashioned direct mailing piece that might generate a mere 1 to 3 percent response."[2]

MOSOP Canada has a letter that can be sent from its Web site to the fax machine of the Canadian Foreign Minister in Ottawa, asking that the Canadian government take more Ogoni refugees from camps across West Africa. (See Exhibits 8–2 and 8–11.) The MOSOP site offers the text of a letter that has already been written for supporters to sign with their name, mailing address, and email address. They may also add their own comments after the main text of the letter. The letter is sent as a form to a computer server in Ottawa, from which a fax is sent to the Minister's office. Because the fax is sent via a local telephone line, supporters of MOSOP across Canada or around the world can send a fax without incurring a long distance telephone charge. MOSOP Canada, however, must pay for the use of the fax server in Ottawa and the cost of programming the form on its Web site.

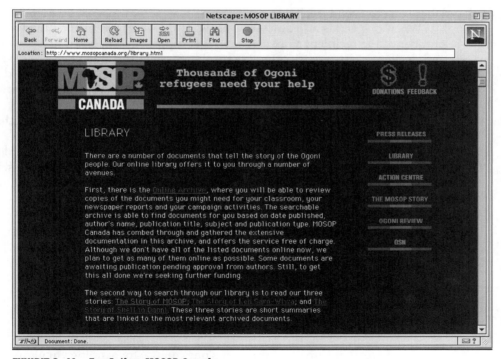

EXHIBIT 8–11 Fax Action: MOSOP Canada

[2]Mark Westlund, email letter to author, 9 September 1997.

Most Internet fax services require that one can send and receive electronic mail. A good example of sending emails as faxes can be found on the Fax the Feds Web site (**http://www.net-efx.com/faxfeds/**). This Web site allows Canadians to send emails that print out on the fax machines of Canadian Members of Parliament. This free service receives approximately 1,000 to 1,500 visitors per month. One can also send emails to the fax machines of all of the foreign diplomatic missions in Ottawa. In this way, someone can send a message of protest to the Nigerian Embassy in Ottawa regarding the treatment of the Ogoni people.

This method of transforming an email into a fax uses a common software programs. The above email-to-fax transformation uses a program called TPC.INT or the "Remote Printing Experiment." This is the progenitor of Internet faxing programs. Using the program is free, but someone (probably at an organization's ISP) needs to set up the program so that it send emails to their proper target. Also, one cannot send a fax anywhere in the world with this service. A group of organizations and individuals have joined together to use this program and provide free sending of faxes for the area they are responsible for. There are only certain areas where one can send free faxes.

When one sends a fax message using TPC.INT, one must include the phone number of the recipient's fax machine. A computer checks the target fax number and decides if any participating fax machines cover the area where one wants to send the fax. If there is a machine in the target area, the message is routed to the appropriate machine for sending. If there is no available fax server in that area, one will receive a message that the fax could not be delivered.

In order to find out what areas in the world may have a fax server that can send faxes, check the TPC.INT FAQ at **www.savetz.com/fax-faq.html**.

To send a fax by email on Fax the Feds, one simply clicks on the minister or embassy's name. This will start whichever email program the sender has. When filling in the details of an email for faxing, one must address the email as follows:

To: remote-printer.info@phonenumber.iddd.tpc.int

The info part of the address is where one fills in information for the cover page. The symbols "/" are turned into a line break, and "_" is read as a space. Here is an example:

To: remote-printer.Arlo_Cats/Room_123@12025551234.iddd.tpc.int

Of course, there are other programs one can use for sending emails as faxes to campaign targets. One must make sure to consult with one's ISP or technical support to make sure that one chooses the most cost-effective and efficient way for sending faxes.

Emails

Sending emails to decision makers from a Web site is incredibly easy. Making a link to a member of Congress, corporate officer, or other influential figure can be accomplished quickly once one knows the email address. The challenge comes with finding the email address. Many public figures have email addresses monitored by staff. The decision makers themselves are not accessible. However, one aim of the campaigner is to find the more private email addresses of those they wish to influence. So, again, it is the research to find the right email addresses that is the challenge for the campaigner.

Also, once decision makers start to get their email addresses bombarded with emails, they may change or cancel their account. People are becoming more protective of their email addresses.

One of the most effective email campaigns was organized by the Electronic Frontier Foundation in 1995. The EFF, a nonprofit civil liberties organization working in the public interest to protect privacy, free expression, and access to public resources and information online, organized the online community to fight the Communications Decency Act section of the Telecommunications Reform Bill. The bill was seen as a restriction on freedom of speech online. The EFF campaign urged supporters to send emails and faxes to key members of Congress, protesting the bill. Over several weeks, more than 20,000 people had sent electronic messages to members of Congress.

Although the bill passed into law, it was eventually struck down for being unconstitutional. There are many campaigning sites that could use fax or email actions on their Web sites. A good example is the Death Penalty Information Center (**http://www.essential.org/dpic**) seen in Exhibit 8–12. The Web site is packed with excellent information about the death penalty issue across the United States, but there is no quick and decisive action that can be taken from the site. A fax service that allowed people to send messages to Texas Governor George Bush before the execution of Karla Faye Tucker in early February 1998 may have been helpful to the cause.

Ready-to-Go Campaign Materials

Many campaigning groups are unconcerned with copyright issues around their information. They want to get their message spread as far as possible. Web sites can offer newsletters, posters, and placards that can be printed from the Web site for mass photocopying and distribution.

In Britain, there is an activist newsletter published on the Internet called Delta, which is an examination of what is happening in the Niger Delta communities in Nigeria, where the Ogoni people live (see Exhibit 8–13). Delta makes it very clear

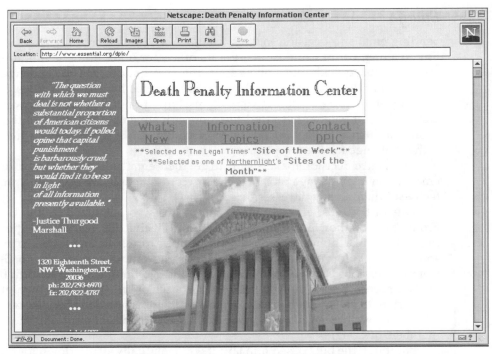

EXHIBIT 8–12   Lack of Email/Fax: Death Penalty Information Center

that their material is "anti-copyrighted," urging people to photocopy and distribute the newsletter as widely as possible.

Signing Up Supporters to a Campaign

A Web site is a great place to canvass for supporters to join campaigning efforts. By getting them to sign up online, a nonprofit organization can stay in touch by emailing them updates, times and places of demonstrations, and further background material in the form of emailed newsletters.

Amnesty International uses its Web site to get people to sign up to its campaign to support the 50th Anniversary of the Declaration of Human Rights. The request is made prominently on the home page. Once getting to the sign-up area, one can sign an online petition that will add the visitor's name to the millions of others to be presented at the United Nations on December 10, 1998, at the General Assembly proceedings to mark the 50th Anniversary of the Declaration of Human Rights. One can also indicate whether he or she would like to receive campaign information updates online.

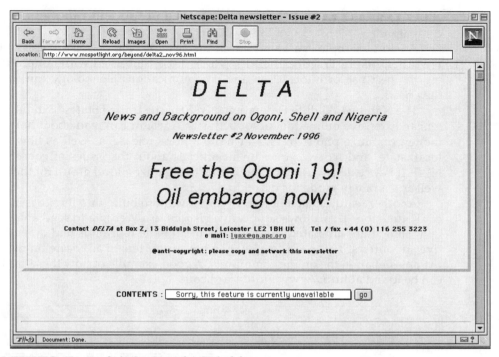

EXHIBIT 8–13   Ready to Go: Campaign Material

One may also want to try and get volunteers to sign up on a nonprofit's Web site. A special area can be created that asks people to leave their name and email if they want to be contacted about volunteering.

Getting Materials to Online Supporters

With a Web site, a nonprofit organization has the ability to send useful and well-designed materials via email to online supporters. For example, MOSOP Canada is now creating a newsletter that incorporates photographs and other information, which can be emailed to supporters that have asked to be informed on a regular basis. It is a cheap and effective way of getting important information to a network of supporters. Some of MOSOP Canada's supporters that will be emailed include 400 individuals who asked Greenpeace Canada for more information about the Ogoni before MOSOP Canada had created its Web site.

One of the most useful things a nonprofit organization can offer online supporters is a toolkit for activist activities taken on behalf of a nonprofit. Many organizations have created "how to" kits so that people will know exactly how to campaign.

A good example can be found on the Benton Foundation's Web site (**http://www.benton.org/Practice/Toolkit**), where those concerned with nonprofits making the best use of information and communications technology can find what they need.

The National Wildlife Federation (NWF) in the United States (Exhibit 8–14) offers an extensive online toolkit for activists. A visitor can read about how to raise money, organize phone trees, and write a press release, as well as how to lobby local, state, and federal government officials about the issues of concern to the NWF. It is an extensive toolkit about how to organize a local group for the NWF, as well as a strategy guide for individual action.

Another feature that a nonprofit might want to build into its site is a "send-a-card" function. This allows supportive visitors to a Web site to send an appealing (and sometimes animated) postcard about an issue to friends and other prospective supporters. This is a cheap way to get supporters to advocate on the organization's behalf in the online community. A good example of how these cards work can be found at **http://www.buildacard.com**.

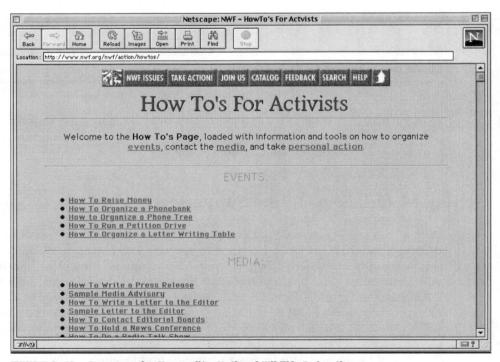

EXHIBIT 8–14   Resources for Nonprofits: National Wildlife Federation

Make a Campaigning Site Appealing

Internet activists are becoming more and more demanding about the Web sites they visit. They want to see a way to take direct action on an issue. They want good background information. They want to see a Web site that is effectively and creatively designed. More and more nonprofit agencies are upgrading their sites, making their graphics more powerful, and adding unique animation—all to appeal to visitors. All nonprofits need to get the Web surfer interested, and effective presentation is a part of the Web site's job.

MOSOP Canada has a powerful black color to most of it. On the home page, there are two powerful animated sequences that appeal directly to the potential supporter.

The first animated sequence are the words at the top of the page, which fade in and out, one after the other. They read:

> Thousands of Ogoni refugees need your help
> Thousands driven from their homes
> Innocents detained and killed
> You can make a difference
> Justice avoided is justice denied
> Fax Ottawa NOW from this site!

Clicking on any of the preceding phrases during the sequence will take the visitor directly to the Action Center, where he or she can fax Canadian Foreign Minister Lloyd Axworthy about the Ogoni refugee issue.

The other effective animation on the home page is the sequence of text and pictures at the center of the screen.

It is clear that using simple animation and effective writing can bring potential supporters into a campaign. MOSOP Canada is a good example of how one can present an issue to the public in a powerful way.

Civil Disobedience Online

Henry David Thoreau, in one of the most famous essays in American literature, "Resistance to Civil Government," stated: "Under a government which imprisons any unjustly, the true place for a just man is also in prison."

Nonprofit organizations often work to change injustice into justice, whether the injustice comes from government, the private sector, or individuals. The mission and mandate of many nonprofit organizations includes the impetus to protest and act to transform the world into one that is safer, fairer, and simply a better place.

Almost all nonprofit organizations work within the boundaries of the law to pursue their mission and mandate, but turning to civil disobedience is often a campaigning option that many see as legitimate. It is important for nonprofit organizations to understand the unique online tools and strategies they can use to campaign more effectively on their issues if legal strategies are no longer effective.

The following discussion of strategies and tactics is in no way endorsing this kind of online behavior, but with Thoreau's quote in mind, these online methods of protest are outlined with the long tradition of civil disobedience in Western democracies in mind.

Perhaps the best example of online civil disobedience has come from the pro-Zapatista movement. On January 1, 1994, there was an indigenous uprising in Chiapas Mexico. Immediately after this uprising, Zapatista communiques began appearing on listservs around the world. Soon thereafter, Web sites, more listservs, news groups, and informal email lists began to grow and coalesce around the Zapatista movement—giving it a chance to survive by creating a growing awareness in the online community about what was happening in Mexico.

The informal online network supporting the Zapatistas turned to online civil disobedience in early 1998. In April of 1998, the Los Angeles–based National Commission for Democracy in Mexico called for protests at Mexican consulates on April 10 to coincide with protests in Mexico City.

Soon after, the Zapatistas called for an online protest to mirror the terrestrial protests. This culminated with a call for a World Wide Web of electronic civil disobedience on May 10 to stop the war in Chiapas.

What is electronic civil disobedience? Stephen Wray is a doctoral student at New York University who has written on electronic civil disobedience. In a paper written for Earth First, he outlines the fact that: "Just as people may physically trespass upon real property, people may trespass upon virtual property on the Net. Just as people may blockade entranceways to buildings, offices, or factories, people may blockade entranceways to portals in cyberspace, to the doors and bridges that allow entrance and egress."[3]

Nonprofit organizations need to think of how they can take the activism of their real world activities and adopt them to the Net. The pro-Zapatista movement has done just that. In January 1998, the Anonymous Digital Coalition issued a plan for virtual sit-ins of five Web sites of Mexico City financial corporations. They issued information about the time zones so people could act together when it was 10:00 A.M. in Mexico City. They instructed people to use their Internet browsers to repeatedly reload the Web sites of these financial institutions. This means that they asked many people to repeatedly strike keys on their keyboards. If many people did it at the same time, then the massive number of reload requests would effectively blockade the Web site.

---

[3]Stephen Wray, in a listserv posting to devmedia@uoguelph.ca, 8 April 1998.

HERE'S HOW A NONPROFIT ORGANIZATION'S SUPPORTERS CAN CONDUCT A 'VIRTUAL SIT IN'

For Netscape Navigator Campaigners:

1. From the *Option Menu* select *Preferences* and set up:
   Memory cache = 0 and Disk cache = 0
   Verify document = Every Time
2. From the *Option* Menu select *Network Preferences,* and activate the No Proxies option.

For Microsoft Internet Explorer Campaigners:

1. From the *View* menu select *Options—Advanced—*and in the *Temporary Internet File Box* select Never

So what are the tools of electronic civil disobedience?

- Arising from the multiple keyboard striking mentioned earlier, there is now software that can automate the reloading requests of a browser—effectively blockading other visitors from reaching a Web site. These small programs are called ping engines. This can be a very effective way to blockade high-traffic sites.
- Another tool is the offshore spam engine. This is a form-driven Web site based in another country that can automatically distribute massive amounts of email to a particular email address. Some organizations are becoming aware of this tactic, and online security can put up barriers against the attacking spam engine.

The two examples outlined above are entranceway tools for electronic civil disobedience. There is one very different tool:

- Intelligent crawlers that crawl through a Web site are being programmed. They are called spiders. These spiders crawl through a site and help categorize and index material on the Web for search engines. Good spider programs move quickly through a site, collecting the information efficiently. However, a civil disobedience spider could be deliberately designed to creep very slowly through a site, causing disruptions to the targeted Web site.

It is important for every nonprofit organization to understand that sending letters online expressing dissent or disagreement with a government or corporation is not illegal. However, automating multiple dispersions of electronic signals causing electronic disruptions can be found illegal. Each organization will have to judge what is appropriate and understand the law.

One of the best places on the Web for more information about online civil disobedience can be found at **www.nyu.edu/projects/wray/oecd.html**.

Finally, a systematic and concerted effort by a nonprofit organization to campaign against the actions of an opponent could lead to a final act of online activism: brand assassination. Brand assassination relies on citizens using search engines to find out information on a particular organization, person, or institution.

When a citizen decides to find out more about an organization or issue they tend to use search engines—these indexes of what's online—the virtual yellow pages of the Internet. Every nonprofit organization has to understand that there may be opponents who will devote time and effort to spread opposing views (sometimes deceitful and devastating) concerning issues or the very reputation of a nonprofit.

On May 6, 1998, the author decided to conduct a search for the NAACP, The National Association for the Advancement of Colored People online using the very popular search engine, Infoseek. What came up was a good example of brand assassination. The first result was a reference to the web site of the NAACP at www.naacp.org. However, the second reference on Infoseek was a web site entitled, "Is the NAACP a racist organization?" which asked why the NAACP remains silent on the widespread abuse of Native Americans as mascots in sports (**http://www.iwchildren.org/naacp.htm**). Whether the visitor agreed with the question or not, the fact is, anyone looking for information on the NAACP could end up at a hard-hitting critique of the NAACP.

In another example on May 6th as well, using the search engine, Lycos, the author typed in Christian Coalition. The first two items brought back by the search engine were actual Christian Coalition sites, but the third was a biting attack on the Christian Coalition of Oklahoma (**www.sirinet.net/~truelife/cc/cc index .html**). The web site uses the Bible to systematically show (from its perspective) how the Christian Coalition falls far short of the Bible's teachings.

Search engines list discussion groups, Web sites, listservs, and many other places on the Net where a particular search topic comes up. Well-concerted efforts by a nonprofit organization's opponents (which may be ideological opponents as well as disgruntled employees, ex-employees, or disgruntled citizens and volunteers) could give online search engine users a shocking introduction to a nonprofit's work. Every nonprofit organization needs to constantly check out what comes up in the major search engines when its name and issues are typed in by citizens. Many nonprofit organizations who don't keep constant tabs on search engines could be unaware of brand assassination going on without their knowing.

CONCLUSION

Campaigning online in the free-for-all of hundreds of thousands of Web sites is a difficult job. However, following the checklist for online activist Web sites will help a nonprofit organization create a place that attracts supporters and will help make change on the issues that it considers important.

Case Study

THE WORLD WILDLIFE FUND USA

INTRODUCTION

The World Wildlife Fund (WWF) USA sees the World Wide Web as a medium ideally built for activism. Randy Snodgrass of WWF USA outlines why:

- Since environmental issues cross nation-state boundaries, the Internet allows global citizens to take action from any part of the world.
- The Internet allows for immediate and flexible activism. If a government, politician, or business leader needs to be pressured, a Web site can put up their fax number or email immediately. Direct mail can take weeks to get to an activist.
- The Internet is a cost effective medium for campaigning. The cost of telephone and mail activism can be prohibitive.
- Every decision-maker in the world has either an email or a fax number and that means a Web site can help an activist to immediately reach and pressure them on an environmental issue.

ONLINE RESULTS

For the last year and a half, WWF USA has been offering online visitors the opportunity to send email and faxes to decision-makers on important environmental issues. They've been generous enough to provide the results of the completed online actions:

WWF ONLINE ACTIONS:

- Save our roadless areas: 805 messages sent (21 wks; 38/wk avg)
- Save the Tongass wilderness area: 1019 messages sent (13 wks; 78/wk avg)
- Save Dillon Creek: 983 messages sent (23 wks; 43/wk avg)
- Protect the Galapagos I: 457 messages sent (14 wks; 33/wk avg)

- Everglades: 235 messages sent (5 wks; 47/wk avg)
- Bryan Amendment (timber roads bill): 454 messages sent (10 wks; 45/wk avg)

There was an average of 47 faxes and/or emails sent each week during these initial online action campaigns. Since those first online campaigns, WWF USA has launched a series of new actions that are attracting more online citizenry to action (these current statistics are combined faxes and emails, where WWF USA has offered both):

- Protect the Galapagos II: 1671 messages sent (2 wks; 836/wk avg)
- Save tigers and rhinos: 4855 messages sent to date (19 weeks; 256/wk avg)
- Protect tropical forests: 1170 messages sent to date (8 wks; 146/wk avg)
- Help protect sea turtles: 3340 messages sent to date (2 wks; 1670/wk avg)
- Save Izembek wilderness area: 140 messages sent to date (2 wks; 70/wk avg)
- Save the Everglades: 1094 messages sent to date (1 week; 1094/wk avg)

There is an average of 678 faxes and/or emails sent each week from these new online action campaigns. That is a 1,500% increase in online activism! What is more, the most current campaign, a Turtle Alert, started in May of 1998 is garnering approximately 1,064 faxes and/or emails sent per week.

INSPIRING THE ONLINE ACTIVIST

Every activist wants to know that their action is making a difference. It is no different whether it is an activist pounding the pavement or an online activist sending emails. The World Wildlife Fund USA has done a very good job of showing every online activist what their electronic action can accomplish. After every online campaign, WWF USA puts up a web page under the heading: Action Results (**http://takeaction.worldwildlife.org/action.htm**) like the following:

Thank you! VICTORY IN THE GALAPAGOS!

In early February, many of you responded to an urgent Conservation Action Network alert asking you to help protect the Galapagos Islands. Your response was tremendous. In just two and a half days, you helped generate more than 600 faxes and e-mails urging President Clinton to express his support to President Alarcon of Ecuador for a pending Galapagos Conservation Law.

We are pleased to report that on March 6, the Ecuadorean government approved the law, a series of sweeping new protective measures for the ecologically rich Galapagos Islands. The law's passage is a landmark in the effort to conserve and protect these singular islands and their unique plants and animals. WWF thanks everybody whose actions helped to save the Galapagos.

For more about the new law, visit our Victory in the Galapagos! section. For more about the islands and the conservation challenges they face, visit our Pressures on Paradise section. You can also visit our Results section to see more positive impacts of WWF's involvement.

Stay tuned for more updates on actions you take through the Conservation Action Network!

Every nonprofit organization that conducts an online campaign should take heed of World Wildlife Fund's example and give their supporters a results page to inspire them to more online activism.

A NEW ONLINE ACTIVIST STRATEGY

This growing success has emboldened WWF USA to create a new and more sophisticated online activist strategy called the Conservation Action Network or CAN. David Housley of World Wildlife Fund USA states that, "We've launched what we're calling the Conservation Action Network (CAN), an electronic (mainly web and email-based) advocacy network. There are 4500 members of CAN to date and we're aiming for 25,000 members. It is a really interesting project and one that we're hoping takes off in a big way."

WWF USA has designed what they are calling a Personal Action Center. Online activists are asked to enter personal information that includes regular contact information like name, address and contact numbers, but then asks for some important new elements:

- They ask each activist how they want their personal introduction to begin on any action email or fax to a decision-maker. A long line of choices like citizen, taxpayer, mother, father, professional etc. are available. The WWF says that, "For example, a letter to a Senator may contain the line 'as a concerned parent and salesperson in your state, I feel that. . . .' Please select from the list of professions below, or feel free to type a word that better describes your vocation."
- Individuals are asked to fill out which environmental issues they would like to receive email notice about.
- Finally, a user name and password are entered.

By filling out this personal information, WWF USA offers every online activist a Personal Action Center on their web site. When a Personal Action Center member decides to come to the WWF USA web site, after filling out their personal information, they'll be presented with a personal greeting, with activist opportunities crafted for them alone. When they want to send an activist email or fax, their personal information will be automatically built into the correspondence.

WWF will allow every Personal Action Center member to personalize the letter-head. It is less effective when every email or fax looks exactly the same. Through this service, every email and fax will be unique and individual. The first Personal Action Center campaign begins on July 8th, 1998. (See Exhibit 8–15.)

GOALS AND PROMOTION

Randy Snodgrass has set goals for CAN that WWF believes are realistic. Since CAN's promotion at the beginning of 1998, WWF USA has attracted almost 4,000 Personal Action Center members from 63 countries. They expect to reach 25,000 by the end of 1998, 50,000 by the end of 1999. They anticipate 100,000 sometime during the year 2000.

To help them achieve their goals, WWF USA has implemented a promotions campaign that includes:

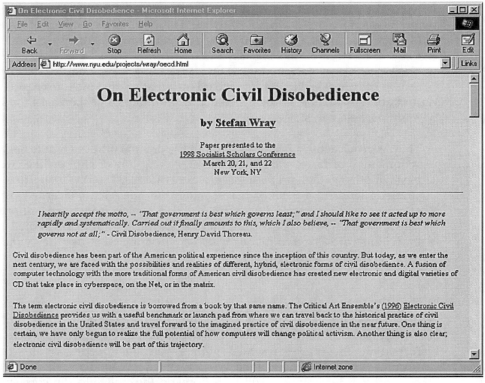

EXHIBIT 8–15   Civil Disobedience on the Net

- Mailing over 25,000 of their most active supporters and asking them to join this online Personal Action Center.
- Launching a print ad campaign in computer magazines.
- Working with search engines like Yahoo to begin an online banner campaign directing online users to the Personal Action Centre.
- Ensuring current print publications highlight the Personal Action Center.

THE FUTURE

Once the Personal Action Centre is underway, WWF USA will turn its attention to Push technology to help its online activism.

Push technology has tried to offer the consumer or customer the ability to get information in a time-sensitive manner—pushed to their computer interface without asking for it at. The problem with Push technology in the nonprofit sector is the fact that it isn't needed for the most part. There is a need for up-to-the-minute information on Wall Street, but neither a cancer society nor a hospital needs this kind of updated-every-five-minutes kind of interface.

However, in the case of urgent environmental and social action, Push technology is probably appropriate for an organization like WWF USA. That's why they are working on what can be called "Push Panda" technology. The WWF Panda is one of the most recognizable logos in the world, right behind McDonald's golden arches, Coca Cola and a handful of other symbols. WWF USA wants to be able to push a small program (along with its Panda logo) onto an activist's computer. The Panda would reside on the computer screen. Whenever an urgent email (perhaps asking the computer owner to take action) is sent by WWF, the Panda will begin to flash, swivel, or move (some kind of animation) in order to get the attention of the activist. That person will instantly know that WWF needs their help. By clicking on the Panda icon they'll go right to their Personal Action Center on the WWF USA site—ready to take action on an important environmental issue.

Appendix 8-A

CAMPAIGNING ONLINE CHECKLIST

The Campaigning Online Checklist has been designed to remind one of the most important issues when preparing a Web site to campaign effectively.

EFFECTIVE AND ACCURATE INFORMATION ABOUT THE ORGANIZATION AND ITS CAMPAIGN

( ) Have you gathered and presented all of the most important information about your nonprofit organization? Tell more about your organization than you would on paper: the publication costs are lower online.

( ) Have you outlined the mission and mandate of your organization?

( ) Is the background to your campaign outlined clearly?

( ) Is there a library of the most important documents for the Web site visitor?

( ) Have you created a Frequently Asked Questions (FAQ) section?

( ) Have you made an Accomplishments section to explain your campaign's progress?

( ) Is there a place where supporters can find out about upcoming events and demonstrations?

( ) Is there an area where journalists can find your press releases and latest news?

A LIST OF CONTACT INFORMATION FOR INSTITUTIONS AND INDIVIDUALS THE CAMPAIGN IS TARGETING

( ) Have you created a place where supporters can find information about the targets of your campaign (i.e., list of numbers and addresses [terrestrial and electronic] for legislators)?

A PLACE FOR CAMPAIGNERS TO EXCHANGE INFORMATION

( ) Have you created a listserv for your supporters?

( ) Is there a discussion area on your Web site for supporters?

( ) Do you need a chat area on your Web site where supporters can share ideas in real time?

( ) Have you investigated using a Web ring to increase the effectiveness of your online campaigning?

( ) Are you a part of the APC family: the IGC in the United States, Web Networks in Canada, or Greenet in the United Kingdom?

A WAY FOR SUPPORTERS TO CONTACT THE NONPROFIT

( ) Is there a feedback logo or mechanism prominently displayed on your home page and connected to an email address?

( ) Is there a staff member who is responsible for answering questions received by the feedback email?

THE ABILITY TO SEND FAXES AND EMAILS TO DECISION MAKERS DIRECTLY OR INDIRECTLY FROM THE WEB SITE

( ) Do you need to set up a fax or email function so that supporters can take action from your Web site?

( ) Have you costed a fax server function with your ISP?

( ) Is the target fax number or email address accurate?

( ) Have you included text for online activists to cut and paste when creating a fax/email to be sent to the target?

( ) Have you ensured that any fax or email sent from your site to a protest target is also duplicated and sent to you as an email to build an activist database?

( ) Have you planned to print the faxes or emails sent in protest and then physically present them to the target of the activism?

CAMPAIGN MATERIALS READY MADE FOR PRINTING

( ) Are there campaign materials you would like to have available for printing online?

( ) Are these materials formatted properly for printing from your Web site?

( ) Have you indicated that your online campaign material is anti-copyrighted and can be copied and spread throughout the Net by campaigners?

( ) Have you included, or linked to, a toolkit that explains how an online supporter can be a more effective online activist?

A WAY FOR SUPPORTERS TO SIGN UP FOR THE CAMPAIGN

( ) Is there an easy way for visitors to sign up to your campaign on your Web site?

( ) Do you have staff and materials ready to service these new members online?

AN OUTREACH SYSTEM FOR SENDING CAMPAIGN MATERIALS TO SUPPORTERS VIA EMAIL

( ) Is it effective to send materials to supporters via email?

( ) Do you have the staff and resources to be able to send these materials via the Internet?

INTERACTIVE AND ANIMATED ELEMENTS TO APPEAL TO VISITORS

( ) Does your Web site make best use of:
    ( ) Simple animation?
    ( ) Powerful graphics?
    ( ) Sound?
    ( ) Video?

ONLINE CIVIL DISOBEDIENCE (OPTIONAL)

( ) If your legal electronic campaigning online is not effective, have you engaged in, or instructed activist supporters, in a form of electronic civil disobedience that includes:
    ( ) Ping engines?
    ( ) Offshore spam engines?
    ( ) Spiders?

Getting Your Message to Stand Out: Marketing Online

The Web site is built. It is beautiful and relevant to the organization's mission and mandate, but it resides on the Internet—a vast electronic landscape filled with tens of millions of voices. How is anyone going to hear about the Web site? How can an organization get anyone to come for a visit?

Every nonprofit organization needs to develop a strategy to bring the public to its Web site. An online marketing strategy needs to be much like any other type of outreach that a nonprofit organization does in the "real world." Online marketing strategies should include:

- Publicizing the Web site in all of your real world publications and products
- Deciding who the nonprofit organization's audience is—and understanding how they are different online than offline
- Looking at the kinds of information that an organization wishes to deliver and knowing how to get it online

Finally, the Web site must reach out to the people the organization desires to contact. Unlike television, where a message is broadcast out to the world in general, the Internet is very personal and private—the media term for this intimacy is *narrowcasting*. This means a nonprofit organization must seek out its audience and attract them to its place on the Net.

PREPARATORY WORK BEFORE MARKETING ONLINE

Information flow is crucial to the survival of every nonprofit organization. An organization usually uses a number of media to communicate information to its stakeholders. Many nonprofit organizations are adept at using printed materials like newsletters, direct mail fund-raising packages, annual reports, and business cards to tell various publics what they do, who they are, and where they can be contacted.

Most nonprofit organizations include their mailing address and telephone numbers on their printed materials. Now, each organization needs to add its email and Web site addresses. If an organization uses television or radio spots, it should add its Web site address to the messages broadcast in each medium.

Exhibit 9-1 highlights how one nonprofit organization, The Arthritis Society of Canada, has made excellent use of its printed materials in getting more people to visit its Web site. The Arthritis Society of Canada sends out a bimonthly magazine to its members and contacts. The subject matter covers a wide range of relevant material for people suffering from arthritis and their loved ones. In preparation of its Web site launch in November 1996, it allocated its Winter 1996 edition to the promotion of the new Web site. The magazine, *Arthritis News,* was 17 pages chock full of information about the new Web site, including the following:

- An introductory article on why the site was built and what it means to users and the organization in the future
- Graphics showing the home page and explaining what is behind some of the content areas on that first page
- An area called "Net Notes" that offered "Quick Tips" and "Close Up"—two content areas that can help new Net users make sense of the Arthritis Society Web site
- Sample copy from all of the major information categories on the home page
- An article called "How to Catch the Wave," which is a quick introduction about how to get connected to the Net

The magazine was meant to introduce members to a wonderful new information resource. In addition, thousands of copies were left in medical offices across the country. Over 20,000 were distributed.

The Arthritis Society of Canada also produced a bookmark that made reference to the new Web site and made sure that all business cards, letterhead, and direct mail fund-raising packages listed the Web site address—**www.arthritis.ca.**

Rob Watts, The Arthritis Society of Canada's Manager of Internet Resources, is quick to point out that, "We didn't have a marketing plan for our web site, except for the printed material we put out—like the magazine, the bookmark and all of our other printed material. Just doing this made an incredible difference to

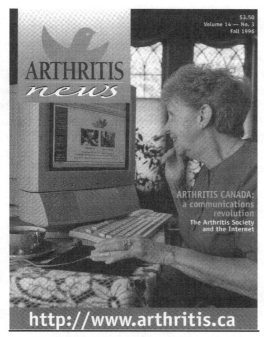

EXHIBIT 9–1   Advanced Promotion of a Web Site: Arthritis Canada.

the number of visitors to our web site—rising from 2,000 a day in November of 1996 to about 7,000 a day one year later, to over 14,000 a day at the beginning of 1998."[1]

However, relying on terrestrial marketing is just not enough. Once a nonprofit organization has covered its marketing of its Net presence in the real world, it is time to turn attention, energy, and proper strategy to an online marketing plan.

FITTING THE MEDIUM TO THE MESSAGE

In order for a nonprofit to understand how to find its audience, the main areas of the Internet must be fully understood, as well as how they are used by different people.

[1]Rob Watts, email letter to author, 3 April 1998.

World Wide Web (WWW)

The WWW is where most of the headline grabbing activity takes place on the Internet. It is populated by two types of people: (1) surfers who are cruising from one site to another looking for interesting information and entertainment; and (2) more settled browsers who have found the handful of Web sites that interest them, and to which they return periodically for updates (see Chapter three for more information on the different behavior of Web users). The Web is likely to be a nonprofit organization's main prospecting area—where they can reach people who are not aware of their organization or to find terrestrial supporters to know an organization they support is now online.

Email/Mailing Lists

It seems that almost everyone has an email address these days. Email is the most personal form of communication on the Internet—direct and person to person. Email addresses may one day be as hotly exchanged in the fund-raising world as real world addresses are today.

The most difficult part of reaching people via email is getting their email address. People are increasingly guarded about giving out their email addresses. A nonprofit organization must decide on a strategy to gather the email addresses of potential supports for a nonprofit organization if they wish to reach them this way.

News Groups

News groups are one of the most open and energetic parts of the Internet. There is a great deal of engaging, sometimes heated, conversation going on here. There is a constant flux of people and interesting content found on the news groups. Tapping into it can be tricky and sometimes perilous, but there is an unmatched potential for prospecting for supporters in this part of the Internet.

It is important for every nonprofit organization to understand that these three main areas of the Internet must be a part of any online marketing plan.

FITTING THE AUDIENCE WITH THE MESSAGE

People's experience of the Internet is largely self-driven and motivated by personal interests. One will find something only if he or she goes looking for it. Unlike television, where a nonprofit is hoping to reach a sympathetic 1% of the viewing population with its message by broadcasting to everyone, on the Internet it is not going to reach those other 99% because they have no interest in the organization's issues, and therefore will not seek out its message.

That means a nonprofit's target audience is much more focused than in a broadcasting medium such as radio or television. It also means that the organization must take steps to get its message directly to its audience. People do not often encounter things "by chance" on the Net. Instead, they find things because they go looking for them.

All of this online behavior could almost be called a walkabout. The nondefinitive nature of the Net means people take a casual, drifting, and sometimes frustrating journey to find what they would like to find. Sometimes, they end up somewhere they did not want to be and they are happier for it—or not.

With this kind of audience and this kind of medium, online marketing becomes vital. Any online marketing plan must put a nonprofit's message in the places where its target audience is most likely to look, so that the people specifically interested in their issues will find out about them. This is not as easy as a nonprofit might think.

That is because the Internet is a wide-open and largely unorganized place, ever expanding and reshaping itself. There is no central organizing body that keeps track of everything that can be found on the Net, so there is no central directory that points the way toward the content that people are seeking. Everyone who is looking for information on the Internet must do the work of finding it themselves.

It takes a lot of legwork to cover the whole Internet in search of a particular piece of information, or even to get an overview of what exists online on a certain topic. There are lots of tools—search engines, directories, and discussion forums—that can help, but one can never be sure that everything has been found. In fact, veteran Internet researchers are often surprised by the discovery of a "new" Web site or information source that has been around for months or even years, but which they have never found even though they have been meticulously hunting down everything on that particular subject.

A nonprofit organization must try to make itself as "findable" as possible on the Internet or else it will miss connecting with people who just do not know how to find it. The next step in a nonprofit organization's Internet marketing strategy is to discover all of the places on the Internet where its audience "hangs out." These are the locations where the organization's message must be presented.

MARKETING STRATEGIES: WORLD WIDE WEB

One of the best ways to get a nonprofit organization's message out onto the Internet is to set up an online "storefront," or home page, that will serve up information about the organization to Internet visitors. Web sites can be as expensive or as cheap as any nonprofit would like. As a general rule, though, the more resources an organization puts into a Web site, the better it will be, both at attracting new visitors and at bringing people back for return visits.

It is also important to remember that a good Web site is a living, growing thing. It requires regular attention or it will quickly become obsolete. Reading through other chapters in this book should provide any nonprofit organization with a number of good ideas to keep its site effective.

You may remember this line from the book and movie, *Field of Dreams:* "If you build it, they will come." Unfortunately, this is certainly not true with Web sites on the Internet!

The World Wide Web is not a very user-friendly place. Take a look, for example, at a relatively simple WWW address: **http://www.interlog.com/~aneilson/ africa.html**. That is the address (also known as a URL [Uniform Resource Locator]) of a single Web page, which could be the home page of a nonprofit organization. In order for people to visit the above Web site, they must tell their browser (Netscape or Internet Explorer) to go retrieve that Web page for the visitor to see.

Nonprofit organizations should negotiate with their Internet service provider (ISP) to try to find a URL that is as short as possible and easy to remember. Another option is to register their own Internet domain. This is a somewhat costly procedure which only larger organizations should consider. A nonprofit organization's Web page, if registered as its own, would then be found at **www.yourorganizationname.org**—which is much easier to remember.

INTERNET LINKS

The most important effort to publicize a nonprofit organization's Web site will take place on the Internet itself. The nature of the WWW promotes *Web surfing*— following links from page to page and from site to site. The best way to draw people to a nonprofit's site is to build links to it from other places on the Internet. That way an organization can bring people in without their having to type out a complicated URL.

It can be a lot of work to set up links to a nonprofit's own Web site. In fact, it is a job that never ends, as new Web sites are continually appearing that may be linked to one's Web site. However, when a nonprofit sets up links leading to its Web pages, it is actually constructing the avenues that Web surfers will use to easily find and visit its website.

There are three main types of Internet links a nonprofit organization can set up.

Search Engine Links

Search engines are by far the most-visited sites on the Web. They are really the yellow pages for the Internet. Unfortunately, there is no search engine for the whole

Internet (yet). The various search engines all cover different areas—with lots and lots of overlap between them, and there are still many sites on the Internet that are not to be found in any of the search engines.

Search engines are quite simply searchable databases of Web pages. When someone wants to locate a Web page on a particular topic, he or she just sends a search request to the search engine and receives back a list of Web pages that the search engine has identified that are related to that subject.

These "search results" lists have URLs programmed into them, so that if people want to visit a Web page found by a search engine, they just have to click on that page's title, and they will be sent straight there. The search engines point the way for seekers of all sorts, linking them to the pages that best match their interests.

The first step in marketing a Web site should be to get the nonprofit's Web site's URL included in the databases of the most popular search engines on the Internet. That way, people who are looking for the nonprofit organization on the Internet will find it in the first place they look—which is almost always one of the popular search engines. Any nonprofit organization can begin by finding out the current inclusion of its site in the most popular search engines.

Position Agent (**http://www.positionagent.com**) is a handy service that lets a nonprofit organization find out what each search engine has as a listing for its organization. The nonprofit must identify the URL of its organization, then it can try different combinations of key words that searchers might use when they are looking for the nonprofit's site. For example, to analyze the current search engine placements of the World Wildlife Fund (WWF) Canada's homepage (see Exhibit 9–2 **http://www.wwfcanada.org**), World Wildlife Canada might try the following combinations of key words:

- "world wildlife fund Canada"
- "wildlife" and "Canada"
- "endangered" and "Canada"
- "wild" and "Canada"

The report back will tell WWF Canada on what page and in what position its URL first occurs in each of the major search engines. Any position in the top five of the first page is a good position. Anywhere other than on the first page indicates that it should attend to that search engine to get its site better placed.

How to Get a Nonprofit Organization's Website Listed on the Search Engines

In order to understand how to get a nonprofit's site well placed on the search engines, one needs to understand how the search engines work. Search engines run programs called *robots* or sometimes *spiders*, which continually travel around the Web looking for new Web pages. They record information about every new Web

EXHIBIT 9–2   WWF Canada Home Page

site that they "discover" and add it to the search engine's database. The robots record all of the text content in the organization's page. The search engine's database then analyzes the page and includes it into its main index, ready to be displayed to Internet searchers.

In theory, when a nonprofit organization puts up a new Web site, all it has to do is wait for the robots to discover it—and it will happen eventually. However, because there are so many new pages added every day, and the robots are continually reviewing Web sites they have already recorded, looking for changes, that there is no way of knowing how long (it could be days, weeks, even months) before the main search engines have located an organization's site.

The best approach is to go the search engines directly and give them the information about the organization's site "in person."

Manual Registration

There are dozens of search engines on the Internet, but the most important 10 search engines account for the vast majority of Internet traffic. If a nonprofit organization gets its site listed on these search engines, it has done most of the work of reaching out to the general Web-surfing population. Exhibit 9–3 lists the world's most popular search engines.

On each of these pages, a nonprofit organization will find a link labeled either ADD A SITE or ADD YOUR URL or something similar. Here is where the organization can manually add its Web pages to each search engine's database. Each nonprofit needs to make sure it is ready to supply a list of key words and a short description of its Web site or organization before it begins registering.

A nonprofit's site will not appear immediately in the search engine's database. When an organization manually registers a Web site, that address is placed in the queue for sites to be visited by the search engine's robots. A nonprofit's site will be added to the database only after it has been visited by a robot, but by manually registering, a nonprofit places its site at the top of the queue.

Once a week or so after a nonprofit's initial registration, its website's listing should be rechecked, using a service like Position Agent (the Internet's first service for monitoring Web site rankings in the search engines) at **http://www.positionagent.com/**) or just return to the same search engines and try the search itself.

Registration Services

An alternative to manually registering an organization's site with each and every search engine is to use a registration service. There are a number of companies that will do all of the fingerwork for a nonprofit. For a fee of less than $100.00 usually,

opentext.net	Open Text
excite.com	Excite
lycos.com	Lycos
webcrawler.com	WebCrawler
infoseek.com	Infoseek
yahoo.com	Yahoo
hotbot.com	HotBot
aol.com/netfind	America Online NetFind
search.com	Cnet Search
looksmart.com	LookSmart

EXHIBIT 9–3   The Web's Most Popular Search Engines

they will register an organization's site with 200 search engines, directories, announcement pages, and other appropriate sites. Results are not guaranteed usually, though some will claim a "Top 10" listing on major search engines. Two registration services are submit-it.com and acclaimweb.com.

A nonprofit's getting its site registered with the search engines does not guarantee a good listing. A Web site must be designed to give the robot programs that visit the site the information they need to properly place a nonprofit's Web site under the correct categories in their search engines' databases.

How to Design a Nonprofit Web Page to Get Listed on Search Engines

The search engines do not treat all of the page's content with equal significance. They give greatest weight to certain sections, which must contain the vital information about a nonprofit organization.

TITLE Key Words

Each Web page in a site should be given an appropriate title. This is not the large, bold text that probably appears at the top of most of a nonprofit's Web pages, but is rather a hidden code that is used to identify the organization's page but does not appear in the main window of a Web browser.

Every nonprofit should ensure that in the <HEAD> section of each of its web pages there is a <TITLE> section that contains a description of that page's content. When a page is visited by the search engine robot, it will record the information in the <TITLE>. This is the text that will be displayed by the search engine when a nonprofit's Web page is listed in a search result. Nonprofits should make their titles as descriptive as possible, and they should all contain an organization's name, because they may appear individually in a search result. For example:

Not good:	"Campaigns"
Better:	"Campaigns—1997"
Better still:	"Greenpeace Canada's 1997 Campaigns"

<META> Tags

<META> tags are codes a nonprofit puts into its Web pages that contain information about that page that an organization does not want to display to the browser, but which can still be read by certain programs and under certain circumstances.

Many of the search engines are able to use <META> tags to fine-tune their information about the Web pages they include in their databases. Search engine robots look for two particular types of <META> tags when they record a nonprofit organization's page's content:

- <META name="description" content="a short statement describing the nonprofit organization">
- <META contained in these META tags will be used by the search engine to more precisely index an organization's Web page—giving greater prominence to the key words the nonprofit has supplied. As well, a nonprofit's customized description will be included on any search results page where the website is listed.

<ALT> Image Tags

If an organization makes use of a lot of images in its site, it may inadvertently be hiding valuable information from the search engines. Search engine robots capture only the text that is contained in a nonprofit's Web page. They are not able to interpret graphic files, and any information that is contained in them is lost to the search engine when it is analyzing the organization's site. This can be a problem with the front page of an organization's site. It is very common for organizations to use big graphic banners on their front page, containing their name and logo. This makes the name prominent to Web browsers, but invisible to the search engine. The remedy for this is to use the ALT function of the <IMAGE> tags that describe the graphic content of each Web page. With the ALT function, a nonprofit can include a text description of an image on its webpage. This text will not appear on its Web page when it is being shown on a Web browser, unless that browser is unable to display images, in which case it shows the ALT text. The search engine robots treat the ALT text in an image file as bona fide content on an organization's Web page, and it is considered alongside all of the other content.

An <IMAGE> tag using the ALT function will look like this:

<img src="image.jpg" alt="description of this picture">

Web Directory Links

Search engines try to catalog everything on the Internet, and the people that use search engines are equally varied. A better targeted subset of Web surfers can be reached via issue-related directories on the Web.

Web directories are nothing more than libraries of links to Web sites that are all related to a particular topic or issue. Some of them are highly focused; others are more general. Some of the largest Web directories have thousands of links, organized into subcategories and usually searchable on key words. Other, smaller Web directories may be just a list of links in no particular order.

Unlike search engines, which employ automatic robots to find new Web pages, Web directories rely on people submitting Websites to be added to their listings. They will review any submissions, most likely by hand, and will consider whether the site is appropriate for inclusion in their directories.

Web directories are particularly good places to publicize a nonprofit's Web site because the visitors to these directories will be already interested in or connected to the organization's issues.

Web directories are not always easy to find. Any nonprofit conducting research for a online marketing plan will have to search out directories on their issues. A nonprofit can try using the Internic Directory of Directories (//**ds.internic .net/ds/dsdirofdirs.html**) to locate web directories that are appropriate to their organization's issues of concern.

Reciprocal Links

Reciprocal links are the most grassroots kind of Web marketing strategy. Numerous other organizations have put up Web sites dealing with the same issues as any nonprofit organization, and have included their own lists of related links. Many of these organizations would be glad to include a link to a like-minded nonprofit organization's home page, and it is only fair that the nonprofit agrees to return the service. To make it easier for a like-minded organization to link to a nonprofit organization, that nonprofit might want to do the following:

- Provide a 25-word outline of what its site is all about that any like-minded organization can grab quickly and put on its Web site
- In conjunction with the text, a nonprofit might want to include an icon or graphic that represents its organization. That icon or graphic can be copied by a like-minded organization and placed on its Web site as a reciprocal link.

The idea is to provide the hypertext coding, graphics, and written text that any linking organization can grab quickly and easily and create an attractive, effective link.

If a nonprofit has links from its home page to other sites, it should make reciprocal links. Also, it should consider setting up links to other sites which have built links to its home page.

The place to find out about any reciprocal links that may already be in place is **www.altavista.com**. A nonprofit should go to that site and enter a search for its site by typing in **link:www.your.domain**. The results of the search may surprise a nonprofit organization when it sees who has already made its own link to the nonprofit's page. In addition to using key word searches, every nonprofit should make a labor-intensive, but useful, manual search around the Web for other sites with whom a nonprofit can set up reciprocal links.

Announcement Sites

There are so many new Web sites being added each day that another kind of Web directory has appeared—the announcement site. Typically, these directories have links to the newest sites that have appeared on the WWW. Like Web directories, they do not have search engine robots, but rather rely on individuals to contact them regarding new Web sites that have appeared. The listing is only for a short duration, sometimes only for a week or two.

Some announcement sites focus exclusively on entirely new Web sites; others will cover the appearance of new pages or resources in existing Web sites. They are great places to announce the launch of a new Web site, or a new Web-based campaign.

To locate an announcement site that may be appropriate for an organization's notices, try using Submit-it's Directory Guide (**www.directoryguide.com**).

Link Exchanges and Web Rings

Finally, there are some variations on the reciprocal and directory links and brief strategies previously outlined.

Link Exchange

Link Exchange is a widespread alternative to the costly advertising banners that a nonprofit may see adorning the search engines and other popular sites on the Internet. There is one link exchange with the exact moniker, Link Exchange (**http://www.linkexchange.com**). It is set up somewhat like a cooperative in which all of the members agree to display (on their own Web site) the graphic ads submitted by other Link Exchange members, free of charge.

The requirements are for an organization to prepare a typical graphic banner ad that will appear on other members' sites, and for the organization to insert a bit of hypertext markup language (HTML) code in the nonprofit's own Web site that will allow other members' ads to appear on their site. The system keeps track of how often a nonprofit's site displays ads for other members, and balances that with the number of times the nonprofit's own ad is shown on other members' sites.

Link Exchange also offers a targeting service (for a small premium), which allows a nonprofit to indicate what kinds of member sites it would like its ad to appear on.

Web Rings

Web rings are a more recent phenomenon on the WWW. They are self-forming associations of related Web sites, all interlinked in a way that encourages Web browsers to move from one site to the next as part of a single community with a specific focus. There are thousands of Web rings in existence already on a wide variety of issues. Ring World is the central index of Web rings. A nonprofit can search for a Web ring on a specific issue, and also find out about starting a new Web ring here (**www.webring.com**).

Email

Email can be a very effective tool for communicating an organization's message—it is personal and content-focused (rather than image/impression focused like the WWW). Its two-way nature makes it an ideal tool for building relationships between an organization and its supporters. Email discussions can take the form of one-to-one communications or can happen as part of an email listing list that includes a larger number of people, all following the same threads of discussion.

An email mailing list is a kind of online discussion club focused on a particular topic. Anyone who has joined the mailing list can contribute a message, and that message is copied to all of the other members automatically. Discussions are carried over from message to message, usually with several different "talks" going on between list members all at the same time. Mailing lists are excellent areas in which organizations can connect with their online supporters. The members of any issue-oriented mailing list are likely to be highly involved and interested in that issue. An organization may use a mailing list to send out public releases, make announcements, network with other organizations, and even canvass for supporters.

There are thousands of mailing lists already in existence. In the case of most organizations, there would be already several mailing lists that are focused on their concerns that they could join. Other organizations may have to consider creating their own mailing list.

A nonprofit organization can find email mailing lists by searching **www .liszt.com**.

News Groups

The primary places to reach the general public are through the Internet news groups. There are many thousands of news groups focused on many different topics. It is necessary for any nonprofit organization to target its online press releases to only those news groups in which people interested in or concerned about the nonprofit's issues are likely to be found. Nonprofits can find news groups that are related to their issues of concern by searching the Dejanews interest finder at **www.dejanews.com**.

Association for Progressive Communications

The Institute for Global Communications (IGC) is the American member of the Association for Progressive Communications (APC)—a global network of environmental, social justice, and human rights organizations. In Canada, Web Networks is the Canadian member of APC and GreenNet is the U.K. sister organization of APC. The APC's members maintain a collection of international conferences, open only to members, where these issues are discussed and information is exchanged. The audience for messages posted to the conferences available through Web Networks is international and activist oriented. These conferences are appropriate venues for project announcements, events coordinating, and information distribution.

MARKETING PLANS—BRINGING IT ALL TOGETHER

The appendix A at the end of this chapter includes the online marketing plan for the World Wildlife Fund of Canada. This real-life sample is built on an understanding of the Net outlined in this chapter and chooses strategies that evolve out of the information in this chapter. It is an effective template that any nonprofit organization would do well to emulate. It is low cost and will work.

For any nonprofit organization to create its own marketing plan, it should remember to do the following:

- Read through whatever marketing plans an organization can get from another organization and study its research methodology and marketing strategies. If a marketing plan can be obtained from a like-minded organization, then all the better because even the links will be relevant (a good place to start is with the World Wildlife Fund of Canada sample at the end of this chapter).
- Fill in each section with information relevant to one's organization.
- If a marketing plan is done by a volunteer, consultant, or staff member, make sure that plan is created in HTML (most word processors allow you to do this).
- Once the marketing plan has been received in HTML, have a staff member, consultant, or volunteer execute the online marketing plan while online. Every Web site, news group, email address, or Internet address should be linked directly from the HTML document to its location on the Web. With a click of the mouse, the executor of the online marketing plan can cover each target spot on the Net in the plan.

It is also important to include the following in any online marketing plan:

- Have a small graphic (as a computer file) that represents the organization (perhaps its logo) delivered to the computer of the person conducting the online marketing plan.
- The coordinator of the plan should also have a 25-word précis of the organization's site along with the graphic. Whenever the marketing plan instructs the coordinator to ask for a reciprocal link, he or she can grab the graphic and prearranged text and send it quickly and efficiently to another site or individual who can put the information online.

CONCLUSION

Nonprofit organizations must be thorough in their marketing strategy and planning for the Internet. By making sure their printed material and real world media communicate their Internet presence, and creating an online marketing plan that takes into account understanding the medium and the audience, any nonprofit should increase the number of visitors who will be able to find its nonprofit organization in this vast Internet environment.

Appendix 9-A

ONLINE MARKETING OF THE WWF CANADA WEBSITE— A STRATEGY PAPER: TEN SPECIFIC RECOMMENDATIONS

BUILDING LINKS TO THE WWF CANADA WEBSITE

In order for people to visit the WWF Canada Website, they must first be able to find it. While there are a number of very important real world steps that must be taken to publicize the WWF Canada Web site address (such as media ads, business cards, etc.), the most important effort to publicize the Web site will take place on the Internet itself. The nature of the Web promotes Web surfing—following links from page to page and from site to site. Building links to WWF Canada's Web pages will present Web surfers with the avenues to easily find and visit this Web site.

There are three main types of Internet links to be developed:

Search Engine Links

Search engines are by far the most-visited sites on the Web. They point the way for seekers of all sorts, linking them to the pages that most match their interests. Marketing a Web site to the general public is best done by concentrating on the 20 most popular search engines and making sure that their databases have the correct information about an organization's site. That way, information seekers will be able to find its home page.

To study the current exposure of the WWF Canada site, Hewitt and Johnston Consultants tested seven popular search engines: Excite, Infoseek, Webcrawler, Altavista, Lycos, Opentext, and Yahoo Canada. The WWF Canada Web site is fairly well marketed to these search engines. Most of the popular engines have at least one entry for www.wwfcanada.org in their databases (the exception was Lycos). Six of the search engines—Excite, Opentext, Infoseek, Yahoo Canada, Webcrawler and Altavista—all return the WWF Canada page reliably for a search on "world wildlife fund Canada." However, when the terms were limited to "wildlife" and "Canada," only Opentext, Altavista, and Webcrawler returned WWF Canada in the top 20 sites. Another further search done on "endangered" and "Canada" netted top 20 results only from Yahoo Canada. Adding more key words to the registry for WWF Canada on these services will increase the chance that a search done on these and other related terms will also return the WWF Canada page among the top links.

Recommendation #1

Add <META> tags to the homepage of www.wwfcanada.org to include (1) a brief description (25 words or less) of WWF Canada's mission and mandate, and (2) a list of key words covering all issues on which the WWF Canada is active. Then re-register the WWF Canada home page with the top 20 search engines. This will incorporate the description text and key words into the search engine databases.

Web Directory Links

A more specific subset of Web surfers can be reached via wildlife- and environmental-related directories on the Web. Visitors to these sites will already be interested in or connected to environmental issues in general. On some of these directories, an entry for WWF Canada would be in a section especially related to endangered species, so the subset of visitors will be even more on topic.

The WWF Canada site is already on one Web directory, though it is listed as an International Organization:

Site Name:	Environment Canada—Green Lane
Page:	Other Environmental Sites and Events
Address:	http://www.ec.gc.ca/other_sites_e.html#intorg

HJC has compiled a list of suitable Web directories to contact and secure an entry for the WWF Canada Web site.

Recommendation #2

The following directories should be contacted with the aim of registering one or more of the WWF Canada Web pages under the appropriate topic areas:

Site Name: Web Networks—Eco Web
Address: http://community.web.net/ecoweb/ecoorglist.html

Site Name: The Amazing Environmental Organization WebDirectory
Address: http://www.webdirectory.com

Site Name: Envirolink
Address: http://www.envirolink.org
Description: EnviroLink Network is the largest online environmental information service on the planet, reaching well over 1,500,000 people in 100 countries. It covers nearly every environmental topic, contains lots of late-breaking news, and is the home for many other environmental organizations.

Site Name: WWW Virtual Library—Environment
Address: http://ecosys.drdr.virginia.edu/Environment.shtml

Site Name: IGC—EcoNet
Address: http://www.igc.org/igc/econet/
Description: Issue Directory on the topic of Habitat and Species—only WWF UK is there

Site Name: Great Outdoors Recreation Pages Nature/Wildlife page
Address: http://www.gorp.com/gorp/activity/wildlife.htm
Description: A U.S. focused site, but it has a section for Canadian wildlife resource links

Site Name: Maple Square, Canada's Internet Directory
Address: http://maplesquare.sympatico.ca/

Site Name: Canada's Schoolnet
Address: http://www.schoolnet.ca
Description: Environment and Geology resource page

Reciprocal Links

Reciprocal links are a more grassroots kind of Web marketing strategy. Numerous other organizations have put up Web sites dealing with the same issues as WWF Canada, and have included their own lists of related links. Many of these organizations would be glad to include a link to the WWF Canada page, and it is only fair that WWF Canada agree to return the service.

The following is an example of a reciprocal link already in place:

Site Name: Canadian Parks and Wilderness Society
Address: http://www.afternet.com/~tnr/cpaws/cpaws.html

A number of sites that are linked from the WWF Canada Links page do not have reciprocal links back.

Recommendation #3

The following site should be approached to set up a reciprocal link in return for maintaining its existing link on the WWF Canada website:

Site Name: Wildlife at Risk (on the Schoolnet)
Address: http://www-nais.ccm.emr.ca/schoolnet/issues/risk/ewww.html

As well, there are a couple of significant Web sites that already have links to the WWF Canada Web page and would be suitable to add to the Links page.

Recommendation #4

Add the following links to the WWF Canada Links page:

Site Name: Alberta's Special Places
Address: http://www.afternet.com/~teal/

Site Name: Pesticide Action Network North America
Address: http://www.panna.org/panna/

HJC has done an intensive scan of the Internet in search of suitable organizations with which to establish reciprocal links.

Recommendation #5

Approach the following organizations with the aim of establishing reciprocal links:

Site Name: Canadian Nature Federation
Address: http://www.web.net/~cnf/

Site Name: Federation of Ontario Naturalists
Address: http://www.web.net/fon

Site Name: Earthroots
Address: http://www.earthroots.org/

Site Name: Greenpeace Canada
Address: http://www.greenpeacecanada.org

Site Name: The Body Shop Canada
Address: http://www.thebodyshop.ca

Site Name: BC Wild
Address: http://www.helix.net/bcwild/

Site Name: The Canadian Institute for Environmental Law and Policy
Address: http://www.web.net/cielap/

Site Name: Friends of the Earth Canada
Address: http://intranet.ca/~foe/

Site Name: The David Suzuki Foundation
Address: http://www.vkool.com/suzuki/index.html

Site Name: Sierra Club Canada
Address: http://www.sierraclub.ca

Site Name: Western Canada Wilderness Committee
Address: http://www.web.net/wcwild/

Site Name: Canadian Wildlife Federation
Address: http://204.191.126.6/cwf-fcf/

Site Name: Canadian Wildlife & Wilderness Art Museum
Address: http://intranet.ca/cawa/

Site Name: The Pesticide Education Network
Address: http://www.ncf.carleton.ca/~bf250/pen.html

Site Name: Canada Animal Network
Address: http://www.pawprints.com/index.html
Description: Pet related, but with a small index on wildlife

Suggestions

- Suggest one possible strategy—create a Canadian Wildlife Directory
- Approach other sites with banner ad ready to be placed on their page, leading to this page

Magazine Web Sites as Reciprocal Links

Commercial magazines in the outdoor/environmental market attract many Web visitors who become regular customers—returning every month to check out the latest online issue. While many of these sites may actually charge for placing banners or links from their site, it may be possible to interest them in a reciprocal arrangement, particularly if the WWF Canada pursues the line of setting up a Canadian Wildlife Directory.

Recommendation #7

Contact the following commercial magazine Web sites to investigate opportunities to set up reciprocal links:

- *Beautiful British Columbia* (**http://www.beautifulBC.com**)
- *Canadian Geographic* (**http://www.cangeo.ca/**)
- *Equinox* (**http://www.equinox.ca**)
- *Explore* (**http://www.explore-mag.com/**)

    Also look for Web sites for the following magazines:

- *Heritage Canada*
- *Outdoor Canada*
- *Up Here*

ANNOUNCING THE WWF CANADA WEB SITE

To announce a Web site relaunch, spread the word into as many places as possible where people who are likely to be interested in visiting the site hang out. In addition to the regular real world press releases and the like that the organization may handle, the announcement should be sent to as many online venues as possible.

News Groups

The primary places to reach the general public are through the Internet news groups. There are many thousands of news groups focused on many different topics. It is necessary to target press releases to only those newsgroups in which people interested in or concerned about wildlife conservation issues are likely to be found. HJC has prepared a list of news groups, grouped into several sections, indicating which groups should be targeted by WWF Canada.

Recommendation #8

The WWF Canada should prepare a text-only version of its press release, announcing the relaunch of its Web site, and post this release to the following news groups:

alt.native
alt.sustainable.agriculture
alt.wolves
alt.save.the.earth
alt.sustainable.agriculture
ca.environment
misc.activism.progressive
rec.animals.wildlife
rec.outdoors.fishing
rec.skiing.backcountry
rec.gardens
rec.hunting
rec.backcountry
rec.camping
rec.bicycles.off-road
rec.birds
rec.outdoors.national-parks
rec.outdoors.camping
sci.bio.ecology
sci.bio.conservation
sci.agriculture
sci.environment
sci.agriculture
talk.politics.animals
talk.environment

Web Networks Conferences

Web Networks is the Canadian member of APC—a global network of environmental, social justice, and human rights organizations. The APC's members maintain a collection of international conferences, open only to members, in which these issues are discussed and information is exchanged. The audience for messages posted to the conferences available through Web Networks is international and activist oriented. These conferences are appropriate venues for project announcements, events coordinating, and information distribution.

Recommendation #9

Post the WWF Canada Web site relaunch announcement to the following Web Networks conferences:

biodiversity
en.pesticides
en.wildlife
en.parks
en.pesticides
forestplan
green.can
web.parks
web.forest
web.announcements
wwf.news

Email Mailing Lists

Email mailing lists are more focused than either news groups or Web Networks conferences. They have small but quite loyal members, whose interests are keenly felt toward the lists they have decided to join. There are a handful of mailing lists whose subject area is related to wildlife conservation issues and would be suitable for WWF Canada input.

Recommendation #10

World Wildlife Fund Canada should post its press release announcing the Web site relaunch to these email mailing lists:

Name: WILDLIFE
Sponsor: International Wildlife Management Working Group
Subject: Wildlife Discussion List
Mail to: listserv@crcvms.unl.edu
Message: subscribe wildlife

Name: natureconnect
Sponsor: Project NatureConnect
Subject: For Personal Connections With Nature
Mail to: natureconnect-request@store-forward.mindspring.com
Message: subscribe natureconnect

Name: CONSLINK
Sponsor: Smithsonian Institute, Washington, DC
Subject: CONSLINK - The Conservation Network
Mail to: listserv@sivm.si.edu
Message: subscribe conslink

Name: BIODIV-L
Subject: Biodiversity and Conservation News and Discussion
Mail to: listserv@cnsibm.albany.edu
Message: subscribe biodiv-l

Name: MARMAM
Sponsor: University of Victoria, BC
Subject: Marine Mammals Research and Conservation Discussion
Mail to: listserv@uvvm.uvic.ca
Message: subscribe marmam

Name: rapid-response
Sponsor: Defenders of Wildlife Rapid Response List
Mail to: majordomo@list.us.net
Message: subscribe rapid-response

Name: RAPTOR-C
Sponsor: The Raptor Center
Subject: Conservation & Rehabilitation of Raptors
Mail to: listserv@tc.umn.edu
Message: subscribe raptor-c

Name: CTURTLE
Subject: Sea Turtle Biology and Conservation
Mail to: listserv@lists.ufl.edu
Message: subscribe cturtle

CONCLUSION

This marketing document gives WWF Canada an excellent resource to use internally to do a better job at getting people to come to its site. The subset of newsgroups that WWF Canada should be involved with can be divided into several categories.

Wildlife Focused News Groups

These news groups are the WWF Canada's "home territory." No one can challenge your right to participate in these discussions, and you are likely to find many allies—and a few foes—here:

rec.animals.wildlife—quite active, plenty of debating; seems dominated by long-standing arguments between a small group of quite opposed minds
talk.politics.animals—lots of involved and articulate debating about animal rights, hunting ethics; some press releases and announcements
alt.wolves—low traffic; some discussions around ethics of captive wolves, some talk of population pressures

General Environment News Groups

These news groups are generally used for discussion and information exchange within the environmental support community. Some news groups have more debating than the others, though the topics of discussion cover a wide range of environmental issues. In these news groups, it is best to assume you are reaching only the "converted," and WWF Canada's involvement should focus around networking with other environmental groups.

- alt.save.the.earth—mixture of press releases, newsletters, and so forth, with a few involved debates on political issues
- ca.environment—not very busy, mostly reactions to media programs and news events
- sci.environment—lots of talk on issues; deep philosophical and scientific talk, some nonsense as well; plenty of announcements/newsletters from organizations
- talk.environment—lots of issues talk, mostly about McDonald's libel case; some press releases from environmental organizations
- misc.activism.progressive—announcements, press releases, newsletters; mostly international politics

- sci.bio.conservation; almost no traffic
- sci.bio.ecology—quite active; some long debates around global environmental issues; also some academic announcements and a few press releases
- alt.native—native politics, but nothing overtly related to wildlife; some press releases

Outdoor Recreation News Groups

These are news groups not directly related to wildlife issues. Their focus is on human enjoyment of the outdoors. There will be voices in these groups that will challenge the WWF Canada's legitimate voice here, but these news groups are the prime areas for outreach to new communities is possible.

- rec.hunting—fairly active, mostly ammo and gun talk; a bit of traffic about move to ban fox hunting in the United Kingdom, one mention of Canada banning lead shot
- rec.backcountry—destinations, advice, equipment, some issues discussions; a few trip reports
- rec.camping—camp equipment talk mostly, some discussion re parks, destinations; no issues talk
- rec.bicycles.off-road—lots of activity; lots of debate about bikes damaging parks
- rec.birds—fairly active, focused on bird sightings, identifications, no issues talk
- rec.outdoors.national-parks—fair traffic; no issues talk, just destinations and the like
- rec.outdoors.camping—mostly talk of equipment and destinations; a bit of issue talk around park management
- rec.skiing.backcountry—not very active; destination focused
- rec.outdoors.fishing—mostly talk of equipment and destinations

Pesticide Use–Related News Groups

These newsgroups have some connection to the use of pesticides, whether in agriculture specifically, or in a home setting.

- rec.gardens—all about gardening details; no issues
- alt.sustainable.agriculture—very little traffic, just a couple of press bulletins
- sci.agriculture—mix of questions on crop science, a bit of genetic engineering debate

Appendix 9-B

MARKETING ONLINE CHECKLIST

This Marketing Online Checklist has been designed to remind you of the most important issues when marketing your nonprofit organization's Internet presence online.

PRINTED MATERIAL SHOULD REFLECT YOUR ONLINE PRESENCE

( ) Have you sent created printed materials (direct mail, newsletters, business cards, etc.) that highlight your Internet addresses?

( ) Have you put your Internet addresses in all mediums (e.g., TV and radio spots)?

( ) Have you decided to concentrate one edition of your newsletter or magazine on your Internet presence, with explanations of content, how supporters can get online, and how they can use your Internet offerings?

MARKETING STRATEGIES

( ) Before you begin registering with the search engines, have you used a service like Position Agent to find out how you are currently listed by the search engines?

( ) Have you registered your domain name with all of the most popular search engines manually?

( ) Have you registered your domain name through a registration service such as submit.com or acclaim.com?

( ) Have you used title key words and <Meta Tags> on your home page to help obtain the most favorable ranking with the search engines?

( ) Have you used an <ALT> image tag to allow search engines to capture the text descriptions resident in graphics you have used?

( ) Have you used a resource like the Internic Directory of Directories to find Web Directories that will be effective places to conduct online marketing?

( ) Have you used altavista.com and entered link:www.your.domain to find out about reciprocal lists that may already exist to your site?

( ) Have you used Submit-it's Directory Guide to find an announcement site that would be an appropriate place to highlight your Internet presence?

( ) Have you prepared a graphic banner and 25 word precis to represent your web site through List Exchanges like www.linkexchange.com/?

( ) Have you investigated the effectiveness and possibilities of online marketing through like-minded Web rings by visiting a site like http://www.webring.com?

( ) Have you investigated the effectiveness and possibilities of online marketing through like-minded email listservs by visiting a site like http://www.liszt.com?

( ) Have you investigated the effectiveness and possibilities of online marketing through like-minded newsgroups by visiting a site like http://www.dejanews.com?

( ) Have you investigated the effectiveness and possibilities of online marketing through like-minded conferences on the International network run by the APC?

▼ Index

A

Accessibility, Web site, 60, 64
ACLU, *see* American Civil Liberties Union
ActiveX, 127
Activism, online, 162–164
ACT UP, 122
Advertising, paid, 12
Affirmative statements, 92–93, 114, 115
Age, user, 31–32, 35
Air Canada, 114
Allen, Nick, 16
Alumni associations, 147–150
Alzheimer Society of Canada, 83, 84, 86
Amazon.com, 99, 110–112
American Cancer Society, 104, 105, 107
American Civil Liberties Union (ACLU), 99, 101, 122
American Heart Association, 102, 107
American Red Cross, 3–5, 19, 59, 94–95, 108–111
Amnesty International, 112–113, 182
Announcement sites, 209, 217
APC, *see* Association for Progressive Communications
Architecture, Web site, 53–55

Archives & Museum Informatics, 155
Arrays, gift, 93–95, 115–116
Arthritis Society of Canada, 37–38, 40, 155, 198–199
Association for Progressive Communications (APC), 178, 211, 219
Auctions, online, 9–16
    celebrity art in, 13–15
    checklist for, 25
    inconsistency in, 12–13
    potential profitability of, 13
    strengths of, 12
    tips for, 10–11
Audience, Web site, 200–201
Axworthy, Lloyd, 185

B

Back button, 67
Backup copies, of Web site, 127–128
Bateman, Robert, 9
Behavior, online fund-raising, 21–23
Benjamin, Walter, 87
Blind links, 69
Bobby, 60
The Body Shop, 9, 162–163

Bookmarks, 67
Bounia, John, 152
Brand assassination, 188
Browsers, 56, 87–88
Bryce, Alana, 108–109
Bulletin boards, members-only, 151–154
Bullet points, 79–80, 89
Business Week, 28

C
Campaigning, online, 161–196.
    See also Marketing, online
    action-oriented, 162–164
    case study, 189–193
    chat areas, 174–175
    checklist for, 193–196
    and civil disobedience, 185–188
    emails, sending, 181
    essential elements of, 164–165
    faxes, sending, 178–180
    feedback, receiving, 178
    future of, 193
    and information, 166–168, 194
    listservs, 169–174
    and local activist units, 168–178
    materials, distribution of, 183–184
    by online communities, 177–178
    signing up supporters, 182–183
    and site appearance, 185
    uncopyrighted material, using, 181–183
    Web rings, 175–177
Canadian Diabetes Association, 13
Caption Center Descriptive Video ServiceÆ
    (DVSÆ), 60
Carlyle, Thomas, 91
Celebrity art, 13–15
Censorship, 34
CERT (Computer Emergency Response Team),
    124
CGI scripts, 135, 176
Champions for Children Foundation, 14–16
Chat rooms, 151–153, 174–175
Children Missing Organization, 176–177
Christian Coalition, 97, 122, 188
Civil disobedience, online, 185–188, 196
Colors, 48, 53, 63

Comic Relief United Kingdom Web, 78, 80
Commission fees, 10
Communications Decency Act, 181
Communities, online, 177–178
Community building, 34–35
Community Collection Crew, 13
Computer Emergency Response Team (CERT),
    124
Contact information, 99, 117, 167–168, 195
Copyright issues, 85, 89
Credit cards, 99, 126
    fear of giving via, 36
    form for, 128
    security issues with, 128–129, 138
Currency convertibility, 106
CUSEEME computer camera technology, 5

D
Death Penalty Information Center, 181, 182
Delphi Internet Services Corporation, 51
Design, Web site, *see* Readability, Web site
Digital certificates, 132–133
Direct donations, 2–5, 24
Direct mail, 48, 76
Discussion areas, 174
Donation coupons, *see* Reply devices
Donations:
    direct, 2–5, 24
    statistics on online, 40–44
Download speed, 51–52
Draught Board, 143–147
Ducks Unlimited, 8–9, 53, 54, 105–106
DVSÆ, *see* Caption Center Descriptive Video
    ServiceÆ

E
Education levels, user, 32
Electronic Frontier Foundation (EFF), 181
Email, 200
    followup via, 110–113, 119
    marketing via, 210
    sending, from Web site, 181
Encryption, 126, 129–132
Erman, Brian, 9–10, 12–13
Essential Action, 170

F

Family Service Association of Metropolitan Toronto, 7–8
FAQs (Frequently Asked Questions), 167
Favorites, 67
Faxes, sending, 178–180
Fax the Feds, 180
Feedback, receiving, 178
Firewalls, 135
Flowcharts, Web, 74–75, 88
Frequently Asked Questions (FAQs), 167

G

Gambling, online, 16–21, 25–26
Garlicka, Malgorzata, 103, 112
Gender, user, 33, 35
Georgia Institute of Technology, 31
Gifts:
    arrays of, 93–95, 115–116
    in memory, 103–105
    types of, 117
Giving culture, 99–100
Global Supporter Network, 153
Gooch, Suzanne, 151
Goods, purchased, 36
Graphics, Visualization, and Usability Center (GVU), 31
Graphics, Web site, 69
Grayscale images, 56, 57
Greenpeace, 22–23, 41–44, 77–78, 97, 99, 100, 104, 133–134, 175
GVU (Graphics, Visualization, and Usability Center), 31

H

Hackers, protection from, 121, 127–128
Hawthorne, Doug, 147–148
<HEAD> section, 206
Hits, 39–40
Home button, 67
Home page, 65–73
    button bar in, 66–67
    links in, 68–72
    menubar in, 65–66
    scroll bar in, 68
    status bar in, 73

    STOP symbol in, 73
    tool bar in, 66–67
    Uniform Resource Locator for, 67–68
Houddini Web Sign Posts, 12
Household income, user, 32–33
Housley, David, 191
Howe, Walt, 51
Howell, Julie, 61–62
HTML, *see* Hypertext markup language
Human memory, 57–59
Hurd, Douglas, 162
Hypertext links, 68–69
Hypertext markup language (HTML), 83–84, 176, 209, 211

I

Icons, 49, 50, 63, 88
IGC, *see* Institute for Global Communications
IISG, *see* Irresponsible Internet Statistic Generator
Images, Web site, 69
Image maps, 69
<IMAGE> tags, 207
Information:
    contact, 99, 117, 167–168, 195
    effective/accurate, 166–167, 194
Info seekers, 59
In memory gifts, 103–105
Institute for Global Communications (IGC), 178, 211
Interactivity, 5, 96–98, 116
InterLotto, 17
International Red Cross, 17–20
Internet membership, 150–151, 159
Internet service providers (ISPs), 123, 125–126, 129–130, 132, 136, 140, 202
Internet Shopping Network, 33
Internic Directory of Directories, 208
Irresponsible Internet Statistic Generator (IISG), 28–29
ISPs, *see* Internet service providers

J

Java, 127
John, Elton, 15
Johnston, Brent, 57

K

Kelly, Kathleen, 4

L

Large gifts, 4–5, 24
Liechtenstein, 17
Links, 202–210
    blind, 69
    on home page, 68–72
    reciprocal, 208–209, 215–217
    search engine, 202–208
    text-based, 68–69
    Web directory, 207–208
Link Exchange, 209–210
Listening to members, 143–147, 156–157
Listing fees, 10
Listservs:
    campaigning with, 169–174
    class/region, 148–149
    members-only, 153–154
Logs, 135
Logo, 48
Lonely Planet, 153–154
Lotteries, online, 16–21, 25–26

M

Mackey, Rhonda, 122
Magge, John, 123, 125, 127–128
Mailing lists, 200, 210, 219–220
Maps, site, 55
Marketing, online, 197–224. *See also* Campaigning, online
    and audience, 200–201
    case study, 212–222
    checklist for, 223–224
    creating plan for, 211–212
    elements of, 197
    with links, 202–210
    preparation for, 198–199
    with search engines, 202–208
    strategies for, 201–202, 223–224
    with various Internet areas, 199–200, 210–211
Martin, Steve, 13–14
Matrix Information and Directory Services (MIDS), 29–30

Members/membership, 139–159
    in alumni associations, 147–150
    case study, 155–156
    chat rooms/bulletin boards for, 151–154
    checklist for, 156–159
    discounts for, 151
    exclusive area for, 140–143
    Internet membership, 150–151, 159
    listening to, 143–147, 156–157
Membership fundraising, 2–3
Memory, human, 57–59
Merchandise donors, 22
Merchandise sales, 7–9, 25
<META> tags, 206–207
Metropolitan Museum of Art (New York), 150–151
Metropolitan Opera, 151
Microsoft Explorer, 67, 69, 73
MIDS, *see* Matrix Information and Directory Services
Mihalicz, Dwight, 17–20
Millions 2000, 19
Mixer, J. R., 161
Monthly donor clubs, 22
Movement for the Survival of the Ogoni People (MOSOP) Canada, 163–167, 169–174, 178, 179, 183, 185
Museum of Contemporary Art (Chicago), 155–156

N

NAACP (National Association for the Advancement of Colored People), 188
Nader, Ralph, 170
Narrowcasting, 197
National Association for the Advancement of Colored People (NAACP), 188
National Center for Accessible Media (NCAM), 60, 61
National Film Board of Canada, 51, 52, 55
National Rifle Association (NRA), 98, 122
National Wildlife Federation (NWF), 184
Nattrall, Paul, 14–16
Navigation, by user, 34
NCAM, *see* National Center for Accessible Media

Negative space, 48
Netiquette, 85
Netscape Navigator, 67, 69, 73
Newsgroups, 200, 210–211, 218, 221–222
News junkies, 59
The New World Foundation, 21
Nissan, 7
Nohr, Marc, 58
NRA, *see* National Rifle Association
NWF, *see* National Wildlife Federation

O
Occupations, user, 33
OCSA, *see* Ontario Community Support Association
Offline surveys, 37
One-time donors, 21
Online Demographics Checklist, 45
Ontario Community Support Association (OCSA), 66–70, 140–143, 152
Ontario Trucking Association, 142–143
Operation Rescue, 122–123
Operation USA, 16
Ottawa Children's Aid Foundation, 13–14
Overused words, 80–83
Oxfam America, 16

P
Paddlers, 59
PAF, 20–21
Pages, Web, 70
Passwords, 125
Payment:
   for access to Web, 35
   methods of, 103–105, 117
Personal Action Center, 191–193
Pictures, 95–96, 116
Planned Parenthood, 122–125, 127–128
Pledges, 5–7, 24
Ploughshares Fund, 48, 49
Plus Lotto, 17–19
Pope, Greg, 98
Position Agent, 203, 205
Pratt, Jane, 94
Premiums, gift, 94, 116

Progressive Conservative Party, 127
Push technology, 193

Q
Quality control, 83–85, 89
Quarterman, John S., 27, 29

R
Race, user, 34
Rainforest Action Network (RAN), 7, 8, 95, 107, 167, 178–179
Ratings, Web site, 38–40
Readability, Web site, 47–64
   checklist for, 62–64
   colors, use of, 53
   flowchart/site map, 74–75
   and grayscale images, 56, 57
   and human memory, 57–59
   and iconography, 49, 50
   logo, 48
   negative space in, 48
   and scrolling, 49–51
   and site architecture, 53–55
   and types of users, 56
Reciprocal links, 208–209, 215–217
"Red-flag" alerts, 127
Registration, 204–206
ReliefNet, 80, 81
Renn, Richard, 4
Reply devices, 91–119
   affirmative statements in, 92–93
   checklist for, 115–119
   contact information in, 99
   and currency convertibility, 106
   donor empowerment in, 106–107
   email followup to, 110–113
   features of effective, 92
   final review in, 109–110
   future of, 114–115
   gift arrays in, 93–95
   interactivity in, 96–98
   leading to, 107–108
   and payment method, 103–105
   pictures in, 95–96
   premiums offered in, 98
   reassuring messages in, 106

Reply devices (*Continued*):
   security concerns, addressing, 99–102
   thank you responses, 108–109
   and type of gift, 103–105
   volunteers, requests for, 105–106
Ring World, 210
Robots, 203

S
Sacks, Oliver, 83
St. Jude Children's Research Hospital, 94
Sales, merchandise, 25
Sample files, 135–136
Sans serif typefaces, 48
Saro-Wiwa, Ken, 162, 163
Satellite Bingo Network, 17
Schneider, Sue, 16, 20
Screensavers, 98
Scroll bar, 68
Scrolling, 49–51, 63
Search engines, 12, 202–208, 212–213
Security issues, 121–138
   checklist, 137–138
   credit cards, 128–134
   Internet service provider, 125–126
   password protection, 125
   risk assessment, 122–123
   tampered/destroyed sites, 121, 127–128
   technologies, Internet, 126–127
   for Web servers, 134–136
seekers, 56
Serif typefaces, 48
Services, purchased, 36
Short, Larry, 38, 39
Site maps, 55, 74–75
Smith, Arthur, 154
Smoot, David, 154
Snodgrass, Randy, 189, 192
Software updates, 135
Speed, download, 51–52
Spending, online, 36
Spiders, 203
Stankiewicz, Julianne, 5–7
Statistics, Internet, 27–45
   age, user, 31–32
   community building, 34–35

credit card information, sending, 36
donations, online, 40–44
education, user, 32
gender, user, 33
goods/services, purchased, 36
household income of users, 32–33
issues, most important, 34
major occupation, user, 33
nonprofit Web sites, 37–43
offline surveys, 37
Online Demographics Checklist, 44–45
pay for access, willingness to, 35
place of access primary, 34
race, user, 34
ratings, Web site, 38–40
spending, online, 36
TV vs. Web, 36
years on Internet, user, 35
Status bar, 73
STOP symbol, 73
Stormship Studios, 60
Storytelling, 85–87
Sun Microsystems, 50, 76
Sunnybrook Health Science Centre, 70–71
Surfers, 59
Surveys:
   offline, 37
   online, 97

T
Tait, Gordon A., 83
Thank you, 108–109
Thor, Asta, 143–144
Thoreau, Henry David, 185, 186
The Thorn Tree, 153–154
<TITLE> section, 206
Tool bar, 66–67
Torn, Rebecka, 142–143
Toronto Hospital for Sick Children, 78, 79, 82–83
Toronto West Park Hospital, 71, 74, 75, 96
Trace Research & Development Center, 60
Transparency, 92
Trenbeth, Richard B., 139
T-shirts, 7, 9
TV viewing, Web use vs., 36

U

UCLA Athletic Fund, 16
UNICEF, *see* United Nations Children's Fund
Uniform Resource Locator (URL), 67–68, 202, 203
United Nations Children's Fund (UNICEF), 92–93, 97, 98, 106, 108, 109, 112
U.S. Department of Justice, 121
Updates, software, 135
URL, *see* Uniform Resource Locator

V

Vancouver General Hospital, 73, 85
Variety Village, 13
Verisign, 132
Virtual Yale Station (VYS), 112, 147–150
Voice software, 5
Volunteers, requests for, 105–106
VYS, *see* Virtual Yale Station

W

Wagner, Melissa, 177
Watts, Robert, 155, 198–199
Web directories, 207–208, 213–214
Web Net, 178
Web Networks, 219
Web rings, 175–177, 210
Web servers, 134–136
Westlund, Mark, 7, 178–179
WGBH, 154

Wheildon, Colin, 63
Wired magazine, 37
World Vision, 38–40, 152–153, 154
World Wide Web (WWW), 2, 200
World Wildlife Fund (WWF), 2–3, 189–193, 203, 212–222
WPLN, 5–7, 98
Wray, Stephen, 186
Writing, for direct mail, 48
Writing, online, 73–90
  bullet points, use of, 79–80
  checklist for, 87–90
  copyright issues, 85
  flowchart/site map, role of, 74–75
  links in, 70–72
  and long vs. short copy, 76–79
  and netiquette, 85
  overused words, avoiding, 80–83
  preliminary tasks, 73–74
  preparing for, 88
  and quality control, 83–85
  storytelling, 85–87
WWF, *see* World Wildlife Fund
WWW, *see* World Wide Web

Y

Yale University, 112, 147–150, 152

Z

Zapatista movement, 18

About the Disk

DISK CONTENTS

Description	Directory	Software Needed
Bookmarks to Internet resources*	BOOKMARK	Internet browser
Checklists saved in RTF (Rich Text Format)	CHECKLST\RTF	Word processor (Most word processors are capable of reading RTF Files)
Checklists saved in Word 97	CHECKLST\WORD97	Word processor (Microsoft Word 97 or above).
Web site design scratch pad	DESIGN	Word processor (Microsoft Word 6.0 or above)
Sample web site donation form	DONATION	Internet browser

The enclosed disk contains a bookmark file with links to over 100 web sites, the checklists printed at the end of each chapter, and a sample web site donation form.

*Note: The bookmark.htm file is also available at http://www.wiley.com/products/subject/ business/nonprofit/johnston/bookmark.htm. The bookmark list will be updated periodically at this site.

In order to use the bookmarks and sample donation file, you will need access to the Internet and Internet browser software. To use the checklists, you will need to have word processing software.

SYSTEM REQUIREMENTS

- IBM PC or compatible computer
- 3.5" floppy disk drive
- Windows 3.1 or later
- Internet browser (Any Internet browser is capable of opening the bookmark.htm file in the browser window. Some Internet browsers can import the bookmark file into your personal bookmark listing.)
- Word processing software capable of reading RTF files (e.g. Microsoft Word for Windows or WordPerfect).

HOW TO INSTALL THE FILES ONTO YOUR COMPUTER

Running the installation program will copy the files to your hard drive in the default directory C:\JOHNSTON. To run the installation program, do the following:

1. Insert the enclosed disk into the floppy disk drive of your computer.
2. Windows 3.1: From the Program Manager, choose File, Run. Windows 95 or higher: From the Start Menu, choose Run.
3. Type **A:\SETUP** and press Enter.
4. The opening screen of the installation program will appear. Press Enter to continue.
5. The default destination directory is C:\JOHNSTON. If you wish to change the default destination, you may do so now. Follow the instructions on the screen.
6. The installation program will copy all files to your hard drive in the C:\JOHNSTON or user-designated directory.

USING THE FILES

Loading Files

To use the bookmarks you can either open the BOOKMARK.HTM file from your Internet browser or import the bookmark file into your personal bookmark listing.

Refer to Help in your browser software for information on importing bookmark files.

To view the sample web site donation form, launch your Internet browser and open the DONATION.HTM page.

To use the word processing files, launch your word processing program (e.g., Microsoft Word or WordPerfect). Select File, Open from the pull-down menu. Select the appropriate drive and directory. If you installed the files to the default directory, the checklist files will be located in either the RTF or WORD97 subdirectory in C:\JOHNSTON\CHECKLST\. A list of files should appear. If you do not see a list of files in the directory, you need to select ALL FILES (*.*) under Files of Type. Double click on the file you want to open. Edit the form according to your needs.

Printing Files

If you want to print the files, select File, Print from the pull-down menu.

Saving Files

When you have finished editing a file, you should save it under a new file name before exiting your program.

User Assistance

If you need basic assistance with installation or if you have a damaged disk, please contact Wiley Technical Support at:

Phone: (212) 850-6753
Fax: (212) 850-6800 (Attention: Wiley Technical Support)
Email: techhelp@wiley.com

To place additional orders or to request information about other Wiley products, please call (800) 225-5945.

For information about the disk, refer to [**About the Disk**] on pages [233–235].